7/85

£2250.   now £315.

WITTGENSTEIN — THE LATER PHILOSOPHY

An Exposition of the
Philosophical Investigations

WITTGENSTEIN -

THE LATER PHILOSOPHY

An Exposition of the "Philosophical Investigations"

by

HENRY LE ROY FINCH

HUMANITIES PRESS

Atlantic Highlands, N.J.

Library of Congress Cataloging in Publication Data

Finch, Henry Leroy.
    Wittgenstein—the later philosophy.

    Bibliography: p.
    Includes indexes.
    1. Wittgenstein, Ludwig, 1889-1951. Philosophische Untersuchungen.
2. Philosophy. 3. Languages—Philosophy. I. Title.
B3376.W563P5324   192   76-46421
ISBN 0-391-00680-0

Printed in the United States of America

Dedicated to

M. R. F.

and in loving memory of

H. J. I. and E. G.

Preface

This book is written on the assumption that what is most needed now in the study of Wittgenstein is an over-all view of his philosophy. We need to have just that kind of an *overview* which he himself made the aim of his philosophy. It is time to find out what holds his thinking together and makes it all-of-a-piece.

Like every great philosopher, Wittgenstein had a single vision of the world. The integrated character of his thought is evident on every page, even when we do not know what the point of view is. It is this singleness of vision which, as time will show, gives his ideas their force and authority.

Wittgenstein's philosophy requires us to "think in a new way," and hence its great difficulty. He is the first philosopher who is really outside of modern philosophy—that is, outside the philosophy of the last three hundred years. In an exact way he is the first philosopher of our times who is not a Cartesian.

We have heard this before about other philosophers. It has indeed been fashionable for a long time, on various provocations, to sound the death-knell for Cartesianism. But when the noise abates, the patient is found to be still there, gasping but alive. Why is it any different this time?

We will see that it *is* different. This time the patient is gone, and the entire situation is changed. It is as if someone else has taken over the institution.

Many philosophers will be reluctant to admit anything so drastic and no doubt will continue their efforts to fit Wittgenstein into the familiar routines. But such efforts, however well-intentioned, are futile and doomed to failure.

In the last chapter of the present book an attempt is made to show Wittgenstein's place in the history of Western thought. This chapter may be read first, but if this is done, it should be borne in mind that it is the rest of the book which substantiates what is said there.

If, as the present writer believes, Wittgenstein stands at the beginning of a new period in Western philosophy, then we will not be able to understand him by trying to fit him into some previous period.

My aim has been, not to give a detailed commentary on every aspect of Wittgenstein's later philosophy, but to establish its general outlines and even the general outlines of both periods taken together. This could only be done by reading, and rereading assiduously, Wittgenstein's texts until their meaning became clear, even if, as was the case, this took many years. We must emphasize what has been said innumerable times before, and will be said innumerable times again, that on every question it is the texts themselves which must have, and will have, the last word.

As in my previous book, *Wittgenstein—the Early Philosophy* (Humanities Press, 1971), the quotations at the beginning of each chapter are intended as a summary of the main ideas of that chapter, as well as food for thought.

For permission to quote at length from the *Philosophical Investigations, Notebooks 1914-1916, On Certainty, Lectures and Conversations on Aesthetics, Psychology and Religious Belief*, as well as other books by Wittgenstein published by them, I wish to thank Basil Blackwell, Oxford. And similar thanks to Routledge and Kegan Paul, and Humanities Press, publishers of the *Tractatus*, for permission to quote from that book.

I should also like especially to express my appreciation to my colleagues in the Philosophy Department at Hunter College of the City University of New York for their assistance in clarifying points and for their willingness to discuss philosophy at any hour of the day or night.

HENRY LE ROY FINCH
New Rochelle, New York
June, 1976.

Acknowledgments

The chapter entitled "Ordinary Certainty" appeared in the *International Philosophical Quarterly*, Vol. XV, No. 4 (December, 1975). Acknowledgment is made to the Editor. Acknowledgment is also made to the following publishers for their kind permission to quote from books published by them: The Macmillan Company and Basil Blackwell for permission to quote from the *Philosophical Investigations;* University of California Press and Basil Blackwell for permission to quote from *Zettel* and *Lectures and Conversations on Aesthetics, Psychology and Religious Belief;* J. and J. Harper and Basil Blackwell for permission to quote from *On Certainty;* Harper and Row and Basil Blackwell for permission to quote from *The Blue and Brown Books;* Basil Blackwell for permission to quote from *Remarks on the Foundations of Mathematics* and *Philosophical Grammar;* Barnes and Noble Division of Harper & Row for permission to quote from *Philosophical Remarks;* all of the foregoing books by Wittgenstein. Also the following publishers for single quotations from the books indicated: Allen and Unwin—J. N. Findlay, *Ascent to the Absolute;* Cambridge University Press—R. B. Farrell, *A Dictionary of German Synonyms;* Dover Press—Spinoza, *Ethics;* Harper and Row—Martin Heidegger, *On the Way to Language;* Humanities Press—Peter Winch, *The Idea of a Social Science;* University of Massachusetts Press—Simone Weil, *Oppression and Liberty;* Open Court—Ernst Mach, *Analysis of Sensations, Popular Scientific Lectures, History and Root of the Principle of the Conservation of Energy;* Oxford University Press—J. L. Austin, *Philosophical Papers;* P. M. S. Hacker, *Insight and Illusion;* Princeton University Press—Hugo von Hofmannsthal, *Selected Prose* and *Selected Verse Plays;* Paul Valery, *Collected Works;* Random House—Wallace Stevens, *Collected Poems;* Prentice Hall—George Pitcher, *The Philosophy of Wittgenstein;* Harold Garfinkel, *Studies in Ethnomethodology;* Macmillan Co. and Allen and Unwin—G. E. Moore, *Philosophical Papers;* Routledge and Kegan Paul—Rush Rhees, *Without Answers.*

Contents

PART IV

CONCLUSION

Abbreviations

The following is a list of abbreviations used to refer to Wittgenstein's writings and to published notes on his lectures arranged in alphabetical order. All references in the text of this book are to sections in these writings or notes, unless the letter *p.* appears, in which case the reference is to a page.

BLB   *Blue Book*, included in *The Blue and Brown Books* (Oxford: Blackwell, 1958).

BRB   *Brown Book*, included in *The Blue and Brown Books* (Oxford: Blackwell, 1958).

LE   "A Lecture on Ethics," *The Philosophical Review*, Vol. LXXIV, No. 1 (January, 1965), pp. 3-26.

MLN   G. E. Moore, "Wittgenstein's Lectures in 1930-33," in Moore's *Philosophical Papers* (N.Y.: Collier, 1962).

MN   *Math Notes*, unauthorized publication of notes on lectures given in the Spring of 1939 (San Francisco, 1954).

N   *Notebooks 1914-1916*, edts. G. H. von Wright and G. E. M. Anscombe, trans. G. E. M. Anscombe (Oxford: Blackwell, 1961).

NFGB   "Notes on Frazer's *The Golden Bough*," *Synthese*, Vol. 17 (1967), pp. 233-53.

NLRB   "Notes on 'Lectures on Religious Belief'," *Lectures and Conversations on Aesthetics, Psychology and Religious Belief*, edt. Cyril Barrett (Oxford: Blackwell, 1968).

OC   *On Certainty*, edts. G. E. M. Anscombe and G. H. von Wright, trans. D. Paul and G. E. M. Anscombe (Oxford: Blackwell, 1969).

PE   "Notes for Lectures on 'Private Experience' and 'Sense Data'," included in *The Private Language Argument*, edt. O. R. Jones (N.Y.: St. Martin's Press, 1971), pp. 232-75.

PG   *Philosophical Grammar*, edt. Rush Rhees, trans. Anthony Kenny (Oxford: Blackwell, 1974).

PI   *Philosophical Investigations*, edts. G. E. M. Anscombe and
        R. Rhees, trans. G. E. M. Anscombe, Third Edition (Oxford:
        Blackwell, 1958).

PR   *Philosophical Remarks*, edt. Rush Rhees, trans. Raymond
        Hargreaves and Roger White (Oxford: Blackwell, 1975).

RFM   *Remarks on the Foundations of Mathematics*, edts. G. H. von
        Wright, Rush Rhees and G. E. M. Anscombe, trans. G. E.
        M. Anscombe (Oxford: Blackwell, 1964).

VWC   von Wright Catalogue of the Wittgenstein Nachlass. This
        material has been deposited in the Wren Library of Trinity
        College, Cambridge, with a microfilm in the Cornell Univer-
        sity Library, Ithaca, New York. A description and number-
        ing of it is given by G. H. von Wright, "The Wittgenstein
        Papers," *The Philosophical Review*, Vol. LXVIII, No. 1
        (1969), pp. 483-503.

T   *Tractatus Logico-Philosophicus*, trans. D. F. Pears and B. F.
        McGuinness (London: Routledge and Kegan Paul; N.Y.:
        Humanities Press, 1961).

Z   *Zettel*, edts. G. E. M. Anscombe and G. H. von Wright,
        trans. G. E. M. Anscombe (Berkeley and Los Angeles: Uni-
        versity of California Press, 1967).

Other Writings of Wittgenstein
Not Referred to by Abbreviations

Letters from Wittgenstein to Paul Engelmann with a Memoir, edt.
B. F. McGuinness, trans. L. Furtmüller (N.Y.: Horizon Press,
1967).

*Letters to C. K. Ogden: with Comments on the English Translation
of the* Tractatus Logico-Philosophicus, edt. with Introduction by
G. H. von Wright, with Appendix of Letters by Frank Plumpton
Ramsey (Oxford: Basil Blackwell, and London: Routledge and
Kegan Paul, 1973).

Letters to Russell, Keynes and Moore, edt. with Introduction by G. H.
von Wright, assisted by B. F. McGuinness (Ithaca, N.Y.: Cornell
University Press, 1974).

Prototractatus: An Early Version of Tractatus Logico-Philosophicus, edts. B. F. McGuinness, T. Nyberg and G. H. von Wright, trans. D. F. Pears and B. F. McGuinness; historical introduction by G. H. von Wright; facsimile of the author's manuscript (London: Routledge and Kegan Paul, 1971).

Ludwig Wittgenstein und der Wiener Kreis: Gespräche, aufgezeichnet von Friedrich Waismann, aus dem Nachlass herausgegeben von B. F. McGuinness (Frankfurt am Main: Suhrkamp, 1967).

PART I

TWO PHASES OF WITTGENSTEIN'S PHILOSOPHY

The Tractatus *and the* Investigations

There was no need of converting the elements of the phenomenal world into eternal elements. . . . The change consisted in the change of aspect.

TH. STCHERBATSKY

You want to make the universe of the possible . . . as inexact as I hold the existential universe to be. But that can't be because the possible is our only *standard* of expression.

CHARLES PEIRCE
(writing to William James)

It is by realizing that even the subtlest of things that one arrives at by analysis are not ultimate in reality that one becomes free from clinging to the products of analysis.

VENKATA RAMANAN

Depth is hidden. Where? On the surface.

HUGO VON HOFMANNSTHAL

CHAPTER 1

The Tractatus *and the* Investigations

i

The initial impression of the *Philosophische Untersuchungen* or *Philosophical Investigations* is likely to be that it is what Wittgenstein himself called it, an "album" of "sketches" (PI p. ix), virtually at the opposite pole from the tightly organized and structured *Tractatus*. But this impression may be very misleading. It may conceal both the enormous amount of care which went into the formulation of the *Philosophical Investigations* and also the unity and structure of the thought which is implicit in it.

The two books—the *Tractatus* and the *Investigations*—are both the results of the most extreme exactitude and care, both put together over long periods of time with constant revision, rewriting and rearrangement, and both reflect the same structured kind of thinking and desire for thoroughness and completeness. But the tones and styles are indeed very different. The *Tractatus* is like a crystal, seemingly unbreakable, or a code which has to be "cracked," its unity broken up into many facets until we see how problematic it is underneath. The *Philosophical Investigations*, on the other hand, is like an ocean which has to be "sounded" again and again until we find its bottom, for there are "depths beyond depths" concealed beneath its seemingly casual tone.

In abandoning his conception of language as an exact calculus, the conception expressed in the *Tractatus*, Wittgenstein did not alter his standards of exactness and thoroughness. Nor was he any the less systematic in working out his ideas. The description of the *Investigations* as an "album" of "sketches" must not mislead us into supposing that the underlying ideas were "fragmentary." The unity of Wittgenstein's point of view was not impaired. The unity was differently understood.

The striking continuity between the two books rests upon un-

1

changed fundamental commitments. While there has been what Wittgenstein himself called a 180-degree turnabout in how he looked at language, even this is more or less on the surface compared to the continuing commitment to such ideas as the *primacy of meaning* and the *immanence of meaning in language.* Here we might say nothing changed, and *these* ideas were simply transposed into a different key. The depth and power of Wittgenstein's philosophy comes from the depth and power of the ideas to which he remained firmly committed throughout.

Wittgenstein's thought may be said to have been intrinsically conservative in this respect—having gained a certain insight, he kept it and built on it, and when he was compelled (as he was in the case of the conception of language as an exact calculus) to change a fundamental idea, then he went over the previous ground to reinterpret it in the light of the change. The landscape is seen in a new light, but it is in effect, the same landscape. And this accounts for the strong sense of familiarity we have in reading Wittgenstein's later philosophy after studying his earlier one.

ii

Just how close Wittgenstein's earlier and later periods are in their general outlines may be suggested by the following table of comparisons. As we study the two phases of his philosophy more and more carefully we will find that the same roles are played by the items parallel to each other in the two columns:

Tractatus	*Philosophical Investigations*
names – objects (T. 3.22, 3.221)	words – uses (PI 30, 43)
pictures (T 2.1-2.2)	instruments (PI 569)
	images – samples (PI 50)
	concepts (PI 569)
	descriptions (PI 291)
logical forms (T 2.102, 3)	criteria (PI 354)
elementary propositions (T 4.2)	language-games (PI 7, 65, p. 224)
simplest propositions (T 4.221)	Ur-phenomena (PI 654-6)
logical simplicity (T 5.4541)	analogical simplicity (PI 130)

forms of objects (T 2.0251)   forms of life (PI 19, p. 221)

all possibilities (T 2.0121)   acting with certainty (PI 211-2)

Es verhält sich so und so. (T 4.5)   *So machen wir's.* (RFM p. 98)
This is how things stand.   *So we do it.*

This table offers much more than merely suggestive parallels. If properly understood, it shows an inner affinity between the two stages of Wittgenstein's thought (or perhaps we might even say an inner "analogical identity"). The finality of logical structure as the essential core of language in the *Tractatus* is replaced by the similar finality of human convention as the last court of appeal. The culminating rubric *So we do it* has the same force in the later as *This is how things stand* does in the earlier. The shift from the pictorial-structural conception to the instrumental-game one (and from logical to analogical simplicity) leaves the requirement that *something* play the role of final prerequisite of language unchanged.[1]

Before we discuss the very important differences between the two periods it is important to look more closely at these similarities. The common factor found in both is Frege's distinction between *meaning (Bedeutung)* and *sense (Sinn)*. In the *Tractatus* this is the distinction between *names* having *meaning* and *propositions* having *sense*. In the *Investigations* the distinction is still echoed in the difference between *uses of words* (which establish *meanings*) and *language-games* (which, in effect, establish *sense*). (Neither of the two latter terms, of course, are to be understood as ontologically simple, but only as heuristically simple, a distinction to be discussed below.)

When the *Tractatus* conception of a proposition as a logical picture began to break down (with the collapse, among other things, of the notion of the logical independence of elementary propositions which could not be squared with the need for ways of expressing the "degree of a quality")[2] this breakdown, as it turned out, could not be

---

[1] It must not be supposed, of course, that the "structural conception" of the *Tractatus* in any way "maps into" the "functional conception" of the *Investigations*. For one thing, "mapping into" is a concept belonging only to the "structure language." And, for another, for the later Wittgenstein there is no *one* function of language, nor even any *one* language.

[2] "Some Remarks on Logical Form" in *Supplementary Volume* IX of the Aristotelean Society (London, 1929, reprinted N.Y., 1964), pp. 162-171.

halted until the notion of elementary propositions itself was abandoned. Wittgenstein was, step by step, forced to *broaden his conception of sense* (in order to maintain his view of its immanence in language). It became necessary to include more and more of the *settings* of words as, in effect, part of their sense. The notion that language *must* be an exact calculus died very hard. Judging from the posthumously published *Philosophical Remarks* and *Philosophical Grammar*, Wittgenstein moved with almost agonizing slowness to the new position that language makes sense only as it is altogether intertwined with different kinds of activities.

Besides the persistence of at least the echo of the meaning-sense distinction the table shows the persistence of the view that thought, language and world must, in some way or another, go together at the very outset (though now this would be understood as action, language and world). There must be something which, in some way, belongs to all three; and this is *logical structure* in the *Tractatus* and *grammatical criteria* in the *Investigations*. (We can no more limit criteria merely to language or to phenomena than we can limit logical form to language or to the world.)

Between *forms of objects* in the *Tractatus* and *forms of life* in the *Investigations* there is another affinity since the former indicates kinds of (meaningful) structure, while the latter indicates kinds of (meaningful) activities. As in the former case we have to accept as given different kinds of structural possibilities (T 2.0123-4), so in the latter we have to accept as given different kinds of activities (PI p. 226). Both are necessary to the workings of language as Wittgenstein understands this in the two different periods of his thought.

As nothing can come between logic and the world in the *Tractatus* (T 5.557) (since the only meaningful world is the world to which language is applicable), so nothing can come between language and the activities carried on with it in the *Investigations* (PI 23) (since these activities are meaningful in this sense because they are already carried on with language). In Wittgenstein's view we cannot *make* language apply to the world any more than we can *make* it apply to our actions. It *is* language because it already has this character. *The complete applicability of language is already given with language,* for this is how Wittgenstein from the start sees language.

This would be nonsense, however, without an equally important corollary which is also maintained in both books: that *the intrinsic meaningfulness of language or its complete applicability does not determine a single actual use of language.* In the *Tractatus* everything is settled up to the final *yes* or *no* (truth *or* falsity), while in the *Investigations* all established practices, rules and conventions do not guarantee that an error will not be made or a rule will not be followed (even in a case where a person may *claim* to be following it).

Despite the 180-degree difference between them, the two books maintain essentially the same view of the presuppositional character of language although this is seen in a very different way, which even involves a different conception of the method of philosophy. We turn now to look more closely at the presuppositionalism and then at the difference in methods.

iii

Standing at the door of Wittgenstein's philosophy (indeed it is the very first sentence of his subsequently published earliest writing, the *Notebooks* of 1914) are the words *Logic must take care of itself.* This sentence, repeated in the next entry and called "an extremely profound and important insight," is indeed like a signature key for all that follows, even when *logic* has broadened into *grammar* and *structure* has given way to *activities.*

Logic must take care of itself. This puts logic in a special place; it is a declaration of *presuppositionalism.*[3] Logic, it says, does not belong to the world which we confront; it is not a fact or part of the phenomena. It is rather what makes it possible to confront any world at all, what we have to take for granted in order to have any world that makes sense. We do not *make* logic, we *presume* it or *require* it. And we cannot *make* language logical any more than we can *make* it conventional or usable. If it is language at all, it is already logical, conventional, usable.

Where does the *a priori* status of logic in the *Tractatus* come from? Wittgenstein's first answer is clear: it comes from logic's dealing with *all possibilities* (T 2.0121). Logic gives us the dipolar arrangement of all possible structures. It is in the early philosophy a certain form of all the possible structures of the world, just that form which

---

[3] This is Wittgenstein's oft commented-upon Kantianism, aimed not at the presuppositions of reason, but of language. It is what makes language possible (rather than what makes science or mathematics possible) which is Wittgenstein's starting point.

the world shares with thought and language. Later the same role is played by grammar, which involves certain kinds of agreement in human action and usage, agreements which establish the everyday world. The preconditions for language being meaningful have changed, but they are none-the-less preconditions.

The statement that *logic must take care of itself* is followed in the *Notebooks* by the sentences: "A possible sign must also be capable of signifying. Everything that is possible is also legitimate." (N. p. 2.) When it comes to language, what we *can* do is what we *may* do. The only intrinsic boundaries are the *impossible*—what by the nature of things cannot be said with sense. We do not establish these boundaries; we find them already within language.

The fundamental perspective here, it is clear, is one belonging to a long tradition in philosophy—that the *actual is intelligible* (indeed *is* anything) *only in terms of the possible*. The possible is not derived from the actual, but is (as this is understood in different ways by different philosophers) the precondition of the actual. It is not *this* relation which is reversed in Wittgenstein's later philosophy, for grammar and forms of life still establish the framework of possibilities for what can be said. (What is reversed is the relation between *signifying* and *using*, for it is no longer a name as such which is the precondition of language, but names are only names when something is done with them.)

The breaking of the spell of language as *essentially* "mirroring" and "representing" did not mean that there was some other way of seeing language clearly apart from seeing it in terms of its possibilities. It only meant that these possibilities were understood differently, no longer in terms of *objects, names* and *referring*, but rather in terms of the contexts of activities which are required for even these concepts really to make sense. (The notion of one ultimately simple description is itself tied to the notion of one essentially correct use of the word *description*.)

In the *Tractatus*, in a way which Wittgenstein later struggled so hard to understand, possibility *became* reality, a super paradoxical sayable and unsayable reality, defining what could and could not be said, the ontological ground of all mappings and projections. This turned out to be illusory when it became clear that *any* projection *could* be done in some other way, so that the hold of the idea of the "only possible final interpretation" was broken.

Possibility then became itself *a way of looking at phenomena* (an *aspect* of phenomena), a way which revealed how language does what it does and also how it misleads us into supposing that it does something else. From this perspective customs, for example, appear not as facts, as anthropology might see them, but as agreed-upon ways of doing things within which language functions. (It is because they are seen as what we are *bound* by, rather than what we are perhaps *caused* by, that they appear as preconditions and not as facts.) While language is a phenomenon, the philosophical description of it cannot leave out its conventionality, in so far as conventions are not merely facts, but also preconditions for making sense in talking about facts. It is in this aspect that conventions embody possibilities.

Wittgenstein has given up trying to *penetrate* phenomena, but not given up talking about their *possibilities* (for to give up this latter would be to give up philosophy).

> We feel as if we had to penetrate phenomena; our investigation, however, is directed not towards phenomena, but, as one might say, toward the *possibilities* of phenomena. We remind ourselves, that is to say, of the *kind of statement* that we make about phenomena. (PI 90.)

To talk about the possibilities of phenomena is still, not only a legitimate way of speaking, but the way that is central to philosophy.

iv

The difference we have been discussing points to the difference in the conception of philosophic method between the earlier and later philosophies. This change of method parallels the change in the way Wittgenstein thought of language. We have two radically different ideas:

(1) language as *logical picture* depicting forms and structures of *objects* through forms and structures of *names;*
(2) language as *human activities*, integrated with *other human activities* through countless different kinds of *uses of words.*

In the first of these conceptions the essential structures of language are hidden by the superficial similarities of the grammars of ordinary languages; we have to dig out these essential structures by using a logically correct symbolism which will prevent mistakes (T 4.1213). In the second case also we have to avoid being misled by superficial grammatical similarities, but now not because they *hide* essential structures, but rather because they lead us to *imagine* that there *are* such hidden essential structures.

The task of philosophy is, in a way, inverted here. Wittgenstein called the first method "analysis" (T 3.201) and spoke of using "a sign-language that is governed by *logical* grammar—by logical syntax" in place of ordinary grammar (T 3.325). The second method he described as "assembling reminders" (PI 127) to bring about "rearrangements" (PI 92; BLB p. 44) which will enable us to "command a clear view of the use of our words" (PI 122).

In the *Tractatus*, as Wittgenstein came to see later, the *need* for clarity was obscured by the *requirement* of *total exactness* (PI 108), so that it even looked as if the two were the same. If the hidden exactness could be found, it seemed, then language would be seen clearly. It was just this picture, however, which, he came to realize, *prevented* seeing language clearly. The requirement of exactness arose from a picture, the picture of language as in a projective relation to the world with the rays of the projection going out from names to simple objects, the simple objects being what the names *meant*, whatever they might *seem* to designate.

The new metaphor which replaced that of language as such a picture was that of language as a box of tools (PI 11), while what replaced the idea of the absolutely simple logical picture was that of the model of the simple language-game (PI 130, 656). At the same time the idea of all *tools* having something in common or all *games* having something in common, which would be the essential meanings of these words, was abandoned. And this reduced the superconcepts of the *Tractatus* such as *name, object, sentence, reference* and *description* to ordinary words, without single, final and correct meanings (PI 97).

How the different kinds of tools and instruments of language are used and how the different games of language played are still, in a certain sense, "hidden," but, as Wittgenstein would now say, hidden in plain view, or *hidden on the surface. We do not have to "dig" to see how language functions; we have to "look" in a new way.*

The new method—Wittgenstein's later method—of revealing the *essence hidden on the surface* attempts to show where such illusions as that which dominated the *Tractatus* come from. Apparent connections and associations of words and pictures have to be dissolved by rearranging them and by inventing new ones, freeing our minds from rigid patterns. The aim is to see what has been in front of our eyes all the time.

Description, of course, is just as important as ever in this later method. But it is not *language* which is to be understood as description, but *philosophy*. And there is not one *right* description, but descriptions for the purpose of removing certain confusions. The point is to stop trying to *explain* language (even explaining it as essentially description) and to be satisfied with ways of looking which remove its bewitchments.

In the course of this new approach and the way of looking at language which it involves Wittgenstein makes use of the *five fundamental ideas* which we listed at the beginning of this chapter and which form the backbone of the *Philosophical Investigations*. These are the ideas of: *use, concepts and images, criteria, language-games* and *forms of life*. These topics will be taken up in that order in subsequent chapters. But first the difference between the *Tractatus* and the *Investigations* needs to be looked at more closely and from a slightly different point of view.

The Basic Change

Is thinking of something like painting or shooting at something? It seems like a projection connection, which seems to make it indubitable, although there is not a projection relation at all.

WITTGENSTEIN (NLRB p. 67)

To regard language as a means for the embodiment or expression of thought is to take a one-sided view of one of its most derivative and specialized functions.

BRONISLAW MALINOWSKI

The human mind can never be understood or handled from outside.

SIMONE WEIL

Man does not stand over against his understanding; he is this very understanding itself.

HEINRICH OTT

CHAPTER 2

The Basic Change

i

The basic change between Wittgenstein's earlier and later philosophies was the giving up of the idea of language as an exact calculus with a world necessarily of a corresponding character. This connection between language and the world seemed like the essential core of any language, what guaranteed the final reference upon which, it seemed, all meaning and sense depended.

That an ideal or perfect calculus might serve as a universal language of science had been the hope of a number of scientifically oriented philosophers. What distinguished Wittgenstein from this group was his respect for ordinary language and his view that such an exact calculus, if it was to be found, had to lie at the heart of ordinary language. This was a far cry from the zeal with which language-reformers attacked the vagueness and ambiguity of ordinary language.

Despite this difference, however, Wittgenstein, it must be said, was just as much in the grip of the idea of an exact calculus as anyone else, perhaps even more so since for him the very possibility of *all* language seemed bound up with it. Indeed in the *Tractatus* an entire metaphysics came into being to support it.

What is not so evident and, in fact, is somewhat concealed in the *Tractatus* is the relation between the idea of language as an exact calculus and the *nature of thinking*. Just how these were thought to be related is brought into the open in the *Investigations*, for there we are able to see why giving up the idea of language as an exact calculus also required giving up a certain conception of understanding, meaning and thinking, and indeed a whole conception of "mental activities."

The large amount of space in the *Investigations* devoted to the topics of *understanding, meaning* and *thinking* (along with certain closely related topics, it is more than half the book), is justified by the fact that the way these were treated in the *Tractatus* was part and

11

parcel of the idea of language as an exact calculus. If the latter went, so did the former, leaving a large hole indeed. Nothing was more important than to find a new approach to these (and other similar) "mental" activities.

We can, however, read the *Tractatus* with the greatest care and scarcely see how important is the difference between the passive, picturing aspect of thinking and the active "meaning and intending" aspect, or exactly what is involved in *projecting the sense of a proposition into a proposition*, the act of thought by which the nature of the world is revealed.

The place in the *Investigations* where we become aware of the intimate relation between the exact calculus and these mental activities is a passage dealing with how it is possible to be misled into supposing that an ideal language is somehow better or more perfect than ordinary language. Then Wittgenstein adds this:

> All this, however, can only appear in the right light when we have attained greater clarity about the concepts of understanding, meaning and thinking. For it will then also become clear what can lead us (and did lead me) to think that if anyone utters a sentence and *means* and *understands* it, he is operating a calculus according to definite rules. (PI 81.)

The words *and did lead me* should not be lightly passed over. We need to ask: How did it so lead Wittgenstein? What was the connection here?

The answer is found later in the *Investigations* in the following passage:

> But isn't it our *meaning* it that gives sense to the sentence? (And here of course belongs the fact that one cannot mean a senseless series of words.) And "meaning it" is something in the sphere of the mind. But it is also something private! It is the intangible *something*, only comparable to consciousness itself. (PI 358.)

Now it appears that it is *meaning it* which gives sense to sentences. Where is this and the very word *meinen* found in the *Tractatus?* It is there, though not called *meaning it*, but rather *thinking the sense.*

> We use the perceptible sign of a proposition (spoken or written, etc.) as a projection of a possible situation. The

method of projection is to think the sense of the proposition.
(T 3.11.)

How the distinction is made between a propositional sign and a proposition appears in the very next sentence:

> I call the sign with which we express a thought a proposi-
> tional sign. And a proposition is a propositional sign in its
> projective relation to the world. (T 3.12.)

At this point we see thinking from both sides—as what is expressed
in the sign and as the projective relation which the sign bears to the
world. It is *through thinking that propositions acquire their exact and
essential natures and complex things become the simple objects of reference which are needed for the senses of propositions.*

What gives exact sense to propositions, no matter how complex
the things referred to may be, is that these things are meant as (and
function in the proposition as) *simple objects* when a thought projects
them as the referents of names figuring in the sense of a proposition.
This special kind of activity, the unique act of "thinking the sense,"
enables language to function because it treats all things, no matter how
complex, as simple by naming them (which is to say, *meaning* them)
in a specific sense required by a particular proposition.

What Wittgenstein's view was in the *Tractatus* he summed up
in the *Blue Book* when he had taken the decisive steps away from it:

> It seems that there are certain definite mental processes bound
> up with the working of language, processes through which
> alone language can function. I mean the processes of under-
> standing and meaning. The signs of our language seem dead
> without these mental processes; and it might seem that the only
> function of the signs is to induce such processes, and that these
> are the things which we ought really to be interested in.
> (BLB p. 5.)

It is the attempt to conceive of "mental processes" in some other way
which occupies so much space in the *Investigations*, for it is now clear
to Wittgenstein that "nothing is more wrong-headed than calling meaning (*meinen*) a mental activity" (PI 693).

ii

Since the logical alchemy "hidden in the medium of the understanding" (PI 102) was in many ways the pivotal feature of the *Trac-*

tatus, providing the means by which complex everyday things were able to be named as logically simple objects, it is worthwhile to look more closely at how Wittgenstein conceived of this as his ideas developed in the *Notebooks*, particularly in the sections written in June, 1915 (pp. 64-71).

Here it is clear that for the young Wittgenstein what was required to have a proposition at all was a *definite sense*, and this meant, in the first instance, a sense capable of being determined to be true or false. What guaranteed such definiteness, according to the *Notebooks*, was the peculiar activity of meaning:

> But the sense must be clear, for after all we mean *something* by the proposition, and as much as we certainly mean must surely be clear. (N p. 67.)

> It seems clear that what we MEAN must always be "sharp." (N. p. 68.)

The example which Wittgenstein gives is "The watch is lying on the table," and he asks: "Does this really have a completely clear sense?" His answer is that it does, *just in so far as what we mean by it goes*, for these complex things (watch and table) function as simple objects for the logical purposes of this sense, *thanks to the activity of meaning them that way*. This is all we need. It is complete definiteness, as is shown by logic being able to work with these sentences just as well as with any others. Logic takes sentences just as they are, but it is Wittgenstein's point that it can do this just because ordinary language already operates on the principle of simple names, and any name functions as a simple name by means of the activity of meaning it, which is what is involved in any functioning language.

Even though, taken alone, the terms *watch*, *table* and *lying on* are vague enough, nevertheless the proposition *The watch is on the table* has a complete and definite sense, when that particular sense is thought, and we may say that it satisfies all the necessary logical requirements, including that of being able to be true or false, permitting truth functions to be set up for it and logical inferences to be drawn from it.

An analogy which seems to be in the back of Wittgenstein's mind is the way in which mathematics applies to ordinary things. So it would seem logic too applies to ordinary things when they are *meant* (*meinen*) as simples, as parts of propositions. In this way the vagueness of ordinary language is justified (N p. 70), or, as he also says, we do not separate the hard from the soft, but we see the "hardness of the soft" (N p. 44).

> For even the unanalyzed proposition mirrors logical properties of its meaning . . . and we work with it in every case exactly as if it were unanalyzable. (N p. 10.)

Any language is able to operate because it operates

> as if in a certain sense all names were *genuine names*. Or . . . as if all objects were in a certain sense simple objects. (N p. 61.)

Through the activity of *meaning the sense* any sense becomes an exact sense.

From this we can conclude that, however vague ordinary language may be, *what is meant can never be vague*. It would seem also to follow that, if a statement is meant to be vague, then this vagueness in turn becomes something definite, since just that is what is intended or meant. (In an analogous way, a photographer intentionally taking a fuzzy or blurred picture, may succeed in getting exactly what he wants, and the fuzziness or blurredness becomes the definite object of his intention—*just what he meant*.)

The *Notebooks* say that every sense is definite because to *mean* something is to mean *something*. As Wittgenstein put it later, looking back:

> The sense of a sentence, one would like to say, may of course leave this or that open, but the sentence must nevertheless have *a* definitive sense. An indefinite sense—that would not really be a sense at all. (PI 99.)

This echoes a *Tractatus* view adumbrated in the *Notebooks*:

> what it (a proposition) does say it says completely, and it must be susceptible of SHARP definition.
> So a proposition may indeed be an incomplete picture of a certain fact, but it is ALWAYS *a complete picture*. (N p. 61.)

Propositions do not wait upon analysis to acquire their core of definiteness because

> even the unanalyzed proposition mirrors logical properties of its meaning. (N p. 10.)

it seems clear that where there is sense there must be perfect order. —So there must be perfect order even in the vaguest sentence. (PI 98.)

A strong Cartesian wind still blows here, particularly in the statement that

It is clear that I *know* what I *mean* by the vague proposition. (N p. 70.)

Here the knowing seems to guarantee the exactness, though it is the activity of *meaning* it which establishes it.

The ontological picture is at one with the epistemological; to say that the world must be definite is to say that it must consist of elements. Or, as Wittgenstein puts it, in his ontological statement *par excellence, the world must be what it is* (N p. 62). Even if the elements are not known, there must *be* elements, for the elements are simply another name for a definiteness not conceivably any more definite. This will-o-the-wisp belongs to what, it seems, *must* be if anything is to be, the familiar in-itself now attached to the state of affairs corresponding to the simplest proposition.

iii

Wittgenstein at any stage would probably have been loath to call *meaning, understanding* and *thinking* "mental processes"—if by this were meant anything of a "psychological" character which could be described factually. Whatever these activities were, they could not be reported upon "factually" since they were presupposed in the functioning of language which included "reporting factually." (To treat them as simply "factual" would be to deliver logic into the hands of psychology.)

That these activities continued to occupy a special place when Wittgenstein returned to philosophy is evident from the Lectures of 1930-33, as noted by G. E. Moore, who reported him as saying that

there was another (sense of "meaning") which he described as that in which it is used as "a name for a process accompanying our use of a word and our hearing a word." By the latter he apparently meant that sense of "meaning" in which to "know the meaning" of a word means the same as to "understand" the word . . . (MLN p. 252.)

The decisive change seems to have come when he ceased to regard *meaning*, *understanding* and *thinking* as processes of *any* kind, however unique, and saw that what we have to do with here are different kinds of language activities besides describing objects. In other words, he was no longer trying to understand language in terms of mental activities, however qualified or veiled, but instead looking at mental processes also from the point of view of language. When the full implications of this were grasped, the notion of thinking or meaning something, which went with the conception of language as an exact calculus, could be entirely dropped.

The new note (possibly even the "kink in thought" referred to at the end of the Moore lectures) was the realization that there is no more in the words *thinking*, *understanding* and *meaning* than there is in the phenomena which they bring together and express and in the language-games which we play with them. In the *Philosophical Grammar* he was well on the way to this when he wrote:

> The mental process of understanding is like the arithmetic object three. The word *process* here and the word *object* there give us a false grammatical attitude toward the word. (PG p. 85.)

In the *Tractatus* the importance of "thinking a sense" lay in its being the means by which even the vaguest proposition acquired an exact sense, so that exactly *that* was meant and no more and no less. This was where the transformation occurred by which *any* language at all acquired the essential exactness which permitted it to *be* a language. Logical possibility, revealed by the activity of thought itself, supplied this essential intended content. As he put it years later:

> The strict and clear rules of the logical structure of propositions appear to us as something in the background—hidden in the medium of the understanding. I already see them (even through a medium); for I understand the propositional sign. I use it to say something. (PI 102.)

The principal accomplishment of the *Investigations*, from this point of view, was to dethrone "mental processes" and bring them fully within the scope of language, rather than allowing them to remain as what language somehow depended upon. To accomplish this it had to be established that there was no "independent reality" in the "inner" direction any more than there was in the "outer" one. We may say that the remnants of the "absolute object" and the "absolute subject" still remain in the *Tractatus* and had to be completely dissolved in order to do full justice to the "linguistic revolution" which that book began.

To put this another way—when the system of the *Tractatus* crumbled, two things went down together: the conception of language as an exact calculus depending upon absolutely simple objects and the allied conception of thinking as a hidden activity by which language acquired this exactness. When the exactness was seen to be a myth, the whole way of thinking about mental activities also was thrown into question.

Taking Wittgenstein's philosophy as a whole, we can see that the anti-Cartesianism expressed in the early philosophy, principally by his abandoning the *thinking self* (T 5.631), could not be completed without dropping also the notion of *meaning, understanding* and *thinking* as mental activities. This is what he summed up in the following quotation from the *Blue Book*:

> Now when the temptation to think that in some sense the whole calculus must be present at the same time vanishes, there is no more point in *postulating* the existence of a peculiar kind of mental act alongside of our expression. This, of course, doesn't mean that we have shown that peculiar acts of consciousness do not accompany the expression of our thoughts. Only we no longer say they must accompany them. (BLB p. 42.)

PART II

LATER CONCEPTION OF LANGUAGE

Meaning and Use

The question "What is it useful for?" was a quite essential question.

WITTGENSTEIN (RFM p. 109)

For the uses of things are the reasons they are used.

EMERSON

To usage belongs the supreme authority for the testing of speech, nor can that which usage condemns be restored save by usage.

JOHN OF SALISBURY

Use has a likeness to the property of the Holy Spirit; provided that use be taken in a wide sense as including also the sense of to enjoy.

THOMAS AQUINAS

CHAPTER 3

Meaning and Use

i

What does Wittgenstein mean by the *use of a word?* This question is as important for understanding the *Philosophical Investigations* as the parallel question "What does he mean by a *name?*" is for understanding the *Tractatus.* The question is all the more important because what Wittgenstein has in mind is something very different from what various other people have meant by the *use of a word.*

Wittgenstein, for example, does not speak of the *use of a word* (1) as grammarians or students of linguistics do, or (2) as most logicians do, or (3) as linguistic philosophers, such as J. L. Austin, do. He does not, in other words, speak of the *use of a word* to bring out linguistic, logical or cultural points about language, but rather to bring out philosophical points of the kind philosophers traditionally have been interested in.

First, he is not concerned with the *use of a word* in terms of ordinary grammar or what are called "parts of speech." The student of linguistics, for example (including members of the latest school of "transformational grammar") may classify all nouns together, all verbs together, etc., overlooking what would be such important distinctions for the logician as those between nouns serving as subjects, predicates or relational terms, and also overlooking what would be crucial distinctions for the philosopher, such as those between nouns having to do with spatial, temporal, mathematical or psychological matters. Wittgenstein is not concerned with the grammatical distinctions which interest the linguist. Nor does he mean by "depth grammar" anything like what the linguist does, since for him the term has also what the linguist would regard as semantic dimensions and not merely syntactic ones.

Secondly the term *use of a word* does not mean for Wittgenstein what it most often does for the logician. Traditionally the logician has been most interested in distinguishing between subjects, predicates, relations, connectives, etc. Or he may speak of words being used to refer, distinguish, relate, qualify, etc. None of this is of primary concern to Wittgenstein. Nor is he interested in developing a "semantic theory" or a "syntactic theory." Language already working is his starting point, and this, of course, is something which is already presupposed by the logician himself in his own language.

Finally this might seem to bring Wittgenstein's notion of the *use of a word* closest of all to such philosophers of language as J. L. Austin. But the impression of similarity here too is misleading, for Wittgenstein's interest and method is very different from Austin's. Austin was concerned with the greatest possible number of distinctions which could be discovered in a specific language (English) to bring out shades of difference in thinking about various topics. He was not trying to see how language (any language) is able to work at all, but rather to explore the conceptual resources of a language, often making use of dictionaries and group consultations. Wittgenstein, on the other hand, wanted to see the "possibilities of phenomena" in such a light that they would no longer generate the philosophical puzzles so familiar to us. He was looking for the *essence* of language, even when his idea of what this would involve had changed completely. Austin might well have approached this by examining the concept of *essence;* Wittgenstein approached it by looking at language in the most general way possible.[1]

With these preliminary indications of what Wittgenstein did *not* mean by the *use of a word* out of the way, we can proceed to examine what he *did* mean by it. To this question there are two broad answers, reflecting the old name-proposition (meaning-sense) distinction of the *Tractatus*, though in a very different way. The first of these is that the use of a word is what can be done with a word as a certain *kind of a word*—such as a color word, a number word, a sensation word, etc. This is the grammatical aspect, revolving around the char-

---

[1] Some of Austin's more strictly philosophical views seem uncharacteristically overstated, such as, for example, his statement (in *A Plea for Excuses*) that "our common stock of words embodies all the distinctions men have found worth drawing, and the connections they have found worth marking in the lifetime of many generations." *Philosophical Papers* (Oxford, 1961), p. 182. Austin gives no reasons for ignoring the possibility that some distinctions and connections which might be worth preserving have disappeared. How does their disappearance show that they were not "worth preserving?"

acter of the word itself and the rules governing its behavior. The second answer, closely intertwined with this, is that the use of a word (and here has to be included also the use of a sentence) is a certain kind of language-activity—such as giving or obeying an order, describing an object or telling a joke. This latter is something like a more general notion of use, and in fact Wittgenstein sometimes speaks of this second notion of use as *kinds of use* (PI 23).

How are *kinds of words* related to *kinds of use?* We have to recognize that the same word can have many different kinds of uses (e.g. the word *water* functioning as a command, an exclamation, a description, etc.), while many different kinds of words can have similar uses (e.g. the words *water, away, ow, help, fine* and *no* all functioning as exclamations, though in very different ways (PI 27)). Wittgenstein seems to have realized that any attempt to classify uses, especially in terms of levels of generality, will always be more or less arbitrary. There is too much overlapping and too many possible ways of doing it. (The attempt to systematize language-games failed and was abandoned in the *Brown Book*.)

Corresponding to the two levels of use are the two leading metaphors of Wittgenstein's later philosophy—*tools* and *games*. Words are compared to tools (PI 11) and also to plays or moves in games (PI 31), the two metaphors running side by side, the first suggesting that words have something like "built-in capacities" being able to perform different functions, and the second that we then use these different capacities in larger kinds of activities. As we cannot, for example, hammer with a saw, except with the greatest difficulty, so we cannot without a similar strain, use the word *pain* as we use the word *red*. Tools, after all, are highly purposive (we might say "almost nothing but purpose"), but this purpose is incomplete if not part of some larger activity. The game-metaphor suggests an activity as self-contained, and it is this aspect of them which seems to be of interest to Wittgenstein (rather than whether games are amusing or have some further purpose). Language, in the way Wittgenstein is concerned with it, cannot be "explained" by something other than itself, since it has no further purpose (PI 496).

The two metaphors of *tools* and *games* are every bit as important to Wittgenstein's later philosophy as the metaphors of *pictures* and *spaces* were to the earlier one. And, of course, each of the two sets of metaphors can be misleading. The qualifications *language*-tools and *language*-games are as important as the qualifications *logical* pictures and *logical* spaces. What both metaphors of *tools* and *games* suggest is that the important thing about a word is what is done with it or can be done with it, but this will involve looking at the word itself *and* at the larger activities into which it fits. Thus, for example, a saw can be described in terms of the action of sawing, but sawing itself is then quite a different activity when it is done in connection with surgery and when in connection with carpentry. (We could very well say that the essential meaning of sawing has changed, even though the tools involved might both be called *saws*.) And, similarly the word *Water!* as a cry of thirst, an expression of disgust or a command to turn on the hydrant has quite different meanings, even though from another point of view, it is the same word. Both levels must be taken into account, the grammar of the word and the language-games in which it functions.

ii

Wittgenstein's shift from a referential-structural to a use-activity conception of meaning involves a new way of thinking about *names*. With this shift it is no longer necessary to think of names as fastening language to the world through meaning simple objects. There is no longer needed such a role for names. Rather Wittgenstein can now say that the word *name* is a way of characterizing different kinds of uses (PI 38). Instead of names being the *basis* of *all* use, the term *name* is a way of grouping a number of different kinds of uses.

As we have already indicated, this is a reversal of the relation between *signifying* and *using*. In the *Tractatus* we can only use words because they signify, or as Wittgenstein puts it, *use mirrors signifying*. In the *Investigations*, on the other hand, different kinds of uses involve different *ways of signifying*, and when we speak of different kinds of referents this means no more than that different kinds of use are involved. Colors, shapes, numbers and relations, for example, are not to be thought of as ontologically distinguishable, but as different kinds of things which are done, and can be done, with language.

Wittgenstein has no objection in the *Investigations* to speaking of "a proper name, the name of a color, the name of a material, a numeral, the name of a point on the compass, and so on" (PI 29). And also he does not object to saying that all of these can be ostensively defined, even though "an ostensive definition can be variously interpreted in every case" (PI 28). It is this latter qualification which is crucial, for what have disappeared are the "core" names which established the inner structural identities between language and the world, required by the pictorial way of thinking about language.

Naming in Wittgenstein's later philosophy is not by itself a use of words. In one place he says it is something like hanging a label on a thing (PI 15), and this by itself has no linguistic significance, since the label *per se* does not even tell us *what* is being labelled, and, indeed, unless it does something more than just stick to something, it is not even a "label." It might just as well have *blown* there. Calling naming a use of words is like calling a tool-box a tool, or, better, a compartment in a tool-box a tool. There is nothing in the world which can be "just labelled," or which is presented to us as an object which corresponds to nothing more than a label (however much a nominalist might wish to imagine that a *particular* is so available).

Even in the *Tractatus* Wittgenstein's view was that there is no *mere naming* or *mere referring* since even the simplest names referred to objects which had forms (or possibilities of combinations with other objects) as part of their intrinsic natures. Sheer existence was not nameable. Or, as Wittgenstein would have agreed at both stages of his philosophy, the way the word *name* is used does not cover the kind of use which the word *this* has (PI 38).

We cannot in Wittgenstein's philosophy get what the nominalist wants—names fastened to particulars in such a way that the name stands for just *this* one unique thing. This may seem to deny the possibility of proper names until we ask ourselves just what proper names name and how they are used. We then recall that we cannot even apply proper names unless we have ways of identifying, so that even in this case it is not the unique particularity which is being named, but rather some assemblage of different recognizable features. Even proper names must have senses or must have uses (PI 79, 87).

A consequence of this is that an ostensive definition explains the meaning of a word only on the condition that the grammar of the word is already known.

So one might say that the ostensive definition explains the use—the meaning—of the word when the overall role of the word in language is clear. (PI 30.)

Just to point at "what the word means" will not accomplish anything unless we already known what *sort* of an object is being pointed at (e.g. a color, a shape, a thing, etc.). Pointing is, in effect, always equivocal since the necessary distinctions cannot be made by the pointing itself (since a number of different features, as it were, always occupy the same spatial locus).

When Wittgenstein asks "What does one have to know in order to be capable of asking a thing's name?" (PI 30), the answer is that we have to know what kind of a thing we are asking for the name of, not in the sense of what species of thing it is, but in the sense of what philosophical grammatical category it belongs to. This is not a question of the classification of the thing, but of something like its "form of meaning." The different "kinds of objects" referred to by such terms as *red, round* and *apple* cannot be distinguished by, as it were, "just looking," any more than we can tell the difference between a bank draft, a police summons and a candy wrapper by "just looking" if we knew nothing ahead of time about these things. We have to know the games within which such pieces of paper function in order even to identify them. And, analogously, the situations in which words function, as well as their relations to other words, is what it means to speak about the "kind of thing" to which a word refers.

The *Philosophical Investigations* open with St. Augustine's description of learning language as a matter of learning names and then immediately contrasts this with Wittgenstein's conception of language as sets of activities as shown by someone going to a store to buy "five red apples." Here are three different kinds of language activities connected with counting, color samples and identifying a kind of fruit, all integrated into the activity of shopping. Wittgenstein wants to show us that calling these three words *names* does not bring out what is involved in their having meanings. It is the *doings* involved that are important and the way the doings are fused in other activities, or *forms of life*.

For Wittgenstein language was always language in operation with its full potentialities of meaning. To do justice to this way of thinking of meaning, he had to begin in the early philosophy with language and world integrated together. And in the later philosophy he had to begin with language and action integrated together. This is what thinking of meaning in terms of use really accomplishes; it makes meaning intrinsically an action.

iii

It is essential to Wittgenstein's whole point of view in the *Investigations* that the term *use* should apply not only to *established use* (in the sense of *usage*) but also to *possible use* (in the sense of what may *not* be commonly established). To accomplish this he makes use of two German words *Gebrauch* and *Verwendung* which are skillfully woven together throughout the text. The two pairs of words *Gebrauch* (and the verb *gebrauchen*) and *Verwendung* (and the verb *verwenden*) represent the two aspects of Wittgenstein's thought about *use*—*use as fact* and *use as act*, or *actual use* and *possible use*.

Although the words *Gebrauch* and *Verwendung* may sometimes be virtually synonymous in German, a careful study of Wittgenstein's text shows him to be sensitive to the shades of difference between the two words and also shows that these differences of meaning are important to him, and have to both be carried along together.[2]

In some places we will find that the difference between use as *Gebrauch* and use as *Verwendung* is related (as so much else is) to the difference, familiar in the *Tractatus*, between the meaning of a word and the sense of a sentence. We find him, for example, speaking of "the use (*Gebrauch*)—the meaning—of the word" (PI 30) and also of sentences with the same *sense* being those with the same *use* (*Verwendung*) (PI 20). This directly connects *Gebrauch* with the *meaning of words* and *Verwendung* with the *sense of sentences*.

The following passage with the two words side by side brings out the same distinction:

> What immediately impresses itself upon us about the use (*Gebrauch*) of a word is the way it is used (*Verwendung*) in the construction of the sentence, the part of its use (*Gebrauch*)—one might say—that can be taken in by the ear. (PI 664.)

In the *Tractatus*, part of the importance of the meaning-sense distinction was that the meaning of a word was regarded as more or less established (given, for example, by the dictionary), while the sense of a sentence is somehow determined by the user (there being no dic-

---

[2] We might say that in his use for the two words *Gebrauch* and *Verwendung* Wittgenstein is perhaps departing from some of the *customary usage* of the words in German in order to take advantage of the *possibilities of use* which they have. And this is just the distinction which the two words themselves embody.

tionary of sentences). Hence there seemed to be a certain liberty in constructing sentences which possibly have never been uttered before, while we almost never find ourselves saying *words* which are totally new.

The distinction is very much broadened when it is expressed in the difference between *Gebrauch* and *Verwendung*, as that between *customary usage* in general and *possible uses*. We do, for example, find Wittgenstein speaking of the use of words as *Verwendung*, but only when the use is other than the customary one. (On the other hand, the "use of a sentence" is always *Verwendung* and never *Gebrauch*, and the "use of language" is both.)

The way Wittgenstein uses the two terms can be summarized as follows:

imaginary uses (PI 6), metaphysical uses (PI 116), "unheard-of" uses (PI 133), and figurative uses (PI p. 215) are all cases of *Verwendung;*
what is learnt (PI 6), practiced (PI 9), and defined (PI 30) are cases of *Gebrauch.*

In addition the following terms are used in connection with *Gebrauch*:

words, numerals, names, signs, signposts, expressions and *rules;*

while the following appear in connection with *Verwendung*:

sentences, questions, orders, reports, expressions, formulae, concepts, descriptions and *rules.*

(The significance of the appearance of *rules* on both lists is discussed below.)

Before we look at the actual texts which embody these differences it may be helpful to summarize the results of such an examination in advance:[3]

---

[3] In R. B. Farrell's *Dictionary of German Synonyms* (Cambridge, 1953), we find "*Gebrauch* approximates closely to 'usage' either as an established way of behavior . . . or in reference to the correct meaning of words" (p. 157); "*Verwenden*: to turn to account, to utilize for some purpose . . ." (p. 381).

Gebrauch	Verwendung
use as *meaning* (PI 30)	use as *sense* (PI 20, 47)
a *custom* (PI 198)	a *doing*
a usage (which may be being carried on now)	a utilizing (which may be finished and over and done with)
something observed (PI 82, 122) taught and learned (PI 6, 9)	something imagined (PI 6, 195) suggested (PI 191, 197)
extended in time PI 138)	comes before the mind (PI 139)

The contrast here is between a *usage* and a *utilizing*, and this becomes clearer if we recall that a *usage may be utilized* and we may say (the sentence is not Wittgenstein's) that we learn the use (*Gebrauch*) of a word in order to have the use (*Verwendung*) of it. While it is possible that a *usage* and a *utilizing* coincide, so that we use a word just as it is ordinarily used, it is also possible that we may use it in some other way, for all kinds of special uses are possible, and, beyond this, new language-games are constantly coming into existence (PI 23).

The best way to see the significance of the distinction we have been discussing is to put some of Wittgenstein's own statements side by side:

(1) We want to establish an order in our knowledge of the *use* (*Gebrauch*) of language . . . (PI 132).
It is not our aim to refine or complete the system of rules for the use (*Verwendung*) or our words in unheard-of ways (PI 133).

(2) The word "agreement" and the word "rule" are related to one another, they are cousins. If I teach anyone the use (*Gebrauch*) of the one word, he learns the use (*Gebrauch*) of the other with it (PI 224).
The use (*Verwendung*) of the word "rule" and the use (*Verwendung*) of the word "same" are interwoven. (As are the use (*Verwendung*) of "proposition" and the use (*Verwendung*) of "true") (PI 225).

(3) In the practice of the use (*Gebrauch*) of language (2) one party calls out the words, the other acts on them (PI 7).
Now think of the following use (*Verwendung*) of language . . . (PI 1).

(4) But assimilating the descriptions of the uses (*Gebrauchs*) of words in this way cannot make the uses (*Gebrauchs*) themselves any more like one another (PI 10).

> Of course, what confuses us is the uniform appearance of words . . . For their use (*Verwendung*) is not presented to us so clearly. Especially when we are doing philosophy! (PI 11).

It would appear from this that *knowledge, practice, learning, teaching* and *description* of use all involve *Gebrauch* or *usage*, while use as something consciously thought of or abstractly considered is *Verwendung*. This way of stating the difference is borne out by the following:

(1) an incorrect account of the use (*Gebrauch*) of a word (PI 345).
the correct idea of the use (*Verwendung*) of the word (PI 305).
(2) It is only in normal cases that the use (*Gebrauch*) of a word is clearly prescribed . . . (PI 142).
In our failure to understand the use (*Verwendung*) of a word . . . (PI 196).
(3) The hypothesis that satisfactorily describes his use (*Gebrauch*) of words which we observe . . . (PI 82).
the picture makes us expect a different use (*Verwendung*) (PI 141).
(4) the "use" (*Gebrauch*) which is extended in time (PI 138).
But can the whole use (*Verwendung*) of the word come before my mind . . . (PI 139)?

These contrasts point to *Verwendung* as connected with *ideas, understanding, expectation* and the *mind*, while *Gebrauch* is what is *prescribed* and *described* and *given an account of*.

The contrast between use as *spread out in time* and use as *grasped in a flash* is of special importance to Wittgenstein and must be examined more carefully, since here we seem to have a head-on collision between two different conceptions of meaning. This is the topic we turn to now.

iv

How is the apparent conflict between meaning as a *practice extended in time* and meaning as *something grasped in a flash* to be reconciled? How *can* something which is extended in time be grasped in a flash? And how does it happen that we say that "we understand what something means suddenly or all at once" and yet our understanding can also be said to be "what we are able to do over a period of time"? From whence arises the sense of strangeness connected with having two such seemingly different ways of speaking about *meaning* and *understanding*?

This subject is discussed in the five sections of the *Investigations* 138-142. The way Wittgenstein approaches it is an excellent example of his later method, particularly that part of his method which consists in finding intermediate cases (PI 122, 161). Finding intermediate cases helps us, for example, to see how two apparently far removed conceptions might both be called "understanding the meaning of a word." Wittgenstein does not say that "using a word in practice over a period of time" and "grasping the use of a word in a flash" *are* the same, for the difficulty is not only that they do not appear to be the same, but that they do not even seem to go together at all. But by looking more closely at the matter we may be able to understand why there is some point to calling them both "understanding the meaning of a word."

What Wittgenstein attempts to show is that "grasping in a flash" and "a practice over a period of time" only give rise to difficulties when it seems that *what* is "grasped in a flash" *is* "a practice over a period of time." Then it seems that something "spread out in time" cannot possibly also be "present in an instant." Two pictures, which it seems ought to fit together, refuse to fit together. While it might seem natural enough to say that we can "grasp a practice," when we stop to think about it, the two pictures appear and *it is they which "collide."*

Looking at this still more closely, we see that the picture of "grasping in a flash" does not seem to apply to "a practice spread out in time" because the picture of "grasping in a flash" leads us to expect a different use of that picture from the one which would be required if it were to be applied to "a practice spread out in time." Apart from this, there is nothing to prevent us from applying *that* picture even in that way. We might, for example, say that the *use* of a word *is* present *in some sense*, and this is just what we do say. The question "How can a practice be present all at once in an instant?" might then be answered by saying: "Ask yourself why it seems strange to think that it could and see if it is not because a picture leads you to expect a certain use of the picture, *as if that were the only possible use of the picture.* Have you not forgotten (or perhaps were unaware) that it is always possible for a picture to be applied in some other way?" In order to make this reply still more convincing we may then suggest a picture which will quite easily apply in both cases without any jarring or collision, a third or intermediate picture.

This is the crux of Wittgenstein's argument as to how the feeling
of collision arises here and how it can be removed. From another point
of view what he is doing is reconciling the two senses of *use* suggested
by the words *Gebrauch* and *Verwendung* discussed in the last section.
The idea of an unbridgeable gulf between two kinds of use (one
"spread out in time" and the other "grasped in an instant") will disappear if we see that no picture *has* to be applied in only one way. As
Wittgenstein came to understand it, this was the very thing which
had been at the bottom of his mistake in the *Tractatus*, for there too
a picture had been allowed to dictate its own application with extraordinary results.

We can now summarize Wittgenstein's argument in four main
steps:

(1) There is no sense in talking about the meaning-of-a-word-that-I-
understand "fitting" the sense-of-a-sentence-that-I-understand (or the
meaning of one word "fitting" the meaning of another word) if meanings are the kinds of uses which are *practices extended in time*. And we
certainly do sometimes understand the meaning of a word when we say
it or hear it, for "we grasp it in a flash, and what we grasp in this way
is surely something different from the 'use' which is extended in time"
(PI 138). This is the initial problem.

(2) Suppose now that what comes before one's mind (or is grasped
in a flash) is a picture (or something like a picture). Then this picture
may fit a possible use of a word (*Verwendung*) in the sense that it
may suggest a use (*Verwendung*). In a similar way a picture of a
cube may suggest what sort of object to use the word *cube* for, even
though the picture *could* be projected in such a way as to make it
fit what we call a triangle (PI 139). A picture may always *suggest*
a use, but it may never *require* a use, for there is always the possibility
of its being used in some other way.

(3) How then in Wittgenstein's own case in the *Tractatus* could a
picture not merely have suggested a use, but, as it seemed, actually
have forced a use on him? The answer is that what it forced on him
was a use in still a third sense, a use in the sense of an *application* (*An-
wendung*). The *picture of an application* might even be confused with
a *picture which is to be applied* (forgetting the crucial point that even
the picture of an application has to be itself applied), so that it looked
as if a certain picture (in the *Tractatus* a picture of an isomorphic

projection) determined its own application in only one possible way. In other words, no picture of an application can take the place of or determine an application (PI 140-141).

(4) The conclusion is that there can be a collision between a picture and the application of the picture (for example, between the picture of "grasping in a flash" and the application of this picture to "what is extended over a period of time") because the picture makes us expect a certain use of the picture and we forget that it is possible to use it another way, and with this realization the feeling of awkwardness of the expression begins to vanish.

The notion of use as an *application* helps us because here is something which can both be grasped as a picture in a flash and spread out as a practice in time. But we do not have to think of an application in this way, for there is nothing wrong with speaking of "grasping a practice in a flash" once we realize that even the picture of an application has to be applied.

The relevance of all this to the *Tractatus* is clear. What went wrong there was that Wittgenstein failed to realize that the picture of the application of a picture was *only a picture too*, and therefore even this picture (of isomorphic mappings), however compelling it was, had itself to be applied and could be applied in some other way. Even a picture of an application cannot determine how that picture itself is to be used. There is always the possibility of doing something else with it. The entire crystalline ontology of the *Tractatus* derived its power from the idea that the picture of an isomorphic mapping itself could only be applied in one way, i.e. the idea that *that* picture determined its own application.

v

Nowhere does Wittgenstein say that "the meaning of a word is its use." He does not restrict the term *meaning* this way. And on the contrary the door is left open for other ways of speaking about meaning:

> For a large class of cases—though not for all—in which we employ the word "meaning" it can be defined thus: the meaning of a word is its use in the language. (PI 43.)

There are two other main cases: (1) meaning as a *physiognomy* (PI 568), and (2) meaning as *intention* (e.g. PI 689-693). Meaning as a physiognomy is meaning found in phenomena, a subject which remains in the background of the *Philosophical Investigations*, but is of great importance in connection with Wittgenstein's views on art and religion.[4] A large part of the *Investigations*, on the other hand, deals with the subject of intention and related questions.

The main point that Wittgenstein makes about meaning as intention is that this is something wholly immanent within language and is not something added to language, which might therefore be considered as separable from language. It is not something "mental" or in the "realm of thought," which is somehow the "inner life" of a language and without which language would be dead.

Before we examine what Wittgenstein has to say about this it is well to consider the difference between meaning as *intention* and meaning as *use*. A main differences is that, while we *describe* use, we do not *describe words and meanings*, we *explain* words and meanings. And when we wish to make clear our intention in using a word, we *explain* it. Explanations make intentions known. Wittgenstein links meaning with explanation, particularly in the opening passages of the *Blue Book* and in the following passage from the *Investigations* which echoes them:

> "The meaning of a word is what is explained by the explanation of the meaning." I.e. If you want to understand the use of the word "meaning," look for what are called "explanations of meaning." (PI 560).

Does explanation, however, come back to use, so that an explanation of a word gives its use? Are definitions, for example, simply statements of how words are used? Wittgenstein says that names can be explained by pointing (PI 45) or by a demonstrative expression (PI 38) or by describing examples (PI 75, 79). In these cases grammars and language-games are implicit and taken for granted. Explanations work because they work within these frameworks.

Explanations, therefore, we might say, are internal to language; they belong to the actual workings of language. They are needed to remove the kinds of misunderstandings which prevent language from functioning, rather than the kinds of misunderstandings (of concern to philosophy) which prevent us from *seeing how* it functions. Hence

---

[4] Meaning as physiognomy is discussed in Chapter 11 in connection with Wittgenstein's phenomenalism.

when asked what we mean by such and such a word, we may give just enough of a definition and examples to indicate what we have in mind and to remove misunderstandings. This may be a very limited indication of use.

The notion of "explaining what we have in mind" may give rise to the picture that what is being explained is an intention or meaning in the sense of an "inner act." And it is this picture to which Wittgenstein is most opposed. Meaning something—in the case where the meaning, as it were, *aims at* something—may not, he repeatedly suggests, be entirely describable as use, but it is also not describable as a mental act, mental process, or inner experience, however rarefied, subtle and private these may be taken to be.

These cases which he considers, have to do with such expressions as "I will go to the bank" (where the speaker *means* or *intends* or *wants to say* the *bank of the river* and not the *bank where the money is*) (Z 183). Or where someone says *March!* and *means* the month and not the command (PI p. 215). In cases like these in which we have two uses of the same expression, we say that the speaker means the one or the other, and then the picture arises that there is a special act or process of meaning which makes the one, rather than the other the one meant. It is this picture which Wittgenstein believes prevents us from seeing clearly how the words *meaning* and *intention* function in these cases.

An explanation or a statement of what we mean by a word, to begin with

> is a definition; not a description of what goes on in me when when I utter the word. (PI 665.)

But Wittgenstein wants to go much further than to bring out that an explanation is not a report of an inner event. He wants to remove all temptation to imagine a mental occurrence as the *source* of the meaning or intention, or as somehow lying beneath or behind the meaning or intention. A temptation certainly exists to create a "myth of meaning" (PI p. 147) or a "myth of mental processes" (Z 211).

> We want to say "Meaning is surely essentially a mental process, a process of conscious life, not of dead matter." (Z 236.)

Then we start to look for such a mental process, for we feel it *must* be there. (Wittgenstein, more than once, warns us against this *must*;

the requirement is a grammatical one, even when it arises from a grammatical illusion.)

Wittgenstein is not, of course, taking the view that mental factors may not be present in cases where we speak of *meaning*, or *intending* or *understanding*. For example, he speaks of the following:

> direction of attention corresponding to a meaning (PI 666)
> something coming before our minds (PI 140)
> my thoughts connecting my words and what I speak about (Z 9)
> experiencing a tendency or readiness (PI 591; Z 33)
> being surrounded by pictures of our intentions (Z 233)
> feeling a word (PI p. 216)
> having a mental undertone (PI 592)

Such mental features may be present, but Wittgenstein's point is that none of them are what we mean by *meaning something;* they may or may not be present, but, in any case, *they* are not the supposed act of meaning something.

The trouble arises from thinking of meaning in this active sense as something which may be separated from language, added to it or taken away from it (as, analogously, and also mistakenly, we think of life as something added to or taken away from a lifeless body (Z 128)). Meaning is not an "extra" which makes language come to life. On the contrary there is no "language" without it, merely empty sounds.

> The mistake is to say that there is anything that meaning something consists in. (Z 16.)
> "Meaning" does not stand for an activity which wholly or partly consists in the "utterances" [outward expressions] of meaning. (Z 19.) (Translator's brackets.)

Certainly, he says, there is a connection between talking about *John* and *meaning* the particular person whom we mean by that name. But the connection is not in the dimensions where we imagine it to be. The connection is not through a mental mechanism (PI 689). And it is not even through thinking, as Wittgenstein himself imagined in the *Tractatus* where he supposed that "to mean it" is "to think it" (PI 692), not having realized that *to mean* and *to think* have quite different grammars (PI 329).

The series of questions which come almost at the end of the first part of the *Philosophical Investigations* dramatically reveal how completely immanent in language, *meaning and intention* and *meaning as intention* are.

> When I make myself a sketch of N's face from memory, I can surely be said to *mean* him by my drawing. But which of the processes taking place while I draw (or before or afterwards) could I call meaning him?
> For one would naturally like to say: when he meant him, he aimed at him. But how is anyone doing that, when he calls someone else's face to mind?
> I mean, how does he call HIM to mind?
> *How does he call him?* (PI 691.)

What this says is that, with regard to meaning and intention, there is *no how. We just do it.* Being able to *think of* somebody is no explanation of being able to speak about him, since the former is no less inexplicable than the latter. The imagined "mental act of meaning" answers nothing because it itself already involves the very intentionality which it is invoked to explain. Language is sufficient to convey meaning, and how it does it is not made more comprehensible by saying that thought or the mind must do it first. Language in operation does it, and that is the end of the matter.

Wittgenstein's position is that meaning and intention and meaning as intention are not mental processes (PI p. 218), or mental actions (Z 51), or experiences (PI 44, p. 217; Z 96). And further:

> Intention is neither an emotion, a mood, nor yet a sensation or image. It is not a state of consciousness. It does not have genuine duration. (Z 45.)

Any attempt to frame an hypothesis or theory or psychological model as to the nature of meaning as intention results in obscuring it. This is what happens when we search for foundations which are illusory instead of stopping at the proper place.

vi

In this chapter we have discussed three basic contrasts to be found in Wittgenstein's later philosophy of language:

(1) the contrast between *tools* and *instruments* of language, on the one hand, and the *games* which are played with these tools and instru-

ments, on the other. (This difference, as was pointed out, is analogous to that between *pictures* (mirroring) and *propositions* (asserting) in the *Tractatus*.)

(2) the contrast between *use* as *usage* (*established use*) and *use* as *utilizing* (*possible use*), which is reflected in the different ways Wittgenstein himself "uses" the two German words *Gebrauch* and *Verwendung*.

(3) the contrast between *meaning as use* and *meaning as intention*. (Here the meaning is immanent in the second case to a far greater degree, for we cannot get outside it to separate it from the act of language at all.)

It may strike us here that in each of these three contrasts there is a similar difference between a more passive and a more active side. Just such a difference is so pervasive in Wittgenstein's philosophy that it penetrates everywhere and does not stop short of the concepts of *language*, *use* and *meaning* themselves.

Perhaps this is not so surprising when we realize that all these differences reflect that most basic difference of all running through Wittgenstein's later philosophy: the difference between *phenomena* and *action* (including that between language as phenomena and language as action).

As the discussion proceeds, we will see that this distinction makes itself felt in many ways: in the difference between describing rules and obeying rules (remembering that the describing is also an obeying); in the difference between describing grammar and practicing it; in language-games as measure and as played. The two sides intermingle because we describe action as a phenomenon, but our description is itself an action.

Although there is certainly little else that is similar between the two philosophers, there is a contrast found in Spinoza which is applicable to Wittgenstein. This is the distinction between *natura naturata* (*nature natured*) and *natura naturans* (*nature naturing*).[5] If we remember that *language* fills up the whole horizon for Wittgenstein as *nature* does for Spinoza, then we will see how in the case of Wittgenstein we

---

[5] Spinoza's distinction is found in Part I, Ch. VIII, *Short Treatise on God, Man and His Well-Being*, trans. A. Wolf (London: A. C. Black, 1910), p. 56. It is also found in Part I, Prop. XXIX, *Ethics*, trans. R. H. M. Elwes (N.Y.: Dover, 1951), p. 68.

might speak of the difference between *lingua linguata* (*language languaged*) and *lingua linguans* (*language languaging*). The distinction is that between language as already established practice and language as action.

There is an autonomy of language for Wittgenstein, similar to the autonomy of nature for Spinoza. This means there is nothing outside of language, or nothing meaningful. Within language there are two sides: *phenomena* (in so far as meaningful) are meanings established or *language languaged*, while actions are meanings occurring or *language languaging*. But the two are never found apart, for there are no meanings established which are not themselves occurring in new language actions, and there are no meanings occurring which can be described other than in terms of meanings established.

Concepts and Images

You said something about a concept. Now what is a *concept? . . . Are you sure there is such a thing?*

JOHN JAY CHAPMAN
(writing to William James)

A concept is always, as regards its form, something universal which serves as a rule.

KANT

The nature of a concept as such is its internal (essential or definitive) relationships with other concepts.

C. I. LEWIS

I have said that the concept itself "is" *nothing more* than the concept, not of any concrete difference that *will* be made to someone, but is nothing more than the concept of the *conceivable* practical applications of it.

CHARLES PEIRCE

CHAPTER 4

Concepts and Images

i

The term *concept* has become so widespread in recent years that it has finally entered the sphere of fashionable jargon, and we find it used by politicians, diplomats, journalists, businessmen and advertisers. As one philosopher has pointed out, the term is now "almost as much of a rag-bag as was the term *idea* in the eighteenth century."[1] Philosophers have contributed their share, possibly even the lion's share, to the popularizing of this word.[2] As the fashion increases, Wittgenstein's comment seems more and more *a propos*: "Concept is a vague concept." (RFM p. 195.)

In the attempt to bring some order into the confusion connected with the term we can recognize three broad types of answers to the question: What is a concept? They are those which are

(1) *psychologically oriented*
    mental capacities (Geach)
    conscious habits (Peirce)
    psychological constructions (Mach)
    abstract representations (Schopenhauer)

(2) *logically oriented*
    predicative expressions (Frege)
    rules of combination or synthesis (Kant)
    signs pointing to invariant relations (M. Cohen)
    propositional functions with one variable (Church)

---

[1] R. I. Aaron, *The Theory of Universals* (Oxford, 1967), p. 188.

[2] Titles of a few recent books in philosophy will show the popularity of the word: *The Concept of Art* (Khatchadaurian), *The Concept of Benevolence* (Roberts), *The Concept of Knowledge* (Batchvarov), *The Concept of Language* (Wilson), *The Concept of Method* (Buchler), *The Concept of Mind* (Ryle), *The Concept of Motivation* (Peters), *The Concept of a Person* (Ayer), *The Concept of Philosophy* (Newall), *The Concept of Pleasure* (Perry), *The Concept of Prayer* (Phillips), *The Concept of Truth* (Armour), *The Concept of Worship* (Smart).

41

(3) *ontologically oriented*
    objective universals (Moore)
    essential characteristics of objects (Werkmeister)
    resemblances between things (Stace)
    distributive objects (W. Sellars)

All three factors, psychological, logical and ontological, tend to be involved in any discussion of concepts, but the emphasis will vary. Wittgenstein's emphasis falls on the *logical* or *grammatical*. Concepts are for him, in the first instance, part of language, or, as he puts it, *instruments of language* (PI 569). They have their home in language and in language-games, and he even calls them "one kind of expedient in the mechanism of language-games" (RFM p. 195). In this respect they resemble sentences (PI 421), descriptions (PI 291), and samples (PI 50), all of which he also calls "instruments of language."

It is a common mistake in discussing Wittgenstein's later philosophy to overemphasize the importance of concepts at the expense of what is equally important for Wittgenstein, language-games. This gives a lopsided picture, since concepts always function for him in language-games, and we do not get their full meanings except in these different settings. Even the same word may function as a concept in one language-game and not in another, for concepts are not found in every language-game (PI 96).

Bearing this in mind, we can proceed to examine what Wittgenstein says about concepts. Perhaps most important is his statement that concepts are *ways in which we make comparisons* (PI 57, 81, 144, 322; RFM p. 16). (Hence what is not comparable is not conceptual.) Along with criteria, which establish standard situations for the use of concepts, they enable us to deal with phenomena in ways which, as Wittgenstein puts it, express the role of the phenomena in our lives.

For reasons to be discussed, we should not think of concepts either as reactions to the characters of phenomena (as if phenomena *had* characters apart from concepts) *or* as attributing characters *to* phenomena (as if the phenomena were known to have no characters apart from concepts). Both these pictures should be avoided. There is, on the other hand, no objection to describing what we do with concepts or what concepts permit us to do, taking phenomena or concepts together, rather than trying to explain one in terms of the other.

It is a fundamental Wittgenstein theme that in the original and normal situation the way phenomena are is not to be separated from the way they are said to be, even though, for example, the statements "This is red" and "This is called red" do not have the same sense and do not appear in the same language-games. We may, nevertheless, say that both statements make use of the same word *red* and, if we choose to say so, the same concept *red*. The word *red* appears to point to the phenomenon of red, but, of course, only points to it in the language-game of "naming colors." The *phenomenon of red* is not separable from the *concept of red* except as the distinction shows up in different language-games.

There is no way of talking about phenomena except in terms of *some* concepts (and this holds true even when we try to talk about phenomena purely as perceived and not as conceived, for this is, as understood by Wittgenstein, *a conceptual distinction*). The basis for asserting any difference between phenomena and concepts could only be in Wittgenstein's terms some alternative way of conceptualizing the phenomena. We are never in a position to compare phenomena as they are apart from any concepts with the way our concepts take them. We do not, in other words, have access to some impossible point beyond both language and phenomena from which we might give a description of the relation between them. Meaning is immanent in language in a way which forbids a pre-linguistically meaningful world.

From this it should be apparent that the word *phenomenon* as used by Wittgenstein bears little relation to the way the same word is used by other philosophers in the traditions, for example, of Kant or Peirce or Mach. He does not mean phenomena as contrasted with noumena or as reduced to something like pure feelings or bare sense data. Rather phenomena are what we speak about with unreduced expression and character. Thus Wittgenstein mentions the *phenomena of thinking* and the *phenomena of hope*. These are not phenomena with their expressiveness removed, but rather retaining their recognizable characters, as human faces do. The phenomena, in other words, are as full and meaningful as our language permits us to say they are. Such a way of taking phenomena and concepts together is just what characterizes Wittgenstein's point of view.

Such an approach may seem not to make room for mistakes, deceptions and illusions. But these are concepts too which have their uses. Knowing, for example, that colors look differently in different kinds of light is part of knowing how to use color concepts and knowing the language-games with them. Similarly, doubting the way things look means that we understand the "language of phenomena," or the way concepts function when we need the distinction between *real* and *unreal*. The phenomena which lead us to conclude that we are deceived may not be the same phenomena as those which lead to the opposite conclusion, but the concepts which we employ and the language-game involved are ones which provide for that kind of mistake.

There are no absolutely correct concepts because there is no world known independently of all concepts with which to compare concepts. Furthermore, alternative concepts are always conceivable. If our interests were different, or if certain very general facts of nature were different, then we would have different concepts than we do (Z 388; PI p. 230). Concepts are like different styles of painting; they are "correct" for what is important to us at different times and in different situations, not correct in some final, absolute sense, just as there is no painting which has no style whatever.[3]

ii

Although a concept for Wittgenstein is primarily an instrument of language, concepts cut across language, thought and world. It is not surprising, therefore, to find Wittgenstein speaking of concepts from all three points of view:

(1) *a concept as the meaning of a word* (PI 532, 135, p. 213)
     analyzing a concept is analyzing the use of a word or describing the use of a word (PI 383, 316, 96)
     learning a concept is learning how to use a word (PI 208)

(2) *a concept as how we think or express* (PI 73, 337; RFM p. 195)
     a picture of the life of a word (PI p. 209)
     the fixed rails along which all our thinking runs (Z 375)
     a medium through which we look at phenomena (PI 177, p. 227)
     the expression of our interests (Z 388; PI 570; RFM p. 155)

(3) *a concept as a way of unifying phenomena* (PI p. 216)
     something felt as a unity, a particular physiognomy (PI 110, 235; Z 376, 392)

---

[3] This question of how Wittgenstein thinks about phenomena in his later philosophy is discussed more fully below in Chapter 11.

what counts as something (PI 68, p. 199)
what we understand under a particular designation (Z 381)

We may summarize this by saying that for Wittgenstein a concept is a way of expressing what phenomena mean to us through words which permit us to take the phenomena in varying patterns of similarity and difference. He compares them to measures that we lay down (RFM p. 130) and to grounds of classification (RFM p. 61). Concepts function as paradigms, permitting comparisons to be made to a standard or in standard ways (PI 55, 385; RFM p. 8; Z 183).

If the word *concept* itself (the concept of a concept) involves us with words, thoughts and phenomena, this means that these three concepts (*word, thought* and *phenomena*) themselves are interrelated and at certain points "run parallel." We are not talking about anything other than concepts here, and certainly not forming hypotheses or theories about language or the psyche or the world. For Wittgenstein concepts are to be described by concepts, including the concept of a *concept*.

This helps us to see why in his later philosophy Wittgenstein was not concerned with (1) finding extra-linguistic ontological features to account for the applicability of concepts to the world, or (2) finding extra-linguistic psychological abilities or capacities to explain how concepts came to be or what they "depend" upon. Both of these traditional concerns, it is clear, he regards as misguided and even illusory.

First of all, trying to find "something in common," for example, in instances of "red" is dismissed in the *Brown Book* as a case of what is called there "reflexive comparison"—a curious effect which makes us imagine that we have to do with two objects where there is only one. It is as if we attempt to take a phenomenon as a paradigm for itself, so that the phenomenon of red, for example, becomes also the justification for calling the phenomenon red (BRB p. 160ff). The same point is made in a somewhat different way in the *Investigations*:

> What is it to *mean* the words "*That* is blue" at one time as a statement about the object one is pointing to—at another as an explanation of the word "blue?" Well, in the second case one really means "that is called 'blue'."—Then can one at one time mean the word "is" as "is called" and the word "blue" as " 'blue,' " and another time mean "is" really as "is"?
> It is also possible for someone to get an explanation of the

word out of what was intended as a piece of information. [Marginal note: Here lurks a crucial superstition.] (PI p. 18.)

What is the "crucial superstition"? The answer, it would seem, is that it is the idea that what belongs to the grammar of the word tells us something about the "nature of the thing." Blue, as a universal, does not tell us about the ontological character of blue, but about the possible ways of using that word.

In a somewhat analogous fashion describing concepts in psychological terms as, for example, "mental capacities" seems to treat concepts as quasi-factual. By the term "mental capacity" we might mean either (1) a psychological phenomenon to which we apply the concept "mental capacity," which would require a criterion to determine what is to count as just this "mental capacity," or (2) an hypothesis, picture or model which we imagine as something like a hidden mechanism (in which case if it is to work as a genuine mechanism we require *two* criteria—one for identifying the mechanism itself and another for recognizing the manifestation it is supposed to explain).

It is true that if we *have a concept* of something, this ordinarily means that we can describe that something or point out examples of it, and consequently there is an ability which we have. But this does not mean that the concept *is* that ability, for there may be no criterion of this ability other than this very describing and pointing out, which are the criteria for saying that we "have a concept." If the identical criteria apply for the supposed particular disposition and for having a certain concept, it is hard to see how anything is gained by calling a "concept" a "disposition," except a spurious sense of "explanation." Actually the concept of *disposition* (and particularly this kind of a disposition) is as difficult to deal with as the concept of *concept*.

Thinking of concepts as *dispositions* or *capacities*, therefore, is from Wittgenstein's point of view, no particular improvement over thinking of them in the more old-fashioned way as *meaning-contents of consciousness*. And in some ways it may even be a retrogression, since the latter way of thinking at least seemed to preserve the formal or paradigmatic character of concepts. As an instrument of language there is no more reason why concepts should be thought of "psychologically" than that sentences or descriptions (which Wittgenstein also calls instruments of language) should be. And indeed all we have to do is to look at the differences between the grammars of the terms *disposition* and *concept* to see how far apart they are. (We can, for example, speak of *adopting* a concept, *revising* a concept, or *dropping* a concept, but we do not speak of *adopting* a disposition, *revising* a disposition or *dropping* a disposition.)

The fundamental Wittgenstein position is that nothing is gained by attempting to ground concepts on something non-conceptual. They may have biological, cultural, historical, sociological and psychological aspects, but these are in the first place of no particular concern to the philosopher,*and, in the second place, merely additional ways of forming concepts.

iii

Wittgenstein says that concepts have their homes in language-games (Z 391). The reason is perhaps because both are standardized aspects of language, forms which may be applied under a great many varying circumstances. There are nevertheless language games which do not involve concepts, and the same words may in some cases function as concept words and in other cases not.

Thus we find Wittgenstein saying:

> It is not in every language-game that there occurs something that one would call a concept.
> "Concept" is something like a picture with which one compares objects.
> Are there concepts in language-game (2) (the builders' language)? Still, it would be easy to add to it in such a way that "slab," "block," etc. become concepts. For example, by means of a technique of describing or portraying those objects. There is of course no sharp dividing line between language-games which work with concepts and others. What is important is that the word "concept" refers to one kind of expedient in the mechanism of language-games. (RFM p. 195.)

This passage suggests that having a concept is like having a sample of what is to count as something or other. Hence just being able to bring a "slab" from one particular pile on command, and not to be able to do anything else with a "slab" at all might not count as having the concept of "slab." It might not fall under our paradigm of "concept." We might, as a minimum, require that someone be able to *describe what a slab is,* or at least *recognize a slab in different settings.*

A non-conceptual use of a word might be one in which a phenomenon or event evokes or is greeted by a single expression without any question as to what it is or what it is *the same* as. The word *red*, for example, used as an exclamation—this is not the use of *red* as a concept, for red is not recognized as an *instance* of red, however much we may be inclined to look at the matter in that way when the word is taken out of any context. Having a word that is a concept in many uses does not guarantee that it is a concept in every use.

This becomes clearer if we consider the case of a person blind from birth. Such a person may have a concept of red, but will not be able to use the word *red* in certain language-games (such as picking out colors, or matching colors, etc.). He may know how to use the word *red* in all kinds of contexts—knowing what objects are or are not red, how red is related to other colors, the theories of electro-magnetic radiations and color-mixing, etc. What would be missing would be the sense experience of red, which we might say does not involve a concept at all. What the blind person could do with language we might call "using the concept of red," while the games he is shut out from might be the "non-conceptual" games. The act of recognizing a color, for example, which the blind person could not do, might be said not to involve the concept red at all.

> If I let my gaze wander round a room and suddenly it lights
> on an object of a striking red color, and I say "Red!"—that is
> not a description. (PI p. 187.)

Certainly I do not have to "have in mind" *what red is* in order to say "Red!" in this case.

Similar points arise in connection with first person expressions of inner sensations such as pain. In talking about other people's pains, doubting whether they have pain, etc., Wittgenstein says we need the *concept* of pain (Z 548). But does one need the concept for saying that one has pain oneself? Since it is Wittgenstein's view that pain is not a private object and there is no question of "identifying" here, we may be better off not to call a pain a concept in this case. And, in fact, this is the point at which Wittgenstein calls the pain an *image* (*Vorstellung*) (PI 300), suggesting that it is the *image* of pain that one calls to mind when one thinks of one's own pain, and not the concept.

If we were trained to express pains by moans (and different moans for different pains), we would not be likely to call these moans con-

cepts. And if I say that I was in pain yesterday, is it the concept of
pain that I am employing or my image or memory of it? (The language-game, of course, I had to learn, here as elsewhere, but is it a
game employing a concept, or one played without a concept?) Someone who was incapable of feeling pain might still learn the concept
of pain, but would be blocked from certain language-games such as
telling the doctor where it hurts. What, it seems, he would lack would
be the *image* of pain (or the *idea* of pain) not the concept of it.

In order to look more carefully into the difference between images and concepts we must first of all see what Wittgenstein has to
say about *images*.

iv

The term *image* is introduced in the following passage:

> It is—we should like to say—not merely the picture of the
> behavior that plays a part in the language-game with the
> words "he is in pain," but also the picture of the pain. Or, not
> merely the paradigm of the behavior, but also that of the
> pain.—It is a misunderstanding to say "The picture of pain
> enters into the language-game with the word 'pain'." The
> image of pain is not a picture and *this* image is not replaceable
> in the language-game by anything that we should call a pic-
> ture.—The image of pain certainly enters into the language-
> game in a sense; only not as a picture. (PI 300.)
> An image is not a picture, but a picture can correspond to it.
> (PI 301.)

When one thinks of pain, this says, one does more than conjure up
the picture of pain-behavior or even the concept of pain, and there
is something more than familiarity with the correct ways of using the
word pain, in addition to all this there is the *image*. We are able to
imagine pain, though not to give ourselves a private exhibition of pain.

How is the concept of *image* being used by Wittgenstein? We can
sum up the main points he makes about it thus:

(1) *there is no bridge between an image and what it is an image of;*
    The difficulty is . . . that the translation of the image into reality
    presents no difficulty at all (PI 386)
    (a) an image is not a likeness, as a picture is (PI 389, p. 177)
    (b) an image does not instruct us about the world (PI 443; Z 641)

(2) *an image is not a kind of seeing, nor is it seen;*
    (a) an image is not a private exhibition; we do not *see* or *possess* our own images (PI 398)
    (b) imaging and seeing are not different "activities" (Z 645)
    (c) an image is voluntary, as seeing is not (Z 637)

(3) *an image can neither be pointed at nor described as a process;*
    (a) this holds whether it is my image or somebody else's (PI 370)
    (b) images cannot be identified (PI 382)
    (c) questions about the nature of images are about the word *image* (PI 370)

In the light of these remarks about images we have to ask now: What is the difference between an *image* and a *concept?* Is it the difference, as some philosophers have said, between a private mental occurrence belonging only to one person and a public meaning familiar to, or at least explicable to, all members of a speech community?[4] This way of putting it would be unsatisfactory to Wittgenstein, for to say that images are private mental occurrences suggests that we are saying something about their nature, while it is his view that what we are really talking about is the way the word *image* is used. An image is no more a private object than a pain is. We do not have a relation to it of the kind that we have to objects (even if it is called a "subjective object").

> What is the meaning of the words: "*This* image"? How does one point to an image? How does one point twice to the same image? (PI 382.)

The differences between *images* and *concepts* (that is, between these two concepts) come out in the different grammars of the two words and the different language-games in which they appear. "Do you have an image (idea) of what I am talking about?" is quite a different question from "Do you have a concept of what I am talking about?"

---

4 Descartes, for example, who probably inherited it from Suarez, distinguished between "the idea as a mode of thought and the idea as a representative content or, as he puts it, between the idea as a formal reality and the same idea as objective reality." Julius R. Weinberg, *Ideas and Concepts* (Milwaukee: Marquette University Press, 1970), p. 43. The idea of an image as an "objective reality" is just what Wittgenstein repudiates, for here is the "private object" which has no role and no reality in his philosophy.

The former asks whether you are prepared to express yourself in a certain way, while the latter asks if you understand the way a word is used in a variety of different contexts. If, on the other hand, we think of an image, as Descartes did, as an "objective subjective reality," then the difference appears to be between two different kinds of objects. But neither *images* nor *concepts* are *objects* for Wittgenstein.

When we say that "Images are private," and "Concepts are public," what we are actually saying is that there are two different grammars. We are calling attention to the difference between the way the word *image* is used and the way the word *concept* is used. We are saying, for example, that we can only compare images through concepts or talk about them in terms of concepts, or sometimes perhaps in terms of pictures.

Bearing this in mind, we have to note that the statements made above about images, which sound as if they were about the nature of images, are actually talking about the *concept* of images or how the word *images* is used. The statements have a grammatical, rather than factual, character. We have access to images in this way—neither "objectively" nor "subjectively," but in terms of the use of a word.

v

The chief difference between *concepts* and *images*, it seems, is that while concepts can be compared and, indeed, are in the most complicated relations with each other, images cannot be compared at all unless they can be expressed either as concepts or pictures.

A large part of the *Philosophical Investigations* is devoted to a study of the relations between concepts, what we might call the *topography of concepts*. Wittgenstein finds a large variety of activities between concepts. They *merge* (PI 544), *cross* (PI 211), *touch* (PI p. 192), *engage with* each other (PI 136), *pass into* each other (RFM p. 157), are *analogous to* each other (OC 21), *correspond to* each other (OC 62), are *distantly related* (PI 574) or *intimately connected* (PI p. 198). (It is a strange landscape indeed, and in one place he even speaks of seeing "bits of concepts, but we don't see clearly the declivities by which one pases into others" (RFM p. 157).)

Most important are concepts which are "intimately connected though not alike," "in closest connection but not of the same kind," "run cheek by jowl and yet do not coincide" (PI pp. 198, 217). These are such pairs as *thinking* and *talking*, *imaging* and *seeing*, *seeing* and *seeing as,* and in addition *is* and *is called, knowing* and *saying, meaning* and *thinking, composite* and *simple.* In all these cases the exact points of the differences have to be carefully disentangled. Being able to do this is perhaps the "skill" which Wittgenstein connected with philosophy in the Moore Lectures Notes (MLN p. 315).

When we turn to *images,* not only is there no such topography, but it is important that *images cannot be compared at all.* We do not inwardly face our own images as "subjective objects"; hence we do not "know" them, "see" them, "possess" them. The "inner façade," so familiar in Western thought, since the beginning of the Augustinian tradition, is gone. Images are described, not because I "observe them in my own case," but because this is how they are manifested; and this itself is a grammatical statement. The Augustinian-Cartesian picture of the subject "knowing" ("apprehending," "being conscious of") its own inner happenings here disappears. (To the extent that this helps to take us "out of the grip of ourselves," it represents a philosophic and human breakthrough of the greatest importance.)

What makes it look as if images are comparable and can be related to each other and said, for example, to be different or the same is that pictures can correspond to images and pictures *can* be compared. But, nevertheless, an image is not a picture, and many images are not replaceable by pictures.

> "Before I judge that two images which I have are the same, I must recognize them as the same." And when that has happened, how am I to know that the word "same" describes what I recognize? Only if I can express my recognition in some other way, and if it is possible for someone else to teach me that "same" is the correct word here. (PI 378.)

Not only can images not be compared with each other, but they also cannot be compared with what they are images of. (For example the image of red and the red in front of me cannot be compared, as Plato realized in the *Theaetetus.*) And this, Wittgenstein says, has a "deep aspect" which "readily eludes us" (PI 387). The image "translates" into reality without any intermediary. But what is *deep* about this? It is that we feel something, not only incomprehensible, but perhaps even a little awesome about a relation so immediate that it cannot be described. (There is no epistemology here.) Understanding in this case is seeing what cannot be understood, and it is this paradox which Wittgenstein calls "the deep aspect." It "readily eludes us" because we readily imagine describing or explaining the relation here. We forget that any theories of this kind already presuppose what they are supposed to be explaining.

Criteria

I am also ready to talk of any x behind my words so long as it keeps its identity.

WITTGENSTEIN (PE p. 254)

"Things" do not carry their "identities" about inside them.

ERIC GUTKIND

In the mere concept of a thing no mark of its existence is to be found.

KANT

It is no accident that Wittgenstein's account of criteria appears to be incoherent according to the conventional wisdom.

GORDON BAKER

CHAPTER 5

Criteria

i

Concepts for Wittgenstein are primarily instruments of language or ways in which language takes phenomena, reflecting, he says, how the phenomena enter our lives and their importance for us. We have, of course, in addition to knowing concepts, to know language-games. And sometimes we need, furthermore, what Wittgenstein calls *criteria*, or ways of deciding the proper occasions for using words.

Criteria have an important place in Wittgenstein's later philosophy because, even if they are only needed when difficulties arise, as some have maintained, they are a way of linking language and the world, other than the pictorial relation of the *Tractatus*. At the very least they fix meanings, when such fixings are needed.[1] And probably no more. It is very unlikely that Wittgenstein thought that semantics needs a *foundation* or that there is any *general theory* of criteria that can be developed. Such views would be foreign to the spirit of his later philosophy and perhaps in principle impossible. Criteria are only needed *when they are needed, not all the time.*

What does Wittgenstein mean by a *criterion?* As he uses the term, it is a phenomenon which has a relation to other phenomena of such a sort that it can serve to identify the phenomena. It is a distinguishing characteristic of a complex, which is raised to the status of being a way of identifying the complex. (In many respects it is like a *landmark* by means of which we mark off territories in our conceptually organized landscapes.)

---

[1] Gordon Baker and P. M. S. Hacker have attributed to Wittgenstein a "criterial semantics," the former in an article "Criteria: A New Foundation for Semantics" in *Ratio* 16 (December 1974), pp. 156-189, and in an unpublished D.Phil. thesis at Oxford "The Logic of Vagueness" and the latter in his book *Insight and Illusion* (Oxford: Clarendon, 1972); especially the last chapter. This has been challenged by J. F. M. Hunter in a review of the Hacker book in the *International Philosophical Quarterly*, vol. xiii, no. 2 (June 1973), pp. 294-8.

A criterial relation, therefore, holds between phenomena when something (which is more or less easy to recognize) is taken as the sign of the presence of a larger complex. Hence we may say that a criterion does not belong either to the phenomena alone or to the language alone, but to both together. And the question of whether this relation holds first between phenomena or between words would certainly have no meaning for Wittgenstein.

Clearly a criterial relation is neither factual (in which one thing is *evidence* for another) nor logical (in which one term *entails* another), but is rather a sign-relation operating between phenomena *and* between words at one and the same time. It might be said that a criterion is a natural sign functioning conventionally, but, of course, both aspects come into existence together. Moaning, for example, when serving as a criterion for pain, is neither evidence for pain nor entails pain, but instead *indicates* pain when and if an indicator is needed and we accept it in that role.

The first point to be emphasized then is that a criterion is a phenomenon taken as a sign of a complex of phenomena when we need to have a "recognizer" for the complex. All criteria, as Wittgenstein uses the word, are, in this sense, criteria of identity or ways of pinning down what we will mean by a word or an expression. They come before facts because they establish what it is we are talking about when we assert facts. Establishing this is not itself making an assertion, but is rather, preliminary to making an assertion. (In this respect criteria are somewhat like the *logical forms* of the *Tractatus*, which establish *possibilities of sense prior to the assertion of facts*.)

A second main point is that a criterion precedes questions of fact because it establishes at the same time both what we may be right about *and* what we may be mistaken about. When we say that a criterion settles how to use a word in doubtful cases, this means that, even if we should be mistaken and what the criterion stands for should *not* be present, the criterion gives us something to be *mistaken about*. Having normally correct or agreed-upon ways of speaking is not only the precondition for being right, but also for being wrong. If, for example, in the presence of criteria of pain we take it that there *is* pain, then if it turns out that we are mistaken, it is still *pain* that we are mistaken about.

Here the analogy with logical forms (which in the *Tractatus* establish the possibility of both truth and falsity) appears again. Criteria by supplying what is accepted as correct ways of speaking give us what we may be *wrong about, deceived about, under an illusion about*. It might, for example, look as if it were raining and not be raining at all, and then it is just *raining* that we had criteria for identifying (asserting it is a language-game) and just *raining* that we were wrong about (PI 354).

The most common error in discussions of Wittgenstein's concept of a criterion lies in confusing what is required for language to function at all (preconditions of meaning) with factual information. Criteria do not supply factual information (even if sometimes they are based on factual information). They supply *means of recognition* and hence ways of determining whether a particular concept is the right one to use under particular circumstances. To settle this we do not have to go in search of facts, but to remind ourselves of how we use words. Thus Wittgenstein asks: When would we call something *reading* (PI 159), or *understanding* (PI 246) or an *image* (PI 239), etc.? Finding a criterion, or fixing one, gives us a way of deciding what to include under a particular concept.

Closely related to the error of thinking of a criterial relation as embodying a factual relation is that of thinking of it as something which establishes the sense of a sentence or justifies making assertions, overlooking that these require language-games. Nowhere in the *Investigations* does Wittgenstein say that a criterion establishes the sense of a sentence or justifies an assertion.[2] (Although this way of speaking does occur in the *Blue Book*, it is dropped in the *Investigations*.) What gives sense to sentences are language-games, not criteria. Applications of words and concepts also have to be distinguished from "making cognitive claims." A child, for example, might learn to call something a tree without learning to make a cognitive claim or to say "This is a tree." He might learn to use the word *tree* in all kinds of language-games without learning *that* one.

Wittgenstein nowhere in the *Investigations* speaks of a "criterial relation" as holding between sentences, and, on the contrary, always

---

[2] One commentator writes: "The sense of a sentence is determined by its criteria" and "the sense of an expression is determined by the conditions which justify asserting it and legitimate a cognitive claim." P. M. S. Hacker, *Insight and Illusion* (Oxford: Clarendon Press, 1972), pp. 263, 303. Professor Hacker's book does not bring out the importance of language-games, and for this reason puts a misplaced emphasis on concepts and criteria, making the *Philosophical Investigations* look too much like the *Tractatus*.

speaks of criteria as criteria for words, expressions, or concepts. By using a word we do not automatically make a claim, since a word can be used for many other things besides that, and, in addition, a word merely by itself or in a sentence doesn't *do* anything except as it functions in a language-game. The notion that we cannot mean anything without making factual claims dies very hard, but it is entirely foreign to Wittgenstein, for whom the presuppositional character of all aspects of meaning is the first commandment.

Criteria for Wittgenstein belong with the *apparatus* of language. They are not part of what we accomplish with language, but one of the ways by which language functions. In one place he calls a criterion a "measure of recognition" (PI 625), and we would not be far off if we thought of it as a device for supplying regularities of usage when these are thought to be necessary.

ii

A common approach to the question of criteria is to regard them as a very special kind of *evidence*, what is sometimes called "non-inductive evidence."[3] But the danger of calling criteria any kind of evidence is that it tends to confuse questions of *meaning* with questions of *truth*, two matters which Wittgenstein always tries to keep separate. In normal usage *evidence* is what counts for or against the *truth* of a statement, while *criteria* are what give *meaning* to expressions. What Wittgenstein saw clearly is that the means for identifying something cannot be the same as the evidence for it, if the evidence is to be evidence *for just that*. And there is no point in blurring this distinction by trying to use the word *evidence* in some peculiar way as if evidence could be a grammatical or logical matter.

It is easy to see how the notion of criteria as "non-inductive evidence" grew up. Criteria are chosen because they almost invariably accompany certain other phenomena and are prominent and constant enough normally to serve as signs of the other phenomena. But *we* have to give them that status in connection with the functioning of

---

[3] In a wide-ranging survey of different views of Wittgenstein's conception of criteria Gregory Lycan observes that "Shoemaker, Kenny, Malcolm and others do not mind saying that criteria are a special kind of evidence." While in the *Blue Book* Wittgenstein does indeed speak in ways which might support this, these ways of speaking are not present in the *Investigations*. See W. Gregory Lycan, "Non-Inductive Evidence: Recent Work on Wittgenstein's 'Criteria'," *American Philosophical Quarterly*, vol. 8, no. 2 (April, 1971), pp. 109-125.

our language, and the status is not of a factual, but of a grammatical character, even though it may be said to hold between phenomena. The kind of separation between language and phenomena to which we are accustomed simply does not apply to criteria, and this is doubtless what has given rise to confusion.

If—to take an example—I try to find out facts about a man named Jones, the facts that I find out are a different matter from what leads me to call him *Jones* (whether I have correctly or incorrectly called him that). In other words, whatever it is I am talking about, or searching for evidence about, is what criteria identify, and this is why criteria are not themselves evidence. If I need evidence, it is already evidence *in connection with something*, and this *something* has already been identified by some kind of criteria. (If I need facts for finding out whether *this man* is or is not Jones, then I have criteria for recognizing "this man.")

That criteria do have a different logical status from evidence becomes apparent when we examine the grammar of the word *criterion* and compare it with the grammar of the word *evidence*. We *set up* criteria (Z 245), *fix* criteria (PI 322), *accept* criteria (PI 182), *define* criteria (PI 253), *regard as* or *take as* criteria (PI 56, 573, 633). On the other hand we do *not* normally *set up, define* or *fix* evidence (except in the unusual cases involving tampering with the evidence, which might almost be understood as negating evidence). The normal use of the word *evidence* is such that we *search for, uncover, find* or *do not find* evidence. This by itself shows that, while at some points there may be parallels between the concepts of criteria and evidence, for the most part they are very different.

We can sum this up by saying that, while there are reasons for selecting the criteria we do (they are perhaps the most conspicuous, the most readily accessible, etc.) we do not normally speak of *reasons for selecting evidence*. Evidence may be *relevant* or *irrelevant*, but it is not evidence because it is *convenient* or *agreed upon*. While we might say that one of the main reasons for selecting criteria is because they are "good evidence" for the presence of phenomena which we take them as criteria of, this would be a somewhat metaphorical way of speaking since taking them as criteria is foregoing interest in them as evidence in order to accept them as indicators, or, again, to use a convenient neologism, "recognizors."

The notion that a criterion is evidence for the *existence* of something confuses questions of *identification* with questions of *existence*. An identification can be wrong, but this is not the same thing as discovering that something does not exist. Nor is asserting that something exists the same thing as identifying it, for in order to assert that something exists we have to already have identified it. And if we identified something wrongly, this is not equivalent to the assertion either that what we have identified wrongly exists or does not exist. Once again the point is that questions of identification have to do with how we are going to use words, while questions of existence have to be settled by looking and seeing.

If criteria are best not thought of as any kind of evidence, would it be any better to take the opposite tack and call them *definitions*? For indeed Wittgenstein himself in two or three places uses the expression "defining criteria." But in most cases it is clear that a criterion is not a definition, and Wittgenstein himself indicates the difference.

In a general way what serves as the mark for the *application* of a concept should be distinguished from what the concept *means*. For example, in case of a doubt, if a yellow color and an ovoid shape are *criteria* for lemons, this does not make the yellow color and the ovoid shape the *definition* of a lemon. This is not the way we use the word *definition*. We usually define a lemon by classifying it as a certain kind of fruit. The criteria, at least in this case, belong to the appearance of the object, not to its name or place in some scheme of classification. We need criteria for *immediate recognition*, not for summing up our knowledge.

In some cases, Wittgenstein indicates, the criteria for using words are far more complicated than any definition (PI 182). And only lengthy investigations can bring out the different criteria which are used in connection with the same word in many different language-games. In such cases no definition could do justice to the vast variety of different uses. And, in addition, we must remember that even concepts like *criteria* and *definition* may themselves involve families of uses with no one single factor present in all of them!

If criteria are neither evidence nor definitions, the tendency to think of them as some kind of strange mating of the two arises out of the feeling that there are only these two choices to begin with, and this is because our point of view conditions us to seeing the distinction between language and the world in this way. But, for Wittgenstein, the traditional philosopher locates his conventionalism in the wrong place, since even the grammatical aspects of language are dependent upon certain very general facts of nature and needs and interests of our own, but none of these are recognized and accepted until they are admitted into language, which in turn depends upon certain common agreements among human beings. No relation between phenomena *has* to be given a linguistic status, but, equally, not every relation *can* be.

iii

What is the logical character of a criterial relation if the relation is neither evidential nor definitional, neither in the traditional sense factual nor linguistic?

We might say that it is a logical relation in this sense: that if a criterion is present, then what-it-is-a-criterion-of must *possibly* be present. But the point is to understand the meaning which Wittgenstein gives to this *possibility* in his later philosophy. For *possibly* does not mean either *empirically* possible, or *logically* possible in the *Tractatus* sense of "all possibilities," or *merely* possible in what has been called the "image-mongering" sense. *Possibly* means in Wittgenstein's later philosophy something like *grammatically possible*—i.e. that it makes sense to say something on the basis of the presence of a criterion.

The criterial relation depends upon and helps to establish consistency of usage, enabling words to have a certain regularity of meaning within flexible limits. Criteria are variable and subject to change, often without notice, but this is in the interests of keeping a certain order among concepts.

A criterion obviously does not guarantee any fact (for nothing linguistic could do that). What it guarantees is a presence *or* an absence, a correct identification *or* a mistake, a success *or* a failure, for it is one of Wittgenstein's basic insights that the two poles in every case always go together. Like a proposition in *Tractatus* a criterion isolates the (in a sense meaningless) question of existence or non-existence, correct or incorrect, from the question of what is possibly present or putatively correct.

Consequently all that is "entailed" by something being a criterion for (someone else's) toothache (the person groaning and holding his cheek, etc.) is that the person either has a toothache or doesn't have a toothache, the toothache being what is constant in both cases. By

using the word *toothache* (which is permitted by the criteria because
this is what we normally say under these circumstances), the matter
is narrowed down to the alternatives of a *yes* or *no* (where *no* in this
case covers the possibilities of deception, illusion and other kinds of
mistakes).

Criteria, we see from this, must be understood in a wider way
than the *Tractatus* manner of speaking suggests, because criteria provide the loci for every kind of "going wrong" (and not just the case
of "falsity"). However a criterion fails, it still sets up a usage which
covers being right and also all these cases of being wrong because,
whichever way it turns out, we are right or wrong *about the same
thing* or *in the same way*. The identification holds through both alternatives.

It is criteria in Wittgenstein's later philosophy which permit the
distinction between appearance and reality to emerge since criteria
provide that which an appearance may be an appearance *of*, a deception a deception *about*, etc. The terms *appearance* and *reality* are by
no means symmetrical (any more than the terms *existence* and *non-
existence*), since the distinction between them operates within the
meaning of the term which in some sense covers them both. There is
a "systematic ambiguity" in the word "reality" as that which "underlies" appearance and hence makes it possible for appearance to *be* appearance and also as that which "negates" appearance or is "contrasted
with" appearance. A similar ambiguity lurks in the word *criteria* since
it establishes both what is to count as appearance and as reality.

Here again we see Wittgenstein's most fundamental commitment
to the distinction between *meaning* and *truth* or *meaning* and *correctness*. In the *Tractatus* the conjunct of existence and non-existence,
supplied by *logical form* and *shown* by a proposition, was always understood as logically prior to the *disjunct* of existence or non-existence,
which was the general form of a proposition and what a proposition
said. Analogously in the *Investigations* the *conjunct* of correct and incorrect, supplied by criteria, is, as it were, logically prior to their *disjunct*. We can always be wrong in taking something as a criterion,
but even in being wrong we will still be making sense because the criterion determines what making sense is in that given case.

iv

A criterion is something in the world established as a sign in language, and this indicates the kinds of situations in which there are *no criteria*, a subject to which we now turn.

When is it that we speak without criteria? Clearly situations in which we are faced with single phenomena, or even perhaps when we are not likely to speak of *phenomena* at all. Then in these cases there is no room for criteria and no need for them. There are five places in the *Investigations* where Wittgenstein speaks of this. There are *no criteria*, he says:

for identifying my own sensations (PI 288, 290)
for identifying my own image (PI 380-9)
for the redness of an image when it is my image (and for sameness when it is mine) (PI 377)
for which color it is "whose image occurs to him" (PI 239)
for determining my saying that "I" am in pain (PI 404)

We want to look now at *why* there are no criteria in these and similar cases.

A principal clue to this is supplied by the following passage:

If I assume the abrogation of the normal language-game with the expression of a sensation, I need a criterion of identity for the sensation; and then the possibility of error also exists. (PI 288.)

This tells us: (1) that in the normal language-game we do not need a criterion and (2) without this normal game we *do* need a criterion, and (3) we need it because the question of identity is then raised and with it the possibility of error.

Why is there no question of identity and no possibility of error in the normal game? The answer would seem to be because there is nothing other than the occurrence itself which could mark the occurrence and hence permit us to judge (correctly or incorrectly) *what* had occurred. In the presence of a simple phenomenon there is, as it were, nothing to identify, for we must remember that in Wittgenstein's view there is no sense in saying that "a thing is identical with itself."

Identity, in this case at least, means for Wittgenstein *identification*, and identification requires being able to play off *what* something is against its sheer occurrence or, alternately, seeming occurrence, thus permitting this latter distinction to be available even if held in abeyance. A criterion is necessary if any such distinction between being right and being in error is to emerge. A criterion is just what permits us to hold something fast over and above being right or wrong about it.

This sheds another light on why, in Wittgenstein's view, there are no criteria for simple phenomena or for one's own inner experiences. It is because in these cases meaning again cannot be separated from truth. In talking about one's immediate experience or one's inner states "whatever we are going to say is going to be the way it is" (and dishonesty is not an epistemological problem but a different language-game). In such cases we literally do not know *what* we are talking about, and indeed we are not talking about anything, since we do not have here a referential use of language. If the nature of what happens is, in effect, the happening itself, referential language cannot get a foothold (though expressive language is not affected).

What tells us whether we are dealing with an object or not (the criterion for the proper use of the concept of *object*) is not the presence of a subject, but the possibility of identifying something so as to be able to refer to it again, and this means the possibility of maintaining the distinction between *meaning* and *truth* and *meaning* and *correctness*. This is the leverage which we need for "objects" and particularly for being able to "recognize" anything where actual doubt may occur.

The two main cases which we have to consider in which there are no criteria are immediate recognition of simple external qualities such as the color red and one's own inner sensations such as a pain.

In the first case the attempt to use one's image of red as a criterion for the recognition of red fails because we are able to pick out red a large part of the time without such an image and also because there is no way of being able to pick out the image. Wittgenstein does admit that sometimes we *do* use an inner image to identify something such as a color, but this he calls a *sample* and puts it in the same category as an actual external physical sample (PI 50; BLB p. 3). Forgetting a color is then comparable to losing such a sample. While a *sample* has something in common with a *criterion* since they both enable us to recognize something, the two appear in quite different language-games. The one is like an imitation or replica, while the other is like a conspicuous feature, trademark or index. Both samples and criteria are instruments of language, but they function in quite different ways.

Something similar holds in regard to inner sensations or states. We have no criteria for recognizing inner sensations or states, but Wittgenstein does not deny that sometimes there may be what he calls "characteristic psychical accompaniments"—as, in one instance he mentions in the case of "sudden understanding" (PI 321). But these are *not* called "criteria," but "tokens" or "characteristics," as when he mentions "sensations characteristic of reading" or "sensations characteristic of cheating" (PI 159). In regard to someone else's reading I need criteria to say that he is reading, and this is why I may be tempted to take such "characteristic sensations" as criteria for applying the word *reading* in my own case. But, Wittgenstein reminds us, this is not the way we learn to say "I am reading," and not what is involved in saying this on any particular occasion.

If we consider an example which may look like a case of "identifying an inner sensation" we may see how Wittgenstein recommends looking at it. Suppose. I am in doubt about whether my sensation is a pain or an itch. We do not have to assimilate this to the picture of "identifying something." I may be uncertain what to say, but this does not mean even possibly being wrong in "recognizing" something, any more than not being able to decide with what words to express certain subtle feelings means that I am unable to "recognize" or "identify" these feelings. I hesitate, not because I "do not know what it is" (the familiar picture toward which we gravitate), but because I am looking for the best "extension" of the feeling or the sensation in words. I may imagine myself "inwardly looking" at the sensation, but this is no more than a picture, and it is precisely this picture of the "inner façade" which Wittgenstein wishes to abolish. The way in which the concept of criteria contributes to this end is in some ways the most important aspect of it.

v

One of the chief uses to which Wittgenstein's notion of criteria is put is to account for the meaning of psychological concepts in a way which avoids falling into either behaviorism (pain is pain behavior) or introspectionism (pain is directly experienced inner sensation). Wittgenstein's alternative undercuts both of these by challenging the premise common to both that we are talking *about* something in stating that pain is or is not an inner sensation. Wittgenstein maintains, as against both, that first-person inner experiences are part of an integral subjectivity, which, in the first person case, is not referred to, but only expressed, and, in the case of others, is recognized by way of *criteria*.

For Wittgenstein it is the picture of the inner object which gives rise to both behaviorism and introspectionism (or mentalism). These are two sides of the same coin because neither doubts that there are inner pains known to a subject, but they only differ on whether *this* is what pain *is*. Wittgenstein, on the other hand, wants to abolish the *mental façade itself*. We can then think of inner experiences as not having the kind of reality which can be referred to, asserted or denied (though he does not object to speaking of them as having names or being described, since both *names* and *descriptions* are terms which may have a wider use than reference to objects). What is proposed is to do away with the self's supposed relation to its own inner sensations, images, states and feelings—the somewhat schizophrenic picture of the "inner theater" which has played such an important part in philosophy. For Wittgenstein this private spectacle is an illusion. It is a picture which could only have occurred to us by imagining a relation which we have to our own inner states, based on the model of the relation which we have to "outer objects." So the façade of the "inner objects" is conjured up.

Wittgenstein's point of view is that there are very different language activities involved in expressing one's own inner states from those involved in speaking about other people's. We need criteria, above all, for deciding what psychological terms to apply to other people's behavior, but we do not need them in our own cases.

Making this distinction between first person and third person language-games and also realizing that criteria are needed for speaking about other people's psychological states meets both the behaviorist's and the introspectionist's requirements: the behaviorist's requirement that observable phenomena are all that are available in talking about other people's psychological states, and the introspectionist's requirement that this is not, however, what we mean by pain in our own case, for, in addition, we may always be wrong about the other. Criteria meet the conditions because they are observable and anchor psychological concepts applied to other people in the phenomena, while at the same time leaving room for error. And at the same time Wittgenstein recognizes that the first person language-game with the word *pain* is a very different one indeed and does not involve the application of a concept or a criterion.

The temptation which is so hard to down is to suppose that to know by criteria is something like an inferior way of knowing, as if a god-like perceiver would be able to look directly into other people's minds and see there the sensations and feelings and other "inner contents" of which the rest of us can only see the outer manifestations. Wittgenstein wishes to suggest that *even for such a god-like observer there would be nothing to see.* If we once understand that we cannot "objectivize" our own inner sensations and feelings, the temptation to imagine that it could even be theoretically possible to "see" someone else's (or for someone else to "see" ours) may disappear. Subjectivity is in a certain sense more inviolable than we have imagined. Inner sensations and feelings are a part of our integral subjectivity in a way which forbids any of this kind of "objectivity." Hence for the god-like observer, looking into anyone's mind, there is *nothing to observe.*

This is an important point (still inaccessible to "depth psychology" for example) since it means that there is no directly objectivizable subjectivity at any level, although, of course, many different kinds of myths may be created for many different purposes. From the point of view of current psychology Wittgenstein's position is almost bound to look like a sophisticated form of behaviorism, in some roundabout way denying the "mental." It will take time to see that what he has done and what is at stake is an intensification of the "subjective" and a placing of it beyond the pseudo-objectivizing of modern thought in a status which restores its importance and inviolability.

Language-Games

Our clear and simple language-games stand as *objects of comparison* . . .

WITTGENSTEIN (PI 130)

ἀτελὲς γὰρ οὐδὲν οὐδενὸς μέτρον.

. . . for nothing imperfect is the measure of anything.

PLATO

We do not wish to ground language in something else that is not language itself, nor do we wish to explain other things by means of language.

MARTIN HEIDEGGER

There are prime phenomena which in their godlike simplicity we must not disturb or infringe.

GOETHE

CHAPTER 6

Language-Games

i

Language-games are the fundamental "units of sense" in the *Investigations*. In this respect they are analogous to the elementary propositions in the *Tractatus*, although they are taken in terms of "heuristic possibilities" rather than "all possibilities." In trying to determine the *sense of a sentence* in the later philosophy we have to bring in the *use of the sentence* in connection with a particular language activity, since even the same sentence can have quite different uses depending on what we are doing with it.

What does Wittgenstein mean by the term *language-game?* Here (as always) we must pay careful attention to his actual words, which are chosen with very great care. In the passage in which the term is first introduced he gives no less than four different meanings for it (PI 7):

(1) "I . . . will sometimes speak of a primitive language as a language-game."
(2) ". . . those games by means of which children learn their native language. I will call these games 'language-games' . . ."
(3) "And the processes of naming the stones and of repeating words after someone might also be called language-games."
(4) "I shall also call the whole, consisting of language and the actions into which it is woven, the 'language-game'."

The key term here is perhaps the word *primitive* (which, in a sense, replaces the word *simple* of the *Tractatus* although Wittgenstein also speaks of "our clear and simple language-games" (PI 130)). What does the word *primitive* mean here? Since he describes language-games as *"different kinds of use (Arten der Verwendung)* of what we call 'symbols,' 'words,' 'sentences'"* (PI 23—Wittgenstein's italics), it seems plausible to regard a language-game as one kind of use of words or sentences.

Thus there is a language-game with colors, or a kind of use of words carried on with such words as *red, blue* and *yellow*. To know this game is to know a certain kind of use. (PI 30.) But the language-game with colors may also be carried on in connection with a great many other language-games, such as reporting sensations, identifying objects, giving orders, etc., etc. In many cases we will not be able to draw any line between the use of words and the use of sentences. What is the difference, Wittgenstein asks, between the report or statement "Five slabs" and the order "Five slabs"? And he replies:

> Well, it is the part which uttering these words plays in the language-game. No doubt the tone of voice and the look with which they are uttered, and much else besides, will also be different. But we could also imagine the tone's being the same. . . . (PI 21.)

If we discuss the use of the word *slab* by itself, we would be dealing with a different language-game from one involving the word *five* by itself. What will count as a single game will depend upon what we take as a single use of words, and this will depend upon the particular case in question. (It is fundamental to Wittgenstein's later point of view that there is no "absolute simplicity.")

The word *primitive* describes a simplified language, more simple than we find in actual use, but this is immediately connected with actual language by referring to it also as the kind of language by which children learn their native tongues. The *Investigations* opens with St. Augustine's simultaneous description of the nature of language and of the way children learn language. Wittgenstein then immediately describes St. Augustine's conception as "a primitive idea of the way language functions" or (a significant shift!) "the idea of a language more primitive then ours" (PI 2). A little further on he speaks of the advantage of studying "the phenomena of language in primitive kinds of use" and then immediately couples this with "A child uses such primitive forms of language when it learns to talk" (PI 5).

This repeated connecting of language-games with the way children learn language is of great importance because it establishes that language-games are not merely devices for describing language, but appear also in the actual practice of language. We are not to think of language-games as the "essence of language" or even as "ideal simplifications," and we are not to go in the *Brown Book* direction of seeing in them an *a priori* system. They are "simplifications," and "explanations," but also "training":

> A child uses such primitive forms of language when it learns to talk. Here the teaching of language is not explanation, but training. (PI 5.)

Even in the imagined case of the "builders' language" the connection with an entire tribe and with children's learning is brought in:

> We could imagine that the language of section 2 was the *whole* language of A and B, even the whole language of a tribe. The children are brought up to perform *these* actions, to use *these* words as they do so, and to react in *this* way to the words of others. (PI 6.)

The step from imagining the "builders' language" as "primitive language" to imagining it as the "whole language" of the participants or of a tribe appears to be the step to imagining it as a language-game. This permits us to consider a single use of language in isolation without having to take into account, for example, the possibilities of errors arising from confusions between different language-games, as would happen if a tribe had more than one language-game.

It might, of course, be supposed that "the means by which children learn their native language" would be a subject for empirical investigations. Is not the philosopher here intruding into the realm of fact, and indeed making assertions which might, upon investigation, turn out to be false? Wittgenstein was well aware of this point, and it is taken into account in his conception of "framework facts" (or those facts which serve to define a world view) as this is discussed in his final book *On Certainty*.[1] The statement that children learn language at least partly by means of such games is, for Wittgenstein, not a factual claim, but part of the framework which defines the way he looks at things.

Although language-games are not factual, but preconditions of facts, they are closely related to facts, as Wittgenstein points out in the following:

---

[1] This subject of "framework facts" is discussed more fully in chapter 13 below.

> If we imagine the facts otherwise than as they are, certain
> language-games lose some of their importance, while others
> become important. And in this way there is an alteration—a
> gradual one—in the use of the vocabulary of a language.
> (OC 63.)

And, in addition, language-games depend upon "primitive reactions" and "characteristic expressions" and would lose their points if these or other facts changed.

> And if things were quite different from what they actually
> are—if there were, for instance, no characteristic expression
> of pain, of fear, of joy; if rule became exception and exception rule; or if both became phenomena of roughly equal frequency—this would make our normal language-games lose
> their point.—The procedure of putting a lump of cheese on
> a balance and fixing the price by the turn of the scale would
> lose its point if it frequently happened for such lumps to
> suddenly grow or shrink for no obvious reason. (PI 142.)

These facts are the ones which we "know for certain," the ones on which we operate in our daily lives, trusting in them because we have never had any occasion not to. These are the certainties of the everyday world, which make up the roads on which we walk.

More than anything else, Wittgenstein wishes to avoid the misunderstanding that language-games are an attempt to *explain* the nature of language and thus to indicate how language might be regularized or improved. He says that, instead, they are set up "as objects of comparison" ("set up" in the sense of "taken as," not of "invented").

> For we can avoid ineptness or emptiness in our assertions
> only by presenting the model as what it is, as an object of
> comparison—as, so to speak, a measuring rod; not as a preconceived idea to which reality *must* correspond. . . .
> We want to establish an order in our knowledge of the use
> of language: an order with a particular end in view; one out
> of many possible orders; not *the* order. (PI 130-1.)

Language-games are a certain way of looking at language. Wittgenstein seems to suggest, not the only way and not even necessarily the best way, but *a* way to arrive at philosophical clarity.

In the early philosophy it was language itself which was understood as a measure of the world. Here in the later philosophy language no longer measures the world, but *we measure language*. Language-games are a particular kind of simplifying scheme, an analogical model, which may be employed pretty much as we choose, to bring out similarities and dissimilarities in the functionings of language to prevent us from being misled by apparent similarities and apparent dissimilarities. Language-games help us to isolate *kinds of use* of words and in this way to avoid puzzles generated by putting together what does not belong together.

This is not, however, the end of the matter, for there is another side to language-games. Wittgenstein also speaks of language-games being played, of them being *there* and of our *noting* them. He says that what happens is a "proto-phenomenon" and we ought to say of it "this language-game is played." The way of speaking in terms of language-games is the way in which we identify the basic thing which happens. Here the phenomenon is not something different from the language-game, but the language-game is the phenomenon.

> You must bear in mind that the language-game is so to say
> something unpredictable. I mean: it is not based on grounds.
> It is not reasonable (or unreasonable).
> It is there—like our life.   (OC 559.)

Is there a conflict between thinking of language-games as "objects of comparison" (and even something which on occasion Wittgenstein *invents*) and thinking of them as "Ur-phenomena" which *are there—like our life*? If the language-games bring an order into the phenomena, it is an order which is perceived as being there, for there is no gap for Wittgenstein between the phenomena and the way of seeing the phenomena. That the phenomena can be seen in other ways also (i.e. that there are other different aspects) does not mean that they have some "independent" character apart from *every* way in which they are seen.

It is characteristic of Wittgenstein's point of view in general that no gap occurs between "the way the world is" and "the way we say it" (except in cases where such a discrepancy actually occurs, and then this, too, is something that we may say). The same principle, it would seem, applies here in the relation between language as a phenomenon and the language-game way of describing language as a phenomenon. That there are different aspects of language as a phenomenon (and different ways of being interested in it) does not discredit any aspect.

We can now summarize the intricate strategy of the opening pages of the *Philosophical Investigations*, leading up to the introduction of the term *language-game* in section 7. First, St. Augustine's treatment of words as being all of the same kind is contrasted with a specific case of *shopping for five red apples* in order to help us see that here there are three very different kinds of words. (In the terminology later to be introduced these will be three different language-games or three different kinds of uses of words—the uses of *five*, of *red* and of *apples*.) At this point then the first primitive language is introduced—the builder's language. In the next section this helps us to see what is right in Augustine's view—that it is an idea of a primitive language (PI 3, 4); the advantage of proceeding in terms of such primitive languages is mentioned (PI 5) and we are reminded that such primitive languages enter into the training of children (PI 6). It is only after all this that we are ready for the introduction of the concept of language-games with the fourfold description of them (PI 7) which is elaborated on in the succeeding pages (PI 7-25). Following this a discussion of names (PI 26-48) leads to the introduction of the second language-game, which is essentially that of Wittgenstein's own *Tractatus* (and also one mentioned in Plato's *Theaetetus*) (PI 48-64), and this opens the way for Wittgenstein to discuss and correct his earlier fixation on this one language-game. So we are led step by step to a reunderstanding of what was actually being done in the *Tractatus*, a reunderstanding in which that becomes one more language-game.

ii

Language-games are fundamental in Wittgenstein's later philosophy. They are the absolute starting point. This means that they can neither be explained nor justified. The idea of trying to account for them (or for language) in psychological, social, epistemological or metaphysical terms has to be given up, for any such accounts will themselves be additional language activities, already themselves presupposing what they are supposed to be explaining. (There is no language-game of explaining language-games, though there is, in philosophy itself, one of describing them.) Language-games are the primary thing, coming before any experience, feeling or imagined reality.

Our mistake is to look for an explanation where we ought to look at what happens as a "proto-phenomenon." That is, where we ought to have said: *this language-game is played.*
The question is not one of explaining a language-game by means of our experience, but of noting a language-game.
. . . Look on the language-game as the *primary* thing. And on the feelings, etc. as you look on a way of regarding the language-game, as interpretation. (PI 654-6.)

Our "feeling" that, for example, there is something that is outside of language does not, this says, have the kind of status that we would like to give it as indicating that there *is* something beyond the language-game. When we attempt to make this meaningful, we are always within a language-game. What is supposed to be accessible beyond the language-game (for example, through an experience of something upon which the language-game rests) always involves us in some other language-game, if not merely an extension of the one we are attempting to "ground." Since language-games provide all ways of speaking, there is no way of making sense outside of them. (In *On Certainty*, as is discussed in a later chapter, this position is modified in a way which overcomes the complete separateness of language-games from each other.)

When we note a language-game or (what is, as we will see, related to it) a form of life, we are *not* noting a fact, something like a "social or cultural fact." We are noting an *agreed-upon activity* which thereby establishes a *possibility of sense*. In one group, for example, there may be a language-game of augury-by-birds, while in another there is a game of telling-dreams-to-a-psychoanalyst and in still another one of writing-reports-on-such-things. Since all language-games stand on the same footing, the attempt to develop theories about the causes for the development of language-games can itself be no more than an additional language-game, whatever else we may imagine it to be. In talking about language-games we are not supplying facts; but, as Wittgenstein puts it, everything descriptive of a language-game is part of logic (OC 57).

Although language-games are a logical precondition (arising out of a certain way of looking at the phenomena of language) they are by no means fixed. There are, Wittgenstein says, countless language-games, countless types of language, and new ones "come into existence and others become obsolete and get forgotten" (PI 23). Not only this, but language-games are, in effect, the veritable innovative point in language. Wittgenstein calls them "unpredictable" and "spontaneous," saying

> Something new (spontaneous, "specific") is always a language-game. (PI p. 224.)

"Newness" belongs to new ways of talking, associated with seeing in some new way. Wittgenstein gives as an example of a new language-game in philosophy the "sense data" way of seeing and talking, which he calls a "grammatical movement."

> What you have primarily discovered is a new way of looking at things. As if you had invented a new way of painting, or, again, a new metre, or a new kind of song. (PI 401.)

That changes may occur in language-games first, and then later in meanings of words is expressed in this sentence:

> When language-games change, then there is a change in concepts, and with the concepts the meanings of words change. (OC 65.)

First, in such cases, we see a whole new way of speaking, and then this leads to perhaps a whole battery of words taking on new meanings. (In the sense data language-game, for example, such words as *impression* or *sensation* acquired different grammars.)

The *spontaneous, originative, primal* character of language-games is one of the most illuminating insights in the *Philosophical Investigations*. It is revealing of Wittgenstein's fundamental point of view that he sees as *fundamental change*, not the discovery of new facts or the development of new theories, but the appearance of new perspectives, new ways of thinking and speaking. (That this is true also in the field of science has lately become more evident with the discussion of the nature of "scientific revolutions.") The ways in which new kinds of "proofs" or new kinds of "numbers" appear in mathematics seem to have much more in common than we might at first imagine with the ways in which new forms and new styles appear in art and poetry. (Wittgenstein's own conception of language-games is, of course, such a new "style" in philosophy).

That language-games are simultaneously the most fundamental precondition *and* the source of the most fundamental newness (and both of these in a way which is connected with *ways of looking*) does not present a problem to those familiar with Wittgenstein's style of thought. (It will be remembered that in the *Tractatus* the composition of elementary propositions could not be given in advance either (T 5.55, 5.557).) These two aspects of language-games shed light on the metaphor of the *game*.

It is sometimes asked why Wittgenstein did not simply speak of language-*activities*, why he insisted on the expression language-*games*. The first answer appears to be because he wanted to stress the formal, rather than the factual character of language, and this in line with the following observation in the *Philosophical Grammar*:

> The explanation of a meaning is no experiential proposition and no causal explanation; but a rule, an agreement. (PG p. 68.)

A game has a certain completeness—it has a beginning and an end; it has a normative character—it is played correctly or incorrectly; and it has a *point*—it allows of success or failure beyond its rules. In addition, games are so various that they have no one common denominator (the concept of game, as ordinarily used, has no fixed boundaries); and games are invented and disappear as a matter of fact. In all these respects games are an apt metaphor for primal language activities. In order to play a game there must be a commitment to a pattern which, as it were, preexists the actual playing (even if this pattern is changed in the course of the playing). And it is there being such a framework in language activities that, above all, the game metaphor brings out.

If Wittgenstein were to speak merely of language-activities, the *formal* aspect of language, which is what interests him, would not come into evidence. Wittgenstein states that he is interested in language as a phenomenon and not as a means to a particular end; in other words, he is not interested in how we bend language to our will, but rather in what language itself does and can do. Individual psychology and specific social considerations are simply not relevant. Language-games are not part of any theory about language, but are *one way of looking at language as a phenomenon*.

Even when a language is invented, as it were specifically for a definite purpose, Wittgenstein comments:

> To invent a language could mean to invent an instrument for
> a particular purpose on the basis of the laws of nature (or
> consistently with them); but it also has the other sense, anal-
> ogous to that in which we speak of the invention of a game.
> (PI 492.)

The language-game is *not* to be understood as a tool (and nowhere
does Wittgenstein speak of *using* language-games); and this is important because the language activity, to bring out what Wittgenstein is
interested in, must be thought of as *self-contained* and having its point
in itself (in addition, of course, to being human creations operating
within human situations). There must be no further *raison d'être* for
the language-game; it must be done for its own sake, or we will not
be able to see its formal nature.

Wittgenstein's "builders' language" is his own prime example of
a language-game, and, therefore, worth looking at more closely. It resembles a game in two important respects: (1) it is an activity which
may be carried on correctly or incorrectly and (2) even if it is carried
on correctly, it may still be done successfully or unsuccessfully. We
are not told whether the stones are already separated or are jumbled
together, how heavy they are, how difficult or easy to carry, how far
they have to be carried, how fast, what the incentives are, what the
status of the participants is in relation to each other, how old, healthy,
cooperative, experienced they are, etc., etc. Within certain broad limits
(which would constitute the "framework of general facts") these things
do not matter. Nor do we need to know the general state of the people who put up such buildings—their culture and environment.

What is it then that does matter? That they are jointly committed
to what can be regarded as a single activity where there are established
inter-locking behaviors, which all together have what we would call
a meaningful character, and the whole thing is carried on by speech.
(We can think of the language-game as merely the language aspect
of the whole affair, or as the language *plus* the activity of the building
(PI 7).) What is essential is that the men (1) can make mistakes—disobey, misunderstand, etc., (2) while carrying on the activity correctly,
may still not do a good job, (3) have had to learn how to function with
language in this particular way. Why do these people give orders and
obey them? There is nothing that would count as an answer from
Wittgenstein's point of view. It is just one of the things which they do.

iii

In order to see the full importance of language-games in Wittgenstein's philosophy we have to recognize that for Wittgenstein it is language-games which embody both the categorical features of the world which philosophers have called metaphysical features, and also the features of knowing which philosophers have called epistemological. In short, as in Wittgenstein's point of view throughout his life, it is the *possibilities of meaning* which establish both the ontological and the epistemological, and not, as in traditional philosophy, the other way around.

What have been regarded as "different kinds of being," in Wittgenstein's philosophy appear as "different ways of speaking" or different language-games. Thus, for example, the differences between a thing, a quality, a relation, a space, a time, a color, a number, a shape, a sensation, an emotion, a motive, an impulse, a disposition, etc., etc., appear as different grammatical possibilities or different language-games. There are different ways of making sense involved with each of these concepts, and this is what the differences between them amount to. We are not, in other words, confronted by "different kinds of realities," but rather by "different possibilities of speaking."

Words of such different kinds have such different grammars, as Wittgenstein sees it, not because the natures of what they refer to are so different (what do we know about what they refer to, except again what we say?) but because these possibilities of making sense have indeed appeared in language. (This should content us; there is nothing more that we need to look for and nothing more that we could find—except more language.)

That all the "metaphysical" foundations of things should appear only as different kinds of uses of language (or different types of language) should discourage us from looking for some further foundation for these types of language themselves. The last stand of the "absolute object" was made in the *Tractatus* where it was only something like an adjunct of logic and where finally it too was dismissed at the end as something which could not really be said in any case.

There is, of course, no objection to the ordinary use of the word *object;* only its metaphysical use has been abandoned. And with it also the "degrees of objectification," by which metaphysicians claim the right to talk "objectively" about all kinds of subjective, ethical, religious and other matters. The term "object" cannot be given any clear meanings when it is used in such ways, even if it appears to have meaning.

In the *Blue Book* Wittgenstein specifically repudiates the notion of metaphysically different "kinds of objects." He says, for example, that those who say that a *sense datum* is a different "kind of object" from a *physical thing*, or that a *number* is a different "kind of object" from a *numeral* are not making a statement like "A railway train, a railway station and a railway car are different kinds of objects," but rather one like "A railway train, a railway accident, and a railway law are different kinds of objects." (BLB p. 64.) This latter sentence involves the differences between a *thing*, an *event*, and a *rule*, and to call these all *objects* is to deprive the word *object* of any meaning whatever.

To speak of concepts embodying "categorical differences," as some philosophers have done, as "the most general concepts with empirical reference" is meaningless for Wittgenstein, since we cannot give any meanings to the supposed different empirical referents except by bringing out precisely the very same grammatical differences which the referents are supposed to account for. We have no *special access* to the referents other than that linguistic access which for some reason we are not satisfied with.

Something similar to what we have been describing as the traditional metaphysical features of the world appearing for Wittgenstein only within language applies also to the epistemological. Thus Wittgenstein says that *doubt* works only in a language-game (PI 288, 24), the kind of *certainty* is the kind of language-game (PI 224), *mistakes* belong to language-games (PI 56; OC 196), *pointing* is part of a language-game (PI 669). This indicates that language-games themselves already involve as part of their sense the kinds of possibilities for knowing and doubting which traditionally were supposed to be the *basis* for what we say, rather than *implicit* in what we say. (This point is supplemented and modified in Wittgenstein's final work *On Certainty* where the question of *a general framework of certainty for all language-games* is discussed.)

Different "kinds of knowledge" (like different "kinds of being") are implicit in different kinds of meaning or different ways of making sense. Here again Wittgenstein reverses the traditional picture. It is not that we have to *know* something in order to *mean* something, but rather *our knowing too must have meaning*, and that comes first. It would not make sense to talk about knowing which was not already a way of making sense.

iv

Language-games, in the dozens of examples which Wittgenstein gives of them, are of such a bewildering variety and crisscross and combine in such an extraordinary number of ways that the very idea of classifying them is ruled out of court right at the beginning.

To give an example of this, Wittgenstein says in one place that "lying is a language-game that needs to be learned like any other" (PI 249). Among his own list of examples which we will discuss shortly, are included "reporting an event," "play-acting," and "making a joke." Using these examples, it is clear that we can make up almost an endless variety of combinations: lying in reporting an event; reporting an event of lying; lying about making a joke of reporting an event; making a joke of lying in reporting an event; play-acting lying about making a joke of reporting an event, etc., etc.

It would appear that some language-games are indeed more "fundamental" that others, and Wittgenstein sometimes speaks of them in this way. But after an abortive attempt in the *Brown Book* to establish some such order, he seems to have realized the futility of it, for the attempt is always open to the ever-present danger of once again, as in the *Tractatus*, getting involved in some ultra-language-game.

When Wittgenstein, nevertheless, comes to give his list of examples of language-games in section 23 of the *Investigations*, it is clear that it is far from a random list. Examination shows that the list is constructed with very great care indeed, and if it is presented somewhat casually, there is still no doubt that it lists fifteen of the very best examples Wittgenstein could find, each one, as it were, being something like a full-blown example of what he in other places mentions as perhaps a less developed language-game or perhaps even just a concept.

If we take a careful look at the language-games on Wittgenstein's list one by one, it may occur to us that we do have here a very effective (if not a fundamental!) list.

Giving orders, and obeying them—
Describing the appearance of an object, or giving its measurements—
Constructing an object from a description (a drawing)—

Reporting an event—
Speculating about an event—
Forming and testing an hypothesis—
Presenting the results of an experiment in tables and diagrams—
Making up a story; and reading it—
Play-acting—
Singing catches—
Guessing riddles—
Making a joke; telling it—
Solving a problem in practical arithmetic—
Translating from one language into another—
Asking, thanking, cursing, greeting, praying—

Whole clusters of games, as we will see, are connected with each of these; and in addition there are all kinds of intermediate cases. Wittgenstein often appears to have chosen the most full-blown ordinary examples, rather than simpler ones which might have come to mind. It is *games in practice* that he is interested in here, rather than artificially simplified ones.

(1) *Giving orders and obeying them*—
It is no accident that this comes first on Wittgenstein's list and that it is also the language-game which comes first in the book and which is discussed at greatest length (PI 2, 8). Indeed the change from the *Tractatus* to the *Investigations* may be symbolized by the fact that "giving orders" is placed first, while "naming objects," the one and only game of the *Tractatus*, only appears as the second example discussed at length in the *Investigations* (PI 48).[2] An indication of why this language-game now comes first may be gathered from two considerations: (1) that *obeying an order* is analogous to *following a rule* (PI 206), and this latter in turn is related to *many* different language-games and (2) *obeying an order*, Wittgenstein says, may be translated immediately into either a proposition, a demonstration or an action

---

2 It was a lecture by the mathematician L. E. J. Brouwer, delivered in Vienna on March 10, 1928, which has been credited by a number of people, who were present, with reviving Wittgenstein's interest in philosophy. Brouwer's lecture on *Mathematics Science and Language* began by describing the three subjects mentioned in his title as "die Hauptfunktionen der Aktivität der Menschheit." This indicates the strongly functionalist and optative character of Brouwer's philosophy, which in itself would have been a challenge to Wittgenstein's still strong structuralism. This matter is discussed further in an Appendix to the present book on *Wittgenstein and Brouwer*.

(PI 459). It is important also that the transition from an order to its execution in action is a basic jump which cannot be further explained (PI 431-3). It should be noted also that *giving and obeying orders* is related to *guiding and being guided by*, which can be involved in a great number of language-games (PI 172), and to *influencing* and *being influenced by* (PI 206, 491), as well as to various games connected with learning such as *repeating after* (PI 7) and *imitating* (PI 285).

(2) *Describing the appearance of an object, or giving its measurements—*

Of all the many language-games in which descriptions figure (as, for example, "description of a body's position by means of its coordinates; description of a facial expression; description of a sensation of touch, of a mood" (PI 24)) this, it seems, still gets special mention. But it is perhaps important that Wittgenstein still does not speak of *describing an object*, but of *describing the appearance of an object*. (We recall the *Tractatus* position that objects can only be named.) To speak of *describing an object* might well involve a different language-game, an hypothesis, rather than a description. It is also significant that *giving the measurements of an object* is included here as belonging to the same language-game as *describing its appearance*. This, if we take it at its face value, suggests that *measurements* are not to be thought of as in any fundamental way different from *appearance;* there would be no basis for thinking of them as, for example, more "primary."

(3) *Constructing an object from a description (a drawing)—*

This language-game appears to be the inverse of the immediately preceding one, since it goes *from* a description *to* an object rather than the reverse. Related to this would be many language-games having to do with *making* things—building, sculpting, manufacturing. Perhaps even the most elementary tool-making might be understood as an instance of this language-game.

(4) *Reporting an event—*

The distinction between objects and events, which in the *Tractatus* was handled by different forms of objects (T 2.0251) here appears as two different kinds of language. By calling something (e.g. a piece of paper) an *object* and something else (e.g. the burning of the piece of paper) an *event* we involve otherselves with different grammars. If

someone tells us that he has seen a red disc flash across the sky, this
might be understood both as a "description of the appearance of an
object" and a "report of an event," and presumably it might happen
that the "description of the appearance of an object" *is* the "report of
an event." Our ability, however, to continue with further questions
such as "How big was the disc?" (asking for further description) or
"When did you see it?" (asking for further report) could serve to
distinguish the two games.

(5) *Speculating about an event—*
This seems an additional step to the immediately preceding game, talking about what *might* have happened or *may* happen or *could* have
happened or *can* happen instead of what *did* happen. If we see an object fall off a table, this is not the same kind of language as if we see
it teetering on the edge and say it *may* fall off. A quite different way
of going wrong would be involved. This language-game would appear to be prototypical for all instances of reconstructing the past or
imagining the future. An element of interpretation would seem to
come in here in a way which is not the case with the previous language-games.

(6) *Forming and testing an hypothesis—*
What would seem to distinguish an *hypothesis* in Wittgenstein's list
from a *speculation* would seem to be the *testing*. Presumably the hypothesis differs from a description or a report in that it asserts some kind
of a connection between phenomena, but it is the testing which lifts
this out of the realm of speculating. In other places Wittgenstein links
hypotheses with "models designed to explain, to sum up what you
observe" (PI 156) as well as with natural laws (PI 325), and in these
cases the models and the laws presumably are subject to tests, for this
is part of the game with hypotheses.

(7) *Presenting the results of an experiment in tables and diagrams—*
Again a game related to the immediately preceding game. What seems
to characterize an *experiment* is that there are results to be presented
in tables and diagrams. The results have to be actual and not merely
imagined. (PI 265). Wittgenstein also undoubtedly has in mind the
distinction, so important to him, between a *calculation* and an *experiment*, where in the former case the outcome is part of the process,
while in the latter it is not. Different kinds of mistakes are possible in

the two cases, since there is no one right outcome for an experiment. We also have to distinguish between experiments and other kinds of investigations since "it takes a particular context to make a certain action into an experiment" (PI p. 188).

(8) *Making up a story; and reading it—*
This might look like two different language-games, but it is certainly Wittgenstein's point that if we know how to do one, then we would know how to do the other. Taking a story *as a story* would be the same in each case. If we do not know what *making up a story* is, then we will not know what *reading a story* is either. Reading a report or reading a newspaper is a different language-game from reading a story because the same words may be taken in a completely different way. The fact that we call both of these cases of *reading* does not mean that they are the same activity in the two cases anymore than buying a house or paying taxes are the same activity because they both involve spending money. (Cf. the long discussion of *reading* in PI 156-71.)

(9) *Play-acting—*
This language-game is obviously related to *pretending* (PI 156, pp. 228-9) and *simulating* (PI 249-50), as well as to *imitating* (PI 285, 450). We might say that it is a full expression of these other games and also the first game which has the element of *play* in it. Pretense for entertainment or edification would have to be distinguished from pretense for deceit, which is another language-game.

(10) *Singing catches—*
This may suggest a prototype of poetry and song, in which rhythm and intonation are especially important. Wittgenstein in several places mentions similarities between language and music as well as between poetry and music. (Cf. PI 527.) He emphasizes in several places the importance of tones of voice (PI 541, 643, p. 214).

(11) *Guessing riddles—*
There are many language-games involving *guessing*: as, for example, guessing the meaning of definitions (PI 32), what time it is (PI 266, 607), what a person means (PI 210), what a person is pointing to (PI 33), intentions or thoughts (PI pp. 222-3). (We cannot, however, *guess* how a word functions (PI 340).) Many things also may appear as *riddles*. Wittgenstein says at one point that "one human being can be a complete riddle (*Rätsel*) to another" (PI p. 223). (Philosophy

also may be conceived as guessing riddles, as witness Charles Peirce's famous essay "A Guess at the Riddle.")

(12) *Making a joke; telling it—*
Wittgenstein is reported to have said that he could imagine an entire philosophy made up only of jokes—a remark which would have been appreciated by a Zen monk or a Sufi sage. Elsewhere he said that if a person (Hilbert) could describe Cantor's transfinite mathematics as a "paradise," he (Wittgenstein) had an equal right to describe it as a joke. Paradoxes might be thought of, not as signs of something "deep," but as something humorous, like trying to make a donkey go in two directions at once. Wittgenstein suggested that grammatical jokes were felt to be "deep" for the same reason that philosophy was felt to be "deep," because they both involved forms of language (PI 111).

(13) *Solving a problem in practical arithmetic—*
We know from Wittgenstein's writings on mathematics that this is for him the "basis" of mathematics. In one place he said, criticizing those who claimed that "Russell somehow got nearer to the bottom of arithmetic," that "a child has got at the bottom of arithmetic in knowing how to apply numbers, and that's all there is to it" (MN p. 68). The word *practical* here is important because of his view that "All the calculi in mathematics have been invented to suit experience and yet they are independent of experience" (MN p. 1). Like language, mathematics is usable and is used, or it is not mathematics.

(14) *Translating from one language to another—*
This is the language-game which includes many kinds of definitions, projections, correlations, transcriptions, decipherings, etc. And it is obviously related to such activities as indexing, cataloguing, briefing, reviewing, etc. We cannot translate from one *language-game* into another, because language-games are independent of each other, but we can translate from one language into another in the many different ways in which we do.

(15) *Asking, thanking, cursing, greeting, praying—*
This is one of the most intriguing of all Wittgenstein's examples of language-games because it may appear at first to be five separate games, perhaps even a miscellaneous collection to round out the list. Further reflection, however, shows that this is one single language-game, which might be called the *ceremonial use* of words, and that it is this lan-

guage-game which is closest to being essential to religion. (It would indeed have been odd if Wittgenstein had not made room for a game of this sort on his list.) What links these five activities, which from certain points of view might appear to be very different, is that they are all language addressed to other persons and might, for example, be addressed to humans or to gods. Understanding one, we very possibly would understand the others. Wittgenstein may have selected them as most representative of innumerable examples of ritual or ceremonial uses of language. (The subject is discussed more fully in connection with Wittgenstein's "Notes on Frazer's *Golden Bough*" in Chapter 12 below.)

Forms of Life

The developmental hypothesis, however, I can see as nothing but the costume of a formal connection.

WITTGENSTEIN (NFGB p. 242)

Only the most naive people can imagine that there can exist in the world anything more important than a convention.

PAUL VALERY

Nothing is more requisite for a true philosopher than to restrain the intemperate desire for searching into causes.

DAVID HUME

Searching for *wisdom*, we may find it in knowing that causal thinking and acting is non-beautiful and hard to justify, and that in the long run it brings disappointment.

L. E. J. BROUWER

CHAPTER 7

Forms of Life

i

No concept in Wittgenstein's later philosophy is more difficult to understand and has given rise to more differences of interpretation that the concept of *forms of life*. The expression occurs only five times in the *Philosophical Investigations*, and nowhere does Wittgenstein attempt to define it. Yet it is of fundamental importance and has to be understood along with the concept of language-games, with which it is closely connected.

Before we explore the meaning of *forms of life* it may be helpful to look at a summary of some of the current interpretations brought together in an article by J. F. M. Hunter entitled " 'Forms of Life' in Wittgenstein's *Philosophical Investigations*."[1] Professor Hunter discusses the following four interpretations, the last one of which he himself accepts:

1 — "A form of life is the same as a language-game, and calling a language-game a form of life is saying that it is something formalized or standardized in our life; that it is one of life's forms."
2 — "A form of life is a sort of package of mutually related tendencies to behave in various ways: to have certain facial expressions and to make certain gestures, to do certain things like count apples or help people and to say certain things."
3 — "To say that something is a form of life is to say that it is a way of life, or a mode, manner, fashion or style of life; that it has something important to do with the class structure, the values, the religion, the type of industry and commerce and of recreation that characterize a group of people."

---

[1] in *American Philosophical Quarterly*, Vol. 5, No. 4 (October, 1968), pp. 233-243.

4 — ". . . the sense I am suggesting for it is more like something typical
of a living being: typical in the sense of being very broadly in the
same class as the growth or nutrition of living organisms or as
the organic complexity which enables them to propel themselves
about, or to react in complicated ways to their environment."

It would be hard to imagine a more "un-Wittgensteinian" list than
this; for these interpretations are completely lacking in the simplicity
which is the hall-mark of Wittgenstein's basic concepts. We sense
immediately that something is wrong. The four interpretations actually represent attempts to take what is a "meaning-concept" and understand it (1) as the same as a language-game, (2) psychologically,
(3) culturally in a superficial sense and (4) biologically. But all these
interpretations miss the point, which is both more obvious and more
simple and yet more difficult to understand. With the exception of the
first one (which does not fit in with what Wittgenstein says about
language-games and forms of life), all these interpretations have a
factual or quasi-factual character, rather than a grammatical or semantic
one. Wittgenstein's understanding of forms of life is not concerned
with anything biological or psychological and also is not restricted to
any particular kind of social or cultural fact. It covers rather all social
or cultural behavior *in so far as it is meaningful.*

Social philosophers (or theorists in sociology) will understand this
best: that what Wittgenstein calls *forms of life* are roughly what they
call "social facts" or "institutional facts"; only for Wittgenstein they
are not "facts," but units of meaningful action which are carried out
together by members of a social group and which have a common
meaning for the members of the group. Wittgenstein does not regard
these as many sociologists do as *facts,* but rather as *forms,* which means
possibilities of meaning, analogous to language-games, but in the area
of human social actions. Forms of life are established *patterns of action*
shared in by members of a group.

In the first instance these are carried on by and with language,
and Wittgenstein gives some examples in the early pages of the *Investigations: shopping, building, fighting battles, calculating.* (The last two
are specifically mentioned as forms of life.) Any action which is established as belonging to a group and which has a common meaning
shared in by the members of that group is a form of life.

To say then that a form of life is a pattern of meaningful behavior in so far as this is constituted by a group is to distinguish it, on the one hand, from behavior which does not have such meaning as, for example, physical or biological happenings, and, on the other hand, from totally individual behavior which, while it may be "meaningful" in some sense, is not an *established group meaning*. Shopping, for example, is something which people do in some societies and which is shared in by them as a meaningful activity. So also are battles, in so far as by this we mean something regularized, "institutionalized" and "common."

It is significant that all of Wittgenstein's five references in the *Investigations* to forms of life mention language, which shows how forms of life are interwoven with language. But it is stressed that it is *speaking* language which is *part* of a form of life (PI 23), and it is language in this sense which cannot be imagined apart from a form of life. Indeed, Wittgenstein even says that to imagine a language *means* to imagine a form of life (PI 19), and we should note this word *means*. If, for example, we try to imagine an actual occurrence of the language-game of giving orders, we have to imagine it in connection with *some* activity. There is no such thing as just giving and obeying orders, as it were in general. The orders have to be *about* something; they have to have a setting in some activity, and this is a form of life.

The inevitable setting of language is some human activity which is meaningful in the terms in which the language with which it is carried out is meaningful. That it *is* carried on with language might be taken as a criterion of meaningfulness, distinguishing what people do that makes sense not only because it is recognizable as a recurrent pattern of behavior, but because it is recognizable as something which makes sense *from the standpoint of those who do it*.

A sheer physiological response or an individually unique response is not, therefore, to be understood as a form of life since it does not represent a recognizable way of acting as an accepted pattern by those who do it. In these cases, for example, an observer would not have to understand a language in order to understand what was going on. Nor would what was going on be a case of some commonly shared regular way of doing things.

To put the matter somewhat differently: a form of life is a possibility of meaningful action shared in by members of a group, and hence repeatable by different members of the group on different occasions, and (within certain limits) in different kinds of circumstances.

These are the activities which we call social or cultural and which
have to be understood if we are to understand what people are doing
and even to make sense out of what they say.

This helps us to see why a form of life cannot *be* a language-
game (as in the first interpretation mentioned by Professor Hunter),
for the same language-games (e.g. giving and obeying orders, or describing the appearance of objects, to mention two of Wittgenstein's
examples), may function in connection with many different forms of
life; as, conversely, many language-games may be united in a single
form of life.

In the case of Wittgenstein's example of *shopping for five red
apples*, for example, we have one meaningful activity or form of life
carried out by means of three different language-games—in this case
counting, identifying colors and picking out objects. The three games
are unified into one meaningful pattern of action. It is easy to imagine
the three games functioning in terms of other quite different forms of
life: as, for example, awarding five red apples, painting a picture of
five red apples, teaching arithmetic by means of five red apples, etc.

In Wittgenstein's highly artificial example of the builders (PI 2)
we have one language-game (giving and obeying orders) and one form
of life (building) inter-fused, but here too we can easily imagine different language-games introduced as additional parts of the same
form of life as, for example, describing the stones or numbering them.
And we can also imagine the language-games (and the stones themselves) as parts of many different forms of life other than building—a
ceremony, a sport, an archeological dig, etc.

Because many language-games may be carried on in connection
with the same form of life and many forms of life may be carried on
with the same language-game it makes no sense to speak of a language-
game as itself *being* a form of life. Nor does it make sense to say what
many have carelessly said to be Wittgenstein's view—that "language is
a form of life." No such statement was ever made by Wittgenstein.
It should not surprise us that a single language activity may occur in
connection with many different social actions and the reverse.

There is an interesting parallel between *forms of life* and *forms
of objects* as these latter figured in the *Tractatus*. In each case we have
to do with *possibilities of meaning* as these are outside of language,
but nevertheless necessary for language. In the *Tractatus* the objects
give the possible structures of the world (which in terms of the pic-

ture conception of language it is necessary for objects to represent), while in the *Investigations* the forms of life give the possible common actions (which in terms of the use conception of language are necessary for common uses). Forms of life are the intelligible settings of language in human affairs as forms of objects were the intelligible structures in the world.[2]

ii

What Wittgenstein means by a *form of life* comes out succinctly in one of his unpublished notebooks.[3]

> our language, characteristic that it is built on regularities of doing (*Tat*) (*Handlung*), fixed forms of life. (VWC 119.)

That language is embedded in acting, which involves also patterns of regularity, making it impossible sometimes to understand the language except in connection with the acting, is a recurrent theme.

> . . . it is not a kind of *seeing* on our part; it is our *acting*, which lies at the bottom of the language-game. (OC 204.)

We are constantly reminded that both language and the activities with which it is connected are *practices*, and they lie beyond being justified or unjustified, in this respect resembling "something animal." (OC 358-9.)

With this in mind we can turn to the five appearances of the term *form of life* in the *Investigations*, giving them here for easy reference:

(1) It is easy to imagine a language consisting only of orders and reports in battle—Or a language consisting only of questions and expressions for answering yes and no. And innumerable others.—And to imagine a language means to imagine a form of life. (PI 19.)

(2) Here the term "language-game" is meant to bring into prominence the fact that the *speaking* of language is part of an activity, or of a form of life. (PI 23.)

(3) "So you are saying that human agreement decides what is true

---

[2] The reader should consult again the table of comparisons between the *Tractatus* and the *Philosophical Investigations* given in Chapter 1.

[3] This notebook is identified as Band XV, date 24/8/37-19/11/37 (Von Wright's Catalogue No. 119). The entry here is quoted by L. A. Schmucker, "Wittgenstein's Remarks on Basic Views," Diss. Univ. of Texas, 1970, p. 114.

and what is false?"—It is what human beings *say* that is true and false; and they agree in the *language* they use. That is not agreement in opinions but in form of life. (PI 241.)

(4) Can only those hope who can talk? Only those who have mastered the use of a language. That is to say, the phenomena of hope are modes of this complicated form of life. (If a concept refers to a characteristic of human handwriting, it has no application to beings who do not write.) (PI p. 174.)

(5) It is no doubt true that you could not calculate with certain sorts of paper and ink, if, that is, they were subject to certain queer changes—but still the fact that they changed could in turn only be got from memory and comparison with other means of calculation. And how are those tested in their turn? What has to be accepted, the given, is—so one could say—*forms of life*. (PI p. 226.)

The first thing that strikes us about these passages is how close a connection they make between language and forms of life. Wittgenstein says that to imagine a language *means* to imagine a form of life, and agreement in language *is* agreement in form of life. This suggests that in practice language is *always* intertwined with patterns of activities (or "regularities of doing"), though, of course, it by no means follows that the reverse is also true, or that all patterns of activities involve language. We should recall here that Wittgenstein even sometimes calls "the whole consisting of language and the actions into which it is woven, the 'language-game' " (PI 7).

The most difficult of these passages to understand is the one having to do with *hope*, the fourth passage cited above. What is the *form of life* which is referred to in this passage? It is the *activity of hoping*. For hoping is expressed in things which people *do* (awaiting someone, writing letters inquiring about them, going to certain places, etc.) These are the "phenomena of hope." Wittgenstein says they are only possible for "those who have mastered the use of a language." But then he indicates that this only means that the concept of hope has no application except for those who *do* have language.

We can here distinguish between the *activities* which are connected with hoping or express hope and the *language* which makes use of the word *hope* and in which people speak about their hopes. It is the former which Wittgenstein calls "this complicated form of life"—various patterns of activities which might be called *hoping behavior*. That this kind of behavior is only possible for people who have language amounts to saying, not that there is a factual connection here, but rather that we simply do not apply the word *hope* to creatures who do not have a language. The dog barking at the door at a regular time every day is certainly "waiting for his master" and "expecting his master," but, we would *not* be inclined to say, "hoping his master will come."

The last passage cited above, which makes the point that "what has to be accepted, the given" are *forms of life* (or patterns of meaningful activities) gives as an example of the impossibility of further "grounding" a form of life the case of *calculation*. This is something that we just *do*, which has no further justification beyond itself. If we try to cast doubts on calculating in general, we find that we can only do it by invoking other means of calculating, and that we cannot get outside the form of life as a whole in order to account for it, or justify it, or challenge it. Forms of life define what makes sense or what it makes sense to do, and there are no further ways of making sense in terms of which to question or to vindicate these. We cannot show how calculating as a whole is justified or unjustified. Without the form of life called *calculating* we cannot even talk about calculating as a whole going wrong.

Some further light may be shed on what Wittgenstein means by *form of life* by considering his much discussed remark that

> If a lion could talk, we could not understand him. (PI p. 223.)

Why is it that we could not understand a lion? Are biologists not making progress in deciphering some forms of animal communication? And could we not say that we understand these? But this is not what Wittgenstein supposes. He is imagining a lion *talking*—that is a lion with a full-fledged language, not English or German, but a "lion-language" comparable to them.

Now the question is: What is to prevent us from translating this "lion-language" into our language the way we translate human languages into each other? Where would the difficulty of understanding lie? The immediately preceding paragraph helps to supply the answer:

> We also say of some people that they are transparent to us. It is, however, important as regards this observation that one human being can be a complete enigma to another. We learn this when we come into a strange country with entirely strange traditions; and what is more, even given a mastery of the

country's language. We do not *understand* the people. (And
not because of not knowing what they are saying to themselves.) We cannot find our feet with them. (PI p. 223.)

This says that even if we have a "mastery of the country's language,"
we still may not understand, because something may still be missing.
What may still be missing is understanding the forms of life, or seeing what they are doing with the language, how it fits into their activities.

If we apply this to the case of the lion, we can see that the real
obstacle will be in not understanding the lion's forms of life. We might
imagine that even if we had understood the lion's vocabulary and grammar (in the superficial sense anyway), somehow managing to translate
them into English, we would still not understand what the lion was
doing with these—what language-games it was playing and what forms
of life it had.

Imagine, for example, that there was some word that was to be
translated as *hunger*. Would this be used by the lion in the language-
activity of *telling-how it feels* or *inquiring-how-others-feel;* or *giving-
reasons* (as giving a reason for going hunting); or *planning-for-the-
future*, etc.? How would it be connected with eating customs, or magic
or religion? The problem would be trying to understand what constituted meaningful activity patterns in the lives of lions with language. When Wittgenstein says categorically we would not understand them, he means that there is not enough in common between
human beings and lions for us to be able to find a sufficient number
of similarities between their forms of life (if they could talk) and
ours, for us to understand them. Lions are already so different from
us in physique and physiognomy that we would not be able to "find
our feet with them" if they were able to express themselves in words.

Wittgenstein considers another example of a case where we would
not even be able to learn a language because we would not be able to
see how it fitted into people's activities. He imagines visiting a strange
country:

Let us imagine that the people in that country carried on the
usual human activities and in the course of them employed,
apparently, an articulate language. If we watch their behavior,
we find it intelligible, it seems 'logical.' But when we try to
learn their language, we find it impossible to do so. For there

is no regular connection between what they say, the sounds
they make and their actions; but still these sounds are not
superfluous, for if we gag one of the people, it has the same
consequences as with us; without the sounds their actions fall
into confusion—as I feel like putting it. Are we to say that
these people have a language: orders, reports and the rest?
There is not enough regularity for us to call it a "language."
(PI 207.)

Here it is imagined that the people "carried on the usual human
activities"—that is, they do things that look like our forms of life.
But we do not know what these activities *mean* to them because we
cannot figure out *how* what they say is connected with them; and,
in addition (and this is the main point of the passage) we cannot even
figure out *what they are saying* because we cannot, see what it has to
do with what they are *doing*.

This example in some ways reverses that of the lion since here
the people behave like human beings and speak in ways that are connected with their behavior, but we are unable to discern the connections; while in the case of the lion what would be for it the meaningful activity patterns to begin with would not be known. We would
not even have the "common behavior of mankind" as the "system of
reference" to interpret the unknown language (PI 206).

The question of whether there are *forms of life* among animals
(that is, whether forms of life include biological "regularities of doing") runs head-on into the question of at what point the word "understanding" no longer applies. When Wittgenstein says "If a lion
could talk, we could not understand him," he is saying that the forms
of life in that case would not be sufficiently like ours to justify the
word "understanding." The fact that we observe what we call "eating
rituals" or "courting rituals" among animals, does not mean that we
"understand" them. At some point a line is crossed where, it seems,
we simply have to observe as if we were looking at natural patterns.
To the poet or animal-lover the animal may still seem to stand on
this side of the line where "understanding" is possible, but even for
them against a background of what is spiritually incomprehensible.

Writing many years before in a different idiom, Wittgenstein
had said in his *Notebooks* of 1916:

This parallelism, then, really exists between my spirit, i.e.
spirit, and the world.

Only remember that the spirit of the snake, of the lion, is
your spirit. For it is only from yourself that you are acquainted
with spirit at all.
Now of course the question is why I have given a snake just
this spirit.
And the answer to this can only lie in the psycho-physical
parallelism: If I were to look like a snake and do what it does
then I should be such-and-such.
The same with the elephant, with the fly, with the wasp. (N
p. 85.)

Although Wittgenstein did not later express himself this way, a good
deal more than merely traces of the idea that we have to find the basis
for understanding others' behavior in terms of what is already meaningful to us remained. In the broadest sense it is just the "common
behavior of mankind" which is already meaningful to us, and it is,
therefore, this which we use as our system of reference (PI 206).

iii

Wittgenstein does not attempt to explain the connection between
language and regular activities or common practices, the connection
which has been of so much interest to social philosophers during the
past few decades. The attempt to find "something in common" between language and social customs and behaviors (something which
might account for their common "meaningfulness") has been a central
theme of a number of different social theories.

A Wittgensteinian sociology would *not* look for "something in
common" between language and social practices (or in his terminology
between language-games and forms of life), for this would lead us
back in the direction of the essentialism of the *Tractatus*. It is just
this which is the mistake of some Wittgenstein-oriented social philosophies as well as of other contemporary schools of social thought
such as *structuralism* and *ethnomethodology*.

Structuralism, for example, regards all kinds of social institutions
and practices, such as kinship systems, mythologies, cooking practices,
codes of etiquette, etc., as "semantic systems" embodying "unconscious
structures" similar to, or the same as, those found in language. Linguistic patterns (such as those discovered by Saussure) as well as binary
codes like those used in cybernetics and information theory are often
put forward as examples of these "unconscious structures." It is not

claimed that they are ontologically primary or, on the other hand, merely heuristic, but rather that they are somehow rooted in the nature of the human mind. Wittgenstein's criticisms of his own earlier structuralism in the *Tractatus* are relevant as objections to these versions of structuralism also. What exactly it is that is being "coded" and what the relation is supposed to be between the "message" and the code when we are talking about the human mind will be found to present insuperable difficulties.[4]

Ethnomethodology formulates its central principle as a "recommendation" that producing and carrying out social practices be regarded as "identical with" doing this in such a way that *accounts* can be given of these social practices by the participants. No inner structure unites the language and the social practice, but only the condition that social practices can always be *reported* on in words.[5] If somebody is unable to give an account of, or report on, what they have done or are doing, then the behavior must be adjudged to be not "social." Here the ethnomethodologist establishes his own meaning for the concept of *giving an account of*, a meaning which varies from the ordinary or everyday meaning, but which is necessary in order to supply the framework for his conception of sociology.

When we turn to a more Wittgenstein-oriented sociology, such as that developed by Peter Winch in his book *The Idea of a Social Science*, we find, surprisingly enough, that here too an attempt is made to put forward "something in common" between language and social practices—in this case *rules*. By altering the ordinary meaning of the word *rules* to cover all kinds of cases of conventional behavior (and even if the people involved would not say that they were "following rules"), Winch is able to find a "basis" for meaning and to make the claim that "all behavior which is meaningful (therefore all specifically human behavior) is *ipso facto* rule-governed."[6] This very un-Wittgensteinian statement unnecessarily limits the notion of "meaningful behavior" by giving the kind of "essentialist" definition which Wittgenstein in his later philosophy wants to avoid. There are "family re-

---

[4]For examples of structuralist analyses in a number of fields see Michael Lane, edt., *Introduction to Structuralism* (N.Y.: Basic Books, 1970).

[5] Harold Garfinkel, "What Is Ethnomethodology?" in *Studies in Ethnomethodology* (Englewood Cliffs, N.J.: Prentice-Hall, 1967), pp. 1-34.

[6]Peter Winch, *The Idea of a Social Science* (London: Routledge and Kegan Paul; N.Y.: Humanities, 1958), p. 52.

semblances" between different cases of what we would call "meaningful behavior," but no reason why they should all involve being "rule-governed." And, indeed, they can all only be brought under this heading by drastically altering what is commonly meant by "rule" and "rule-governed." Winch falls between the two stools of Wittgenstein's early philosophy and his later philosophy by treating the ideas of the later philosophy in a way reminiscent of the earlier one. But he is not alone in doing this.

Winch thinks that understanding Wittgenstein's notion of a *form of life* has something to do with epistemology, for he says "epistemology will try to elucidate what is involved in the notion of a form of life as such," and he adds "Wittgenstein's analysis of the concept of following a rule and his account of the peculiar kind of interpersonal agreement which this involves is a contribution to that epistemological elucidation."[7] This is a misunderstanding of Wittgenstein on several counts, for "following a rule" *is itself a form of life*, and, although it may, in addition, help us to describe some other forms of life, Wittgenstein never says that it is a practice to be found in connection with *all* forms of life, as Winch seems to suggest. There *is* no epistemological basis or content to the notion of forms of life. This is why Wittgenstein says they are what has to be accepted, the given (PI p. 226). It is characteristic of Wittgenstein's philosophy *not* to try to understand meaning in terms of knowledge (or epistemology), but instead to reverse this relation and think of knowledge in terms of meaning.[8] There is no problem about how we know language-games or forms of life; we learn them (by means of other language-games), and they belong to what we take for granted, the activities in which we share.

What holds language-games and forms of life together is not rules, but a still wider context presupposed by both of them, the context of everyday life and everyday certainties which Wittgenstein discusses in his last book *On Certainty*. As Wittgenstein brings out in this last book, this wider context is not something we "know," but is rather the framework in terms of which our knowings and doubtings and

---

7 *Ibid.*, p. 41.
8 This matter of the reversal of the relation between *meaning* and *knowledge* (*grammar* and *epistemology*) is discussed more fully in the last chapter of the present book.

judgments and investigations take place. It is what "stands fast" as the language and circumstances in which our knowledge and questions are cast. This should not be understood as either a psychological or a sociological thesis, but rather as a way of looking at what makes it possible for even these activities to have sense.

There are other important respects in which Wittgenstein-oriented social theory, as formulated by Winch and others, differs from the point of view of Wittgenstein. One of these is the tendency, common to many anthropologists, to compare the science and technology which is dominant in our society with the magic and religion which is dominant in primitive societies (instead of comparing our science and technology with primitive science and technology and our magic and religion with primitive magic and religion). This leads to many misunderstandings including the idea that primitive peoples are attempting (unsuccessfully) to do with their magic and religion what we (successfully) do with our science and technology—namely, influence and control the course of nature.

Malinowski, who did not make this mistake, pointed out long ago that primitive peoples do not allow their magic and religion to interfere with the "technical" requirements of constructing canoes and planting yams, any more than we allow our magic to interfere with our construction or planting. In his "Notes on Frazer's *Golden Bough*" Wittgenstein points out that primitive peoples do not have the bizarre ideas about the course of nature which anthropologists sometimes attribute to them, when the anthropologists are under the impression that magic and religion are to be thought of as a kind of primitive science. And, in addition, he points out that primitive magic and religion are still very much alive in us as shown by our ability to understand what they are all about in a visceral or instinctive way. We could (and often do) construct magic rituals for ourselves, and our ability to do this shows a common relation.

Isolating each culture by itself as a self-contained system, as some sociologists and anthropologists are wont to do, does not find any particular support in Wittgenstein's point of view. Nor is there any particular reason for saying that we have to "understand" an entire culture in order to "understand" a single magical or ritual practice. On the contrary, by comparing primitive customs with customs familiar to us (for example, in connection with initiation or death or marriage) we may be able to find in ourselves a "sense" for what primitive people are doing, once we cease looking at them through rationalist spectacles.

A Wittgenstein sociology, oriented, as Wittgenstein's philosophy is, to the question of meaning, is possible if we free ourselves not only from the self-congratulatory myths of the Frazer school, but also from the causalism of Durkheim, the functionalism of Malinowski and the neo-structuralism of Levi-Strauss and others. Most of all, however, we must give up trying to "explain" meaning, either in terms of *rules* or *giving accounts*. These things do not clarify Wittgenstein; they distort him.

PART III

WITTGENSTEIN'S WORLD-VIEW

Solipsism—Old and New

Might I not ask: In what sense have you *got* what you are talking about and saying that only you have got it? Do you possess it? You do not even *see* it.

WITTGENSTEIN (PI 398)

If the perception of sight is present before your sight, you should be able to point out to me which is your perception of sight and describe it to me.

Surangama Sutra

You must confess, Monsieur Descartes, that to say "I am" is to say absolutely nothing. . . . If "I am" means anything, "I am not" tells us neither more nor less.

PAUL VALERY

Parallels all things are; yet many of these are askew;
You are certainly I; but certainly I am not you.

A. C. SWINBURNE

CHAPTER 8

Solipsism—Old and New

i

We cannot pretend that any part of Wittgenstein's philosophy is easy to understand, but a special enigma attaches to the question of solipsism, an enigma so central that it affects the whole of his philosophy. From the start Wittgenstein saw something with regard to this question which is both extremely obvious and extremely elusive. Those who believe that everything in philosophy should be easy to understand will try to ignore it. But others will find that this is what accounts in large part for the feeling they have in studying Wittgenstein of something both very clear and very obscure, a tantalizing feeling of a *new kind of clarity*.

What we have is a radically new perspective, and the chief difficulty is that it is a perspective which has no precedent in Western philosophy. One way to approach it is to say, however, that there is in Wittgenstein a new kind of solipsism, what might be described as a "public solipsism" in place of the familiar "private solipsism." (We might consider dropping the word *solipsism* altogether, but we do not do so because we want to indicate that Wittgenstein is not concerned merely with "refuting solipsism," but rather with an alternative point of view which has to be understood. We will close the door to any genuine understanding of Wittgenstein if we do not see his own kind of solipsism.)

The trouble with the traditional solipsist, Wittgenstein suggests in a number of places, is that he *does not go far enough*. If the traditional solipsist were to carry through his position all the way (instead of truncating it by trying to "explain" it by making comparisons which cannot be made), he would find himself freed from a prison, which, in a sense, is a creation of his stopping halfway. Wittgenstein knew that it is possible to escape from this halfway house because he had gone

105

the whole way out of it early in his career. He had come to see what
is correct and what is incorrect in solipsism.

What is correct in solipsism, he saw, is not the Cartesian self and
the Cartesian privacy, with which it is usually associated, but an in-
communicability which is, we might say, *wholly public*. The solipsist
is right in recognizing the absolute uniqueness of the experience of
the *I*, but he is wrong in supposing that there is anything "private"
about this. The world as it confronts the *I* is indeed incommunicable
in just that way in which it is experienced by the *I*, but this is not
because the *I* is private, or this first person experience is private. It is
because of the nature of language, which is a "measure" of the world,
and not the "experience" of the world.

We can do without the Cartesian thinking, representing self, which
is a mere superstition and illusion (N p. 80; T 5.631). This does not
remove what is correct in solipsism (the unspeakable immediacy) but
it frees the solipsist from his prison because it shows that it was not
his solipsism which put him there. He is freed into a new openness.
And it is Wittgenstein's task to point this way.

> What is your aim in philosophy?—To show the fly the way
> out of the fly-bottle. (PI 309.)

The fly is the old-fashioned solipsist who needs to give up the Cartesian self and needs to be shown the way to do it. Wittgenstein does
not say his aim is to *find* the way out, because he *knows* the way out.
His aim is to *show the fly* the way out. That it is the old-fashioned
solipsist that is the fly is shown by the way the same metaphor is
stated in the "Notes for Lectures on 'Private Experience' ":

> The solipsist flutters and flutters in the flyglass, strikes against
> the walls, flutters further. How can he be brought to rest?
> (PE p. 256.)

The traditional solipsist, the fly in the fly-bottle, sees himself as
a locked-away private self with a private experience of the world, accessible only to himself. He is in the grip of that picture, which is,
as it were, implicit in the Cartesian point of view. He has not discovered
that the "first person world" and the "first person experience" (wrongly
identified by these terms since there is no "person" involved in this)
do not belong to anybody, but are, rather, overwhelmingly public.
What it is that "I alone" claim to see or experience I cannot say, *not*

because it is mine alone, but because it is nobody's and everybody's, literally incomparable and unsayable. For the fly to escape from the fly-bottle is to be propelled into an openness where the immediacy which seemed to be the private possession of the fly is, if anything, intensified in its immediacy by being dissociated from its supposed privacy. What it is that put the fly into the bottle was not the main point at all.

Wittgenstein underwent an experience as a young man which seems to have taught him that there is no self in the Cartesian sense.[1] From that time on he attempted to express this in his philosophy—first in the *Tractatus* in the doctrine of the single metaphysical *I* at the limit of the world (T 5.64) and at the end in the *Philosophical Investigations* in the attempt to show that there are no private objects of inner experience, as the Cartesian doctrine seems to require.

In what sense was Wittgenstein himself a solipsist? This is the question which has to be clarified and answered before his philosophy will become intelligible. And the reason is that this is the main place where we have to do with the "outside" of language and hence with the necessary complement of Wittgenstein's entire philosophy of *panlinguism.* We will never see how language could be *everything* for him until we see its *immediate limits.*

It is a striking and illuminating point that two of the most careful students of Wittgenstein give opposite answers to the question: Was he a solipsist? John Findlay declares him "the one absolute solipsist

---

[1] The experience was connected with seeing a performance of *Die Kreuzelschreiber,* a play by a lesser-known Austrian playwright, Ludwig Anzengruber (1839-1889). The crucial scene in this play occurs at the beginning of the Third Act when one of the characters describes the realization that has freed him this way:

Whether you are lying six feet deep in the earth beneath the grass or whether you have to face this many more thousand times again—nothing can happen to you—you belong to all of it and all of it belongs to you. Nothing can happen to you. And this was so wonderful that I hollered to all the others around me: Nothing can happen to you. . . . Now be joyful, joyful—Nothing can happen to you. (*Gesammelte Werke* (Stuttgart, 1898), Vol. 7, p. 279.)

What happened to Wittgenstein on seeing this play seems to have remained with him. In the "Lecture on Ethics" of 1929 or 1930, for example, he seems to be echoing it in speaking of an experience of "absolute value" "in which one is inclined to say 'I am safe, nothing can injure me whatever happens.'" (*Philosophical Review,* Vol. 74, No. 1 (January, 1965), p. 8) For the biographical facts see Norman Malcolm, *Memoir* (Oxford Univ. Press, 1958), p. 70; and W. W. Bartley, *Wittgenstein* (Philadelphia: J. B. Lippincott Co., 1973), p. 44.

who has ever existed," while Rush Rhees says "Wittgenstein has never held to solipsism . . ." First, the Findlay quotation:

> It is one of the immense ironies of philosophy that what may be called Wittgenstein's refutation of solipsism and solipsistic language, at which so many British and American philosophers have grasped with so much enthusiasm, is the invention of a philosopher who is probably the one absolute solipsist who has ever existed . . . (J. N. Findlay, *Ascent to the Absolute* (London: Allen and Unwin, 1970), p. 156.)

Then Rhees:

> Wittgenstein has never held to solipsism, either in the *Tractatus* or at any other time. (Rush Rhees, *Without Answers* (London: Routledge and Kegan Paul, 1969), p. 43.)

As we may suspect, both of these are right and both wrong. Wittgenstein both was and was not a solipsist. He was not a Cartesian "private solipsist," but he was what we have been calling a "public solipsist." If the only solipsism we can imagine is the Cartesian kind, then we will agree with Rhees; but if we can also recognize the absolute uniqueness of the I-world without the Cartesian self, then we will understand Findlay.

The two points are stated very clearly in the *Tractatus*, for there Wittgenstein says that *what solipsism means is correct* (T 5.62), and he also says that there is no subject which thinks or entertains ideas (T 5.631). The *I* that is needed to express what is correct in solipsism is only an extensionless point (T 5.64). Here is the separation between what is correct and what is incorrect in solipsism:

> correct is the *uniqueness* of "first person" experience
> its total immediacy and indescribability
> the impossibility of comparing it to anything else
> incorrect is the *ownership* or *privacy* of this
> its belonging to anyone
> the supposed metaphysically private world which goes with it

What solipsism means and what is correct about it "cannot be *said*, but makes itself manifest" (T 5.62). But have we not just said what it means and what is correct about it? This is an important point, for not even the concepts of *uniqueness*, *immediacy* and *indescribability* really apply (since there would have to be something that they apply to and in this case there is nothing). And, of course, in addition, the expression "first person experience" is seriously misleading since, as Wittgenstein later brought out, *I* is not a person.[2]

The totally unique world of immediate experience (which is not a world and not an experience!) in no way requires the Cartesian self. This is a phantom which gives the illusion of getting some kind of philosophical hold on the immediacy, but at the price of total isolation of each individual. Wittgenstein's position, in an ungrammatical nutshell, is that *I is nobody*. This, of course, is just the ungrammatical mixture which the private solipsist conjures up when he says things like "Only I can experience my experience" or "There is no other world but mine." Even Descartes's statement "I am" makes no sense, since if it did make sense "I am not" would make just as good sense, a point made, not by logicians, but by the poet Paul Valery.[3]

At the beginning of his career the problem appeared to Wittgenstein in quite conventional terms. In the *Notebooks* we read:

> There really is only one world soul, which I for preference call *my* soul, and as which alone I conceive what I call the souls of others.
> The above remark gives the key for deciding the way in which solipsism is a truth. (N p. 49; cf. T 5.62.)

Twenty years later we find in the "Notes for Lectures on 'Private Experience'" this:

> I want to describe a situation in which I should not be tempted to say that I assumed or believed that the other had what I have. Or, in other words, a situation in which we would not

---

[2] The difference between *I* and *person* is discussed more fully in section iv below.

[3] P. F. Strawson is right in speaking of Wittgenstein's "hostility to privacy," but wrong in speaking of his "hostility to immediacy," in "Review of the *Philosophical Investigations*," reprinted in G. Pitcher (edt.), *Wittgenstein: The Philosophical Investigations* (Notre Dame, Ind.: University Press, 1968), p. 22-65. Wittgenstein is not hostile to immediacy, but only to the idea that it can be expressed in language. It might better be said that he wishes to recover a genuine immediacy. On the other hand, he is indeed hostile to privacy, though, of course, it must be remembered that it is metaphysical and not factual (or contingent) privacy that he is hostile to. The "intermediary" of an intrinsically incommunicable inner private experience has to be discarded in order to release the full impact of the immediacy of the world without this inner cushion. It is, in short, philosophical privacy which blunts immediacy by hiding it, concealing indeed "something glorious" (PI 610).

speak of *my consciousness* and *his consciousness.* And in
which the idea would not occur to us that we could only be
conscious of our own consciousness.
The idea of an ego inhabiting a body to be abolished.
If whatever consciousness (there is) spreads over all human
bodies, then there won't be any temptation to use the word
'ego.' (PE p. 239.)

These passages are juxtaposed because they are both so uncharacter-
istic. They appear to be advancing a thesis. But there is nothing to be
argued about or *proved,* only something to be *seen,* a point of view
from which certain ways of speaking would no longer occur to us.

The source of misunderstandings is clear, for nothing but the
"privacy" can be seen from the familiar point of view. From that
familiar point of view Wittgenstein is *bound* to seem like some kind
of a behaviorist and something (the self, the subject) will appear to
be lacking. We get then the eerie feeling, so brilliantly described by
John Hems:

There are no subjective realities in Wittgenstein's world.
One imagines a sort of haunted ballroom—music in the air,
the echo of conversation between dances, and *no dancers.*
("Husserl and/or Wittgenstein," in *International Philosophical
Quarterly,* Vol. viii, No. 4 (December, 1968), p. 566.)

To this we have to reply: We are so used to having subjects bandied
about as though they were a special kind of object that when somebody comes along who has so much respect for subjects that he refuses to talk in this way, then it appears as if he has *left something out.*
Is Wittgenstein's world the haunted ballroom? Or is it perhaps that
the ballroom has been haunted for a long time by Cartesian ghosts,
and it is Wittgenstein who is trying to "dehaunt" it?

Which is the haunted ballroom—the Cartesian one or the Wittgensteinian one? It depends on our perspective. From where most of
us are standing—the Cartesian perspective—it will appear that Wittgenstein is attacking an important "reality," the "subject," the "inner
world" (that "inner world" which acquired such a preeminent epistemological status in Descartes). But from another point of view—Wittgenstein's—the question is rather one of the "recovery of genuine subjectivity," the integration of the human being and the rejection of
the Cartesian inner split.

It is perhaps most ironical that to the Cartesian it appears that it is Wittgenstein who objectifies the subject! Thus Professor Hems states:

> Wittgenstein, having adopted a total objectivism as his point of view, is bound to finish up objectifying the subject. (*Ibid.*, p. 578.)

So "real" has the Cartesian picture become that without it we appear to have no subject at all. The absence of the Cartesian pseudo-subject appears now to leave us with no subject. In other words, we have become so used to a pseudo-subject, that when somebody proposes looking to see *who the real people in the ballroom are*, he seems to be denying that there *are* any real people in the ballroom.

Wittgenstein's philosophy throughout consistently rejects the Cartesian ballroom because for him it is the haunted one, but the way he expresses this changes in very important ways. In this chapter we will discuss this development—how the "metaphysical subject" of the *Tractatus* (the extensionless point which was the only epistemological subject of the early philosophy) metamorphized into the "grammatical I" of the *Investigations* and how "my world" of the *Tractatus* (which was the "living in the present") became the "aspect" of the world which was still "something glorious" in the *Investigations*.

ii

How is the *I*, and with it what is correct in solipsism, to be understood, if not in terms of the Cartesian self? Corresponding to the two different periods of his philosophy, Wittgenstein gave two different answers to this question:

(1) In the *Tractatus* the *I* is a transcendental condition, a limit poir´ for the world, making it altogether as a whole *my* world, but not altering it in any way whatever (T 5.64). This means that the I is a precondition for the world *being experienced*, but this *being experienced* does not register as any additional fact. All supposed differences between *I*'s which are actually differences between persons, emerge as factual (psychological) differences, belonging to the common sayable world. The only genuine *I* has no content and is not discernible. The world is all that can be described, and everything can be described, except that *myness*. The *I* is merely the "experience operator" or "first person marker" bounding the world and exactly analogous to

the eye as the geometrical limit of the visual field. (T 5.632-5.6331.)[4]
(2) In the *Philosophical Investigations* the *I* is no longer a metaphysical condition, but a *grammatical* one. The word *I* at this point appears as having a totally unique grammar. It is a word which is not
reducible to any other word and which is *not a name in any sense*.
It is neither the name of a person, an inner self, a stream of events, a
bundle of memories or feelings, *nor* a metaphysical limit point. The
metaphysical *I* becomes the uniqueness of a certain use of language,
a use which could even be carried on with a different vocabulary than
the third person one, though nothing would be gained by this (PI
403; cf. BLB pp. 58-9).

We want to examine these two phases in detail, but also to look
at the transitional phase between them, when the idea of "primary
experience" was introduced, and a distinction was attempted between
the *I* as subject and the *I* as object.

First to look at the *Tractatus*. To say as Wittgenstein did that the
I is an extensionless point without content is to say that the *I* is such
that it is able to be used without having to attach a subscript to it and
without there being any describable difference between different *I*'s as
I's. What makes one person's experience different from another lies
among the facts and can be described and hence belongs to the common world. What does not lie among the facts or in the common
world is only one thing—the *myness* of experience (that it is all *mine*).
That cannot be described and is not part of the world. All differences
between persons or between experiences are not differences between
I's, but between facts.

What the metaphysical *I* is doing in the *Tractatus* is vividly expressed in the "Notes for Lectures on 'Private Experience' " where
Wittgenstein imagines someone asking him:

> "But aren't you neglecting something—the experience or what-
> ever you might call it—? Almost *the world* behind the mere
> words?"

---

[4] Wittgenstein's entire discussion of the "metaphysical subject" in the *Tractatus* is under the influence of Ernst Mach's notion of the "visual field" with the
eye at its limit. This is Wittgenstein's model for thinking about the first person
world (T 5.6331). See Ernst Mach's *Contributions to the Analysis of Sensations*
(Jena, 1886; English trans., Chicago: Open Court, 1897).

And his reply is:

> ... Couldn't I say: If I had to add the world to my language it would have to be one sign for the whole of language, which sign could therefore be left out. (PE pp. 233-4.)

This notion of "one sign added," which is a way of expressing what is correct about solipsism, is also mentioned in the *Blue Book* thus:

> When I think about it a little longer, I see that what I wished to say was: "Always when anything is seen, something is seen." I.e., that of which I said it continued during all the experience of seeing was not any particular entity "I," but the experience of seeing itself. (BLB p. 63.)

What the solipsist is getting at is not something which affects the world or what I can say about it. It does not interfere with my ability to understand others or their ability to understand me. And this despite the fact that I try to express the uniqueness of my experience by saying things like: "The only world that is real for me is the world I experience" or "There *is* no experience but my experience."

In the 1930's when Wittgenstein returned to philosophy he started on a new tack. He began to speak of *primary experience* and *primary experience language*, or first person reports. This might then be compared with *private experience* and *private experience language*. When the metaphysical framework of the *Tractatus* collapsed, some new way had to be found to express what is correct in solipsism and to distinguish it from what is incorrect. And this is where the distinction between a *primary language* and a *private language* began to emerge.

The difference between them can be seen by comparing the ways they deal with the difference between "I have a toothache" and "He has a toothache." In a *private language* a toothache is seen as a psychological event or state which I alone know and refer to directly in my own case and know and refer to only indirectly in another person's case. In a *primary language*, on the other hand, toothache may be expressed by an entirely different word in my case from the word used if it is somebody else's. We are on the road to seeing that the word *toothache* functions in two entirely different ways when it is my toothache and when it is someone else's. And this is a way of bringing out the uniqueness of the *I*, while separating it from the unnecessary picture of privacy.

Wittgenstein's fundamental point here is that the difference between so-called first person and third person statements cannot be described by any comparison between them whatever, since any comparison puts them on the same level, while the point is that they are *totally incomparable*. (This is, of course, what the old-fashioned private solipsist kept forgetting when he made the comparisons implicit in "I alone know . . ." or "I alone experience . . .") In the Moore Lecture Notes we find this:

> He (Wittgenstein) said that solipsism is right if it merely says that "I have toothache" and "He has toothache" are "on quite a different level," but that "if the solipsist says that he has something which another hasn't, he is absurd and is making the very mistake of putting the two statements on the same level." (MLN p. 305.)

This is the reason why the difference between so-called first person and third person statements must be entirely shown by the use itself since it cannot be brought out in any other way. And one method of dramatizing this is by actually introducing different words in the two different kinds of language:

> If I were to reserve the word "pain" solely for what I had hitherto called "my pain" and others "L.W.'s pain," I should do other people no injustice, so long as a notation were provided in which the loss of the word "pain" in other connections were somehow supplied. Other people would still be pitied, treated by doctors and so on. It would, of course, be *no* objection to this mode of expression to say: "But look here, other people have just the same as you!"
> But what should I gain from this new kind of account? Nothing. But after all neither does the solipsist *want* any practical advantage when he advances his view! (PI 403.)

The fact that *nothing* would be gained from this new way of speaking repeats the *Tractatus* point in a new form that what is correct in solipsism cannot be said. The impossibility of saying meaningfully that my pain and other people's pains are the "same" illustrates their incomparability.

After the "metaphysical subject" has been discarded the difference between the *I* way of speaking and other ways of speaking will eventually come down to differences between language-games. Even the notion of primary experience or a language of primary experience has been dropped in the *Investigations* because even this would be making a comparison and so in a certain sense attempting to "objectivize" what is correct in solipsism. The new approach will have to be in terms of the grammar of the word "I," which is what we now turn to.

iii

The main emphasis in the later philosophy to express what is correct in solipsism falls on the grammar of the word "I" and especially the differences between this word and the word *person*. We can see this already in the Moore Lecture Notes of 1930-33:

> he (Wittgenstein) said that "what characterizes 'primary experience'" is that in its case "'I' does not denote a possessor." In order to make clear what he meant by this he compared "I have toothache" with "I see a red patch"; and said of what he called "visual sensations" generally, and in particular of what he called "the visual field" that "the idea of a person doesn't enter into the description of it, just as a (physical) eye doesn't enter into the description of what is seen"; and he said that similarly "the idea of a person" doesn't enter into the description of "having toothache." (MLN p. 302.)

It should be noted, in passing, that Wittgenstein is still willing to call first person reports of our own inner states "descriptions," and that he continued to speak this way to the end, broadening the word "description" to cover reports about even what we cannot "refer" to.

Moore goes on to tell of Wittgenstein saying that

> the word "I" or "any other word which denotes a subject" is used in "two utterly different ways," one in which it is "on a level with other people," and one in which it is not. This difference, he said, was a difference in "the grammar of our ordinary language." As an instance of one of these two uses, he gave "I've got a match-box" and "I've got a bad tooth," which he said were "on a level" with "Skinner has a match-box" and "Skinner has a bad tooth." . . . But in the case of "I have toothache" or "I see a red patch" he held that the use of "I" is utterly different. (MLN p. 303.)

Following this up, in the *Blue Book* he speaks of two different uses of the word "I": its "use as object" and its "use as subject" (BLB pp. 64-71). On the one hand, we have statements like "I have grown six inches" and "I have a bump on my forehead," and, on the other, statements like "I see so-and-so," "I think it will rain" and "I have a toothache." Wittgenstein says that cases of the first kind "involve the recognition of a particular person" and, in addition, "the possibility of error has been provided for," while in cases of the second kind "there is no question of recognizing a person" and "no error is possible" because what we might be inclined to call an error is "no move of the game at all" (BLB p. 67).

Wittgenstein first makes the point in the *Blue Book* that *I* is not the name of a person and should not be confused with a person:

> To say, "I have a pain" is no more a statement *about* a particular person than moaning is. . . . The word "I" does not mean the same as "L.W." even if I am L.W., nor does it mean the same as the expression "the person who is now speaking." But that doesn't mean: that "L.W." and "I" mean different things. All it means is that these words are different instruments in our language. (BLB p. 67.)

It is clear that "my name" cannot be substituted for the word "I" even if I am the speaker. That it also cannot mean the same as "the person who is now speaking" can be seen from this example: If L.W. says "L.W. has a pain," and someone then asks "Who is L.W.?" L.W. might reply "I am L.W.," which is an exchange which could not take place if "I" and "the name of the person who is now speaking" had the same meaning. Nor does the word "I" point to the person who is now speaking (any more than a finger pointing to the sun also points to itself or the mouth which is speaking is part of what is said).

> The mouth which says "I" or the hand which is raised to indicate that it is I who wish to speak, or I who have toothache, does not thereby point to anything. . . . The man who cries out with pain or says that he has pain, *doesn't choose the mouth which says it.* (BLB p. 68.)

In the *Investigations* Wittgenstein again emphasizes that *I* is not the name of a person. (PI 404-414.) Here the point is made that I never have to use criteria to identify who *I* is as I sometimes have to do with persons. When I say "I am in pain," I am not saying *who* is in pain because, as he well puts it, "in a certain sense I have no idea who is" (PI 404).

It may help to see the force of this if we put it in a traditional philosophic way (remembering that the paradoxical aspect comes, in Wittgenstein's view, from mixing up language-games). Thus we might say "I am not the person who goes by my name," and this might be used to give information to someone by a man who had been travelling incognito. But in a philosophic usage (as, for example, by Indian philosophers in the Upanishadic tradition) it would be a way of calling attention to the universality of the *I*. Similarly a statement like "I do not know who I am" might be said by someone suffering from amnesia, but as a statement in philosophy it tells us that *I is not a who*. And this is what Wittgenstein tells us in the following:

> It would be possible to imagine someone groaning out: "Someone is in pain—I don't know who!"—and our then hurrying to help him, the one who groaned. (PI 407.)

It might be said, however, that even if I do not have to know who I am myself in order to use the word "I" correctly, I do say "I am John Smith" and thus tell others *who I am*. Wittgenstein refers to this:

> "I" is not the name of a person, nor "here" of a place, and "this" is not a name. But they are connected with names. Names are explained by means of them. (PI 410.)

Even in cases of telling other people *who I am* Wittgenstein maintains that there does not *have* to be a connection between *I* and *person* and *who*. In order to show this (and thus complete the separation of *personal identity* from *I*) he imagines the following case: a group of people standing in a circle and among them I, and then, without the people being able to see what happens, one or the other person is given an electric shock. We can imagine a case where "I could feel the shock even when someone else is electrified." In *that* case my feeling the shock would *not* be the criterion of who was being electrified. This would establish that there is no logical connection between *I* and *person* even in this case (PI 409).

This example parallels my being able to feel a toothache in someone else's tooth, discussed at length in the *Blue Book*:

It is conceivable that I feel pain in a tooth in another man's mouth; and the man who says that he cannot feel the other's toothache is not denying *this*. The grammatical difficulty which we are in we shall only see clearly if we get familiar with the idea of feeling pain in another person's body. For otherwise, in puzzling about this problem, we shall be liable to confuse our metaphysical proposition "I can't feel his pain" with the experiential proposition "We can't have (haven't as a rule) pains in another person's tooth." (BLB p. 49.)

Here the metaphysical proposition attempts to express what is felt as a peculiarity of the grammar of the word "I," and this is to be distinguished from the factual question that I might, for example, be hooked up to another person's brain and be able therefore to say with sense that "I feel his pain." Whatever the method used, it is indeed conceivable that I could feel another's pain in the sense of feeling a pain in his tooth, but not conceivable (because not grammatical) that when I say "I am in pain" I could mean the same thing as when I say "He is in pain."

Wittgenstein makes it clear that persons have names and identities and pains and sufferings (e.g. PI 302, 404) whereas (in a manner of speaking) *I*'s have none of these things— first because there are no separate *I*'s (the word "I" is not used in that way), and, second, because these cannot be attributed or ascribed to an *I* (again because the word "I" is not used in that way).

This point of view has been described as a no-ownership one since I do not have or own my feelings, thoughts or images, or, putting it another way, *I is not a possessor*. Opponents of the view, such as P. F. Strawson, have argued that we *do* ascribe states of consciousness to ourselves since, as Strawson puts it, to deny this is "incoherent; for it involves the denial that someone's states of consciousness are anyone's."[5] All that can be said about this is that Strawson has missed the point,

---

[5] P. F. Strawson, *Individuals, An Essay in Descriptive Metaphysics* (London: Methuen and Co., 1959), p. 98.

This book, which in many ways is a compromise between traditional Cartesianism and Wittgenstein, falls between two stools. On the one hand, it attempts to distinguish between bodies and states of consciousness as Descartes did, while, on the other, insisting that they always go together in a *person*. This, however, fails to recognize the more fundamental difference, pointed out by Wittgenstein, between *person* and *I*.

which is that *I* is not *someone* or *anyone*, and what we say about a person (even about ourselves as persons) we do not say about *I*. There remain different language-games and different grammars for *person* and *I*.

Since Wittgenstein's position remains unfamiliar and misunderstood, there is perhaps some justification for expressing it in a way which is ungrammatical and misleading, but which nevertheless makes the point of how vast the gulf is between *persons* and *I*:

Persons have identities	I has no identity
persons have names	I has no name
persons have bodies	I has no body

It is the expressions *my identity*, *my name* and *my body* which seem to bridge this gap, but we should remember that *my* in these cases means "the person who is now speaking," while *I* does not mean this. I may say "I am in pain" to call attention to myself, but I am still not speaking about a person any more than if I moaned with pain. *My name* means "the name of the person who is now speaking"—certainly not "the name of my *I*."

iv

From the discussion thus far it might seem that the main difference between the *Tractatus* and the *Investigations* on the question of solipsism was a matter of transposing a metaphysical point into a grammatical one. But the difference is more complicated because if the metaphysical subject goes, so does the distinction between the metaphysical subject and the "empirical self" and with it Wittgenstein's whole way of handling the psychological in the *Tractatus*.

There is a "psychological self" in the *Tractatus*—not the metaphysical subject which makes all the world *my world*—but a composite of psychological states, which Wittgenstein regarded as the subject matter of psychology (T 5.542). The "superficial psychology of the present day" is only wrong in calling this a soul, because it is composite rather than a unity (T 5.5421). Whenever there is a reference to a person, Wittgenstein seems to have thought, we can substitute references to psychological states, which are simply facts like other facts though of a different form.

Thus the statement "I have a toothache" in the *Tractatus* was as much of a description as "He has a toothache"—the main point be-

ing that in both cases the structural descriptive character was to be
separated from the *myness* of it, in whichever direction this went, toward my own states or toward other people's. The two directions
seem to have been on a par so far as the possibility of description went.
The important distinction was drawn between what can be expressed
in language and what cannot be, whether this applied to one's own
experience or to another's.

The will was handled in much the same way. On the one hand,
there was the *phenomenal will*, which is simply part of the facts and
brings about factual changes (T 6.423), and, on the other hand, there
is the *ethical will*, which is not part of the world at all and never shows
itself *qua* ethical in the world at all, since the world is *nothing but
facts*. Wittgenstein seems to have thought of the phenomenal will at
first as nothing but *wanting* and, as he says in the *Notebooks*, this is
just on the same level as other facts, for

> what happens, whether it comes from a stone or from my
> body, is neither good nor bad. (N p. 84.)

The ethical will, on the other hand, has no foothold among the facts,
and in this sense I am *completely powerless*.

> I cannot bend the happenings of the world to my will: I am
> completely powerless. (N p. 73.)

I can change facts through the phenomenal will or my wanting, but I
cannot introduce the ethical as such, because all that happens ever is
just more facts. Hence the ethical will is powerless.

What is especially important about this, and often overlooked, is
that Wittgenstein regards the difference between voluntary and in-
voluntary as itself a *factual difference*, not requiring any reference to
a subject. The difference, for example, between my being able to control certain bodily movements (hands, arms, head, etc.) and not being able to control others (heartbeat, stomach digestion, etc.) is for
him a phenomenal difference since it can be noticed and described and
hence there is no need to bring in the subject in order to distinguish
them.

This helps to explain an otherwise obscure passage in the *Tractatus*:

> If I wrote a book called *The World as I Found It*, I should have to include a report on my body, and should have to say which parts were subordinate to my will, and which were not, etc., this being a method of isolating the subject; for it alone could not be mentioned in that book. (T 5.631.)

We may wonder how reporting on what parts of my body are subordinate to my will and what parts are not could be a way of showing that in an important sense there is no subject, "for it alone could not be mentioned." It would seem that a subject is exactly what would have to be mentioned. For Wittgenstein, however, if the distinction can be made, it must be phenomenally available and the subject (or the will as the ethical) is never phenomenally available.

All facts, whether they are bodily facts that I will, or bodily facts that I do not will, Wittgenstein says in the *Notebooks*, must be at an equal distance from me (N p. 88), and this means that these differences must be factual and describable or phenomenally available. What is not mentioned then and is never phenomenally available will be the subject or the will as the ethical. This is what has to be always at an equal distance from everything, including my body, and has to confront the world as its equivalent (N p. 88).

It is these distinctions between the *metaphysical subject* as an extensionless point and the composite *psychological self*, and between the *phenomenal will* which moves the body and other objects and the *ethical will* which has no effect in the world whatever—it is these distinctions which are dropped in the later philosophy. This then involves a wholly new examination of psychological concepts and "first person language" which is indeed what takes up the largest part of the *Philosophical Investigations*. All these ways of thinking about the psychological and the physical and the willed and unwilled have to be rearranged. The main line has to be drawn between first person psychological statements and third person ones, rather than between both of them and the metaphysical *I*.

v

Three of the most enigmatic passages in the *Investigations* have to do with the question of immediacy and "immediate experience" and show how Wittgenstein continued to think about the question of solipsism after the lengthy discussion in the *Blue Book* (BLB pp. 58-74).

These three passages may be thought of as summarizing his views. They are (1) the discussion of the "visual room"—the room with no outside and no owner (PI 398-401); (2) the example of the aroma of coffee and the impossibility of describing it—notes which, Wittgenstein suggests, "say something glorious, but I do not know what" (PI 610); and (3) the discussion of how the translation of an image into reality "presents no difficulty at all," a matter which has a "deep aspect" which "readily eludes us" (PI 386-9). We want to examine each one of these passages, taking as our example the color red.

(1) In looking at the color red we are tempted to say: "At least I have something when I look at red which no one else has" (i.e. the *experience* of red, the *feeling* of red). This makes it seem that, being in the presence of red, I am in possession of its qualitative reality—just what *I* am experiencing.

To this Wittgenstein's reply is: "Why do you say you have it? You do not even see it" (i.e. you see the red; you do not see what is supposed to be yours alone, *your seeing of the red*). The *seeing* cannot be seen, for there is no outside to the seeing:

> Can one not add: "There is here no question of a 'seeing'— and therefore none of a 'having'—nor of a subject, nor therefore of 'I' either"? (PI 398.)

Now Wittgenstein asks: "What is this thing that we are speaking of, this 'it' that we do not have or possess?" And he says that it is, for example, if you are sitting in a room, the "visual room." This is the room which has no owner and no outside. It *cannot* have an owner. In the *Tractatus* this "visual room" was exactly analogous to *my world* or the world of first person experience, and both of them seemed like a kind of discovery,

> but what its discoverer really found was a new way of speaking, a new comparison; it might even be called a new sensation.
> You have a new conception and interpret it as seeing a new object. You interpret a grammatical movement made by yourself as a quasi-physical phenomenon which you are observing. (PI 400-01.)

This is a criticism of the *Tractatus* way of trying to express what is correct in solipsism by analogy with the "visual field," as something like a new kind of object. But, on the other hand, as a new way of speaking, a new conception or new way of looking at things, it might even have value and be of great use. Hence Wittgenstein is not repudiating the points he made with regard to what is correct in solipsism (no possessor, no owner); he is simply saying that they are to be understood, not in a metaphysical sense as in the *Tractatus*, but rather as a new (recommended) way of speaking and looking at things. What is valid here is now an "aspect."

(2) In looking at the red color or smelling the aroma of coffee, we are tempted to say: "There is something here which cannot be described, something that is being left out, the *sheer qualitative given*." And now if we are not careful we will get the idea that there ought to be some way to get that into language. But the point that is being made is much stronger than that we cannot do it. It is that *nothing* is being left out, for there is nothing that can be said to be "being left out." There is nothing we *cannot* do, even if various pictures and the misuse of language suggest that there is. It makes no sense to speak of the failure of description, or the failure of language or any other failure.

But what is "glorious" about this? For here is where Wittgenstein appends the words:

> I should like to say: "These notes say something glorious, but I do not know what." These notes are a powerful gesture, but I cannot put anything side by side with it that will serve as an explanation. (PI 610.)

The notes say that we are in the total presence of the unsayable, and that the greatest beyond we can imagine is too close to be said! If we will "let go" of the world then something entirely new will be revealed. A new "turning point" is very close. Is this "something glorious"?

(3) When we look at the red color, we may, finally, be tempted to say: "This is the same color as I imagined when you asked me to imagine a certain shade of red. So there must be something in common between what I imagine and this color. They must be related in some way."

To this Wittgenstein, in effect, replies: "You are talking as though you stood outside of both of them and could compare them and see how they are related. But that isn't what happens when you recognize the red you see as being the same as your image. There is no in-between, no intermediary, no *way* to do this.

> The difficulty is not that I doubt whether I really imagined anything red. But it is *this*: that we should be able, just like that, to point out or describe the color we have imagined, that the translation of the image into reality presents no difficulty at all. (PI 386.)

The difficulty is that the color and the image are *too close* and there is no room for any *connection* between them. And this is what makes us uneasy.

Why does Wittgenstein add here

> The *deep* aspect of this matter readily eludes us. (PI 387.)

Perhaps because we tend to assume that there is some connection between the image and what it is an image of. While what is *deep* is that the image can do what it does *without any connection* with what it is an image of. We are simply unable to answer the questions which Wittgenstein asks:

> How do I know from my *image* what the color really looks like? How do I know that I shall be able to do something? that is, that the state I am in now is that of being able to do that thing?

To sum up this discussion of the three enigmatic passages: in them Wittgenstein was making these points:

(1) no experiencer, no possessor
(2) nothing that cannot be described
(3) no connection between image and world

Our tendency in each case is to add something to fill up what seems to be a kind of void. Wittgenstein's philosophy urges us to "look again." For the philosophy of "no metaphysical self" and "no metaphysical object," oddly enough, does not result in losing something, so much as in gaining something. (What has been said of other great thinkers and artists is true of Wittgenstein: he showed us how to give up something without giving up anything at all!)

That there is an unheard "language of things" outside of our language, whose words we do not know and whose meanings we cannot fathom, appears to have been one of the thoughts which haunted Wittgenstein. This idea was most eloquently expressed in an essay by Hugo von Hofmannsthal called "The Letter of Lord Chandos," with which Wittgenstein may have been familiar since it was published in Vienna in 1902.[6] The letter purports to have been written by Lord Chandos, the "younger son of the Earl of Bath," to Francis Bacon, "apologizing for his complete abandonment of literary activity." It ends with the following paragraph:

> You were kind enough to express your dissatisfaction that no book written by me reaches you any more, "to compensate for the loss of our relationship." Reading that, I felt, with a certainty not entirely bereft of a feeling of sorrow, that neither in the coming year, nor in the following nor in all the years of this my life shall I write a book, whether in English or in Latin: and this for an odd and embarrassing reason which I must leave to the boundless superiority of your mind to place in the realm of physical and spiritual values spread out harmoniously before your unprejudiced eye: to wit, because the language in which I might be able not only to write but to think is neither Latin nor English, neither Italian nor Spanish, but a language none of whose words is known to me and wherein I may one day have to justify myself before an unknown judge.

The anti-Cartesian revolution which began in the *Tractatus* with the labelling of the Cartesian thinking self as an illusion and the establishment of what is correct in solipsism by a universal *I* which is a single point, culminates in the *Philosophical Investigations* with the demonstration that there is no "inner doubling" or "inner façade" of private objects of the kind required by the Cartesian points of view. With this Wittgenstein's overthrow of Cartesianism is complete. We turn now to his attack on Cartesian privacy.

---

[6] "The Letter of Lord Chandos" is included in Hugo von Hofmannsthal, *Selected Prose* (N.Y.: Pantheon, 1952), pp. 129-142. The relevance of this letter to Wittgenstein was first pointed out by Allan Janik, and mentioned by Stephen Toulmin in an article entitled "Ludwig Wittgenstein" in *Encounter*, Vol. xxxii, No. 1 (January, 1969), p. 66. Herman Broch in his Introduction to the English translation says that Hofmannsthal held the belief that

> As long as objects are to you merely an antithesis to your "I" you will never grasp their real essence. . . . You may succeed, however, if you are able to divest yourself of your "I" . . ." (p. xi.)

Privacy—Attack on the Inner Facade

Always get rid of the private object . . . This private exhibition is an illusion.

WITTGENSTEIN (PI p. 207, 311)

Who doubts that he lives and remembers and understands and wills and thinks and knows and judges?

ST. AUGUSTINE

The grand mistake is to think that we have *ideas* of the operations of our minds.

BERKELEY

The minute you are two it is not philosophy that is through it is you.

GERTRUDE STEIN

CHAPTER 9

Privacy—Attack on the Inner Facade

i

Wittgenstein's discussion of private language has been perhaps the most controversial part of his philosophy. The few pages dealing with this subject (PI 243-315) have been pored-over, analyzed and re-analyzed so much that many are simply tired of the subject. Yet it remains the central argument of Wittgenstein's philosophy, the place where his attack on Cartesianism is most strongly focused. And it is certainly the case that Wittgenstein's philosophy will not carry the day without this argument.

What should be clear at the outset is that the main point of the private language discussion is not to establish something about language (e.g. that language is necessarily "social"). Wittgenstein is after much bigger game than that. He is out to establish something about so-called "inner experience," to break down the Cartesian way of thinking of this, and thus to change in a fundamental way our conception of ourselves. There is an attack on the prevailing philosophical conception of the self implicit in the attack on the possibility of a private language, and it is this which gives the project its importance.

Wittgenstein's position is that our own inner sensations, states and feelings are not *private objects* "known" only to the person who "has" them. This is not, of course, to deny the "reality" of these inner sensations, states and feelings. Nor is it to maintain that they are only "real" if they are public. It is only to insist that the words *object* and *know* are misused in this case and give rise to (and are produced by) a thoroughly misleading picture. The "inner façade" which I alone observe is, for Wittgenstein, an illusion. But this is not to say that there are no *inner sensations* or *inner states*, for these terms do not lose their usefulness for being thought of in a different way. It is the *private* object and the picture of the *inner process* which Wittgenstein wishes to dissolve, and not the reality or importance of the "inner life."

127

Before we turn to the argument itself it is important to clear up a very fundamental matter of terminology. By the time he wrote the *Philosophical Investigations* Wittgenstein had broken the hold of two terms which cast an almost magical spell over the *Tractatus*. These were the terms *name* and *description*. He had come to see that these words do not have the single ultimate ontological meanings which they were given in that book. A name can function in some other way than *naming an object* and a description in some other way than *resembling what it describes*. The "freeing" of these two words was at the same time the freeing of Wittgenstein from the *Tractatus* conception of language.

If we are not to suppose, as the *Tractatus* did, that a *name means an object* (by the nature of the word, the nature of thought and the nature of the world) how then are we to think of a name? Wittgenstein sees the question altering from "How does a name refer?" to "How is a connection set up between a name and what it is a name of?" And with this goes the further question (in a sense replacing the question about the nature of the world) "How is the connection learned?"

> How do words refer (*beziehen*) to sensations? . . . how is the connection between the name and the thing set up? This question is the same as: how does a human being learn the meaning of the name of sensations? of the word "pain" for example? (PI 244.)

If instead of a name being connected intrinsically with an object we set up connections, then we can give a meaning to the word *pain* without necessarily connecting it with an object. But something must still be presupposed:

> what is presupposed is the existence of the grammar of the word "pain." . . . (PI 257.)

A name does not *create* grammar, but already presupposes grammar. (The parallel condition in the *Tractatus* was that objects have forms, i.e. intrinsic possibilities of combination.)

The new conditions for a name are (1) that we can *learn* how to use it and (2) that it has a *grammar* which is already established (i.e. that we know what kind of a word it is or what language-games it functions in). If these two conditions are met—however they are met—we have names that can do a great deal more than refer to objects.

Something similar applies to the word *description*. Again by the time of the *Investigations* this word had been freed from its single meaning of "logical similarity" (combinations of names corresponding to combinations of objects). This may be *one* meaning of the word *description*, but it is not "what a description essentially is." Wittgenstein points out that many different things are called *descriptions* and that we describe such different matters as events, mathematical formulae and states of mind, and there is no reason to suppose that all of them have "something in common." There is no objection to speaking of "describing pains" if we can get it out of our heads that this means that pains must therefore be objects or combinations of objects.

It is Wittgenstein's aim to show that pains are *not* objects and that if we name them or describe them (for we may still say that we name them and describe them), we are not naming or describing objects.

ii

There are two aspects to Wittgenstein's argument against a private language or two ways in which it is expressed. He argues that (1) we cannot imagine or invent an absolutely private language which would be able to function as a language and (2) no existing language or part of an existing language would be able to function if it *were* such a private language or based upon such a private language.

The first version has this form: We begin by imagining a language that only I can understand because its meanings come only from my imagined references to my own private sensations (PI 243), and then we see that *even I* could not understand such a language, and *even I* would only *appear* to understand it (PI 269). In other words, what Wittgenstein shows is that the supposed private language (which is totally private by definition) *would not even be a language for the person who had it,* but only empty sounds or meaningless marks. The point is *not* that no one else could understand it (for this is assumed from the start), but that *even I* myself could not "understand" it.

In the second version, Wittgenstein argues that if the only source of meaning for the word *pain*, for example, were reference to my sensation of pain, the word would not be able to function as a word at all. But the word pain *does* function as a word, and, therefore, we can conclude that its meaning *cannot* derive from reference to a private sensation, but must arise in some other way, one possibility being that it arises as a new piece of pain behavior, or a learned additional way of manifesting pain. All this has to be shown.

We now state the argument in a more expanded form which covers both versions:

1 — Wittgenstein's aim is to show that the *picture* of sensations as private objects is only a picture and a false one if applied in such a way as to suggest that there really *are* such objects.
2 — He does this by showing that if inner sensations were private objects (as this picture taken in this way makes it seem), the person who has the sensations would be able to refer to them privately in a way which no one else could understand.
3 — But we cannot refer to our own sensations in this way as objects (for reasons to be discussed).
4 — Therefore, they are not private objects.
5 — And, therefore also, the private language which we began by assuming to be possible is not possible.
And more widely:
5 — The objectification of ourselves to ourselves, which the name-object picture, applied to inner sensations, suggests, is a fiction.

The pivotal point is point 3. For the entire weight of the demonstration falls on showing that it is not possible to refer to inner sensations as objects because the minimum conditions for intelligible reference to objects are not, and cannot be, met in this case.

What are these minimum conditions which would have to be met if we were to be able to refer to our own inner sensations as objects? Very slowly and with a great many interpolations to guard against misunderstandings, Wittgenstein lays out the answer. The gist of it is that even the simplest sign requires a grammar to be a sign at all, and that means in this case a *criterion of identity*, which is just what is lacking in the case of a presumed reference to one's own inner sensation as an object.

We must pause here to recall that, for Wittgenstein, there is no such thing as "pure naming" in any case whatever. Naming has to make sense. As he puts it:

one forgets that a great deal of stage-setting in the language
is presupposed if the mere act of naming is to make sense.
(PI 257.)

Sheer reference does not even occur in the *Tractatus* since there are
different kinds of objects and we always refer to an object of some
form or other and *never* to just an object. There is "grammar" (possibilities of combination, ways of making sense) or the word is not
even a name. This matter is simply restated in the *Investigations*.

The minimum grammar needed to refer to sensations as objects,
if it were possible to refer to them in such a way, would be a criterion
of identity (PI 253). This is required in order to be able to say of
a pain that it is the *same* as another pain. The crucial point is that this
criterion of identity cannot be furnished by a sensation itself or by
a memory of some previous sensation because sheer reference (which
in any case is a meaningless notion) cannot provide it, and nothing
else is available.

Why cannot the sensation itself be the criterion of its own identity? For this is what we try to make it when we attempt to *point
to it inwardly* (PI 275), *cast a sidelong glance* at it when we are doing philosophy (PI 274), or try to impress it on ourselves by *inwardly
staring* at it (PI 412). But none of these "ceremonies" can give us a
basis for recognizing whether something is or is not the same on some
other occasion.

To return now to the two versions of trying to make a sign refer
to an inner sensation as a private object:

1 — the case where we *invent* a sign which we write down every time
   a certain sensation occurs—*the diary case;*
2 — the case where we already have a word (say for example, the word
   pain) and know how to use it and then try to understand its meaning as deriving from reference to a private object—*the beetle in the
   box case.*

In the first version we suppose that every time a sensation occurs
we put down some arbitrary sign in a diary (PI 258). The problem
then, as Wittgenstein outlines it, is not that something does not happen and we do not go on writing down signs, but that we cannot give
any sense to the notion that anything *recognizable* occurs. What allows us to take an occurrence as an occurrence of what we have

agreed upon with ourselves that the sign is to stand for? What tells us that this is a *bona fide* instance of what we are supposed to be taking note of and not an occurrence of *something different?* There *is* no way of telling, for whatever we *imagined* to be the same, or whatever *seemed* to be the same, would do as well as anything. It would be like a game in which every move was at the same time the rule which was supposed to justify the move. (We would not call it a *game.*) So each use of the sign in the diary settles for itself what is correct (And we would not call it a language.)

In the second version where we already have the word *pain*, and it looks as if we know *what pain is* (from emphatic first-hand experience) we may feel that this is already identification enough! Why should we need any criterion of what pain is since we can remember experiences of pain and how horrible they were? Yet there is a mistake here for we do not give ourselves any private exhibition of pain (PI 311). That is not what happens when we call to mind what pain is. We do not summon up the actual feeling. For neither the *concept* of pain, nor the *image* of pain, nor the *memory* of pain functions in the way which it would have to if the meaning of the word *pain* were to be the actually privately experienced pain identified in that way.

To see that this is so we make the additional assumption that there are no natural manifestations of pain (PI 256) which would permit the word to acquire its meaning in the way in which Wittgenstein suggests it might normally do (PI 244). And now we have the situation vividly illustrated by the example of the beetle-in-the-box. Everyone, we are asked to imagine, has his own private box with something in it which is supposed to serve as *his meaning* for what the word *beetle* means to him. But since nobody knows what is in anybody else's box, it cannot be *this* which people are talking about when they are talking about beetles. In fact it wouldn't matter if the boxes were empty; nothing would be changed.

> The thing in the box has no place in the language-game at all; not even as a *something*: for the box might even be empty.— No, one can "divide through" by the thing in the box; it cancels out whatever it is. (PI 293.)

If, analogously, the only source of meaning of the word *pain* were references to each person's totally private pain, there would be no common meaning for the word at all. But since there palpably is a

common meaning for the word, we have to consider some other way
by which it might have this meaning, and Wittgenstein suggests that
one possibility (for there may be others) is that words like pain

> are connected with the primitive, the natural, expressions of
> the sensation and used in their place. A child has hurt himself,
> and he cries; and then adults talk to him and teach him ex-
> clamations, and, later, sentences. They teach the child new
> pain-behavior.
> "So you are saying that the word 'pain' really means cry-
> ing?"—On the contrary: the verbal expression of pain re-
> places crying and does not describe it.   (PI 244.)

So powerful is the picture of pain as a private object that we
have come to think that this is what pain *really is*. Challenging this
then seems to be denying the painfulness of pain (i.e. that it *hurts*), or
the frightfulness of being in pain. It seems to be saying that there is
nothing psychological here, that pain is nothing. To this Wittgenstein
replies:

> Not at all. It is not a something, but not a *nothing* either!
> The conclusion was only that a nothing would serve just as
> well as a something about which nothing could be said. We
> have only rejected the grammar which tries to force itself on
> us here. (PI 304.)

Pain can be everything we say it is without it needing to be a subjective object. We can even use this picture of naming something, if we
do not forget that it is just a picture and that it does not correspond
to "the way things are."

iii

A common idea is that inner sensations are identified by means of
memory and that it is memory which provides us with something like
a way of recognizing a sensation. Could it not be memory which supplies the criterion of identity which Wittgenstein says is needed for
me to be able to say that this is the same sensation today as the one
I had yesterday or the day before? Plato, it will be remembered, examined this question in the *Theaetetus* and pointed out that appealing
to memory does not solve the problem, but only restates it because if
we use a memory to recognize a sensation, then, he asks, what do we

use to recognize the memory? Wittgenstein makes the same point in a different way and with a number of added considerations.

It is clear, to begin with, that memory cannot be what is at work in *every* case since we can conceive of a person who could not remember what the word *pain* means, but, nevertheless, continued to use the word as everyone else does. On this Wittgenstein comments:

> Here I should like to say: a wheel that can be turned though nothing else moves with it, is not part of the mechanism. (PI 271.)

This, of course, is a logical point: that how we use a word is logically distinguishable from what we say it means or what memory we say we have of what it means. If the use is correct, the memory, which may or may not be present, becomes irrelevant.

A second related point is that if memory were in principle the basis for identifying our sensations, this would require that memory be always available as the last court of appeal or that to which we were committed in the end for settling what our sensation is. But memory plays no such role. We do not treat it as the last court of appeal, and, in fact, it frequently deceives us. Referring to trying to remember different shades of color, Wittgenstein asks:

> Aren't we as much at the mercy of memory as of a sample? (PI 56.)

He even suggests that one way to shake the private object fixation is this:

> Always get rid of the private object in this way: assume that it constantly changes, but that you do not notice the change because your memory constantly deceives you. (PI 207.)

One answer to the unrealiability of memory might be to try to appeal to another memory to validate the first one. But this will not help, for the new memory, too, may just as well be wrong. And it also involves another logical or grammatical error because memories do not stand in corroborating relations to each other. Wittgenstein says it is

> As if someone were to buy several copies of the morning paper to assure himself that what it said were true. (PI 265.)

This example has been challenged on the grounds that it *would* make sense to buy different copies of the morning newspapers if they were copies of different papers or perhaps even different editions of the same one. But this misses the point that in the case of memory we have no way of telling whether we have several copies of the same edition, or different editions or different papers. Lacking criteria for the sameness and difference of memories, how can we tell whether we have two memories of the same occurrence or two memories of different occurrences? Such confusions actually happen, but all that is necessary to establish Wittgenstein's point is that they *can* happen and we can never be sure that they have not happened, for we have no grounds for settling such a question one way or the other.

This is the place at which Wittgenstein points out that there is no such thing as a justification in imagination, for this would be no justification at all, since

> justification consists in appealing to something independent.
> (PI 265.)

To those who might say: "When I say 'I am in pain' I am at any rate justified *before myself*," Wittgenstein replies:

> What does that mean? Does it mean: "If someone else could know what I am calling 'pain,' he would admit that I was using the word correctly"?
> To use a word without justification does not mean to use it without right. (PI 289.)

In appealing to inner sensations as if they were objects, we are attempting to use them to justify what we say, in a situation where actually the inner sensations cannot play that role, and no justification is possible. And the same thing applies to memories of inner sensations, for these memories too have to stand without justification.

Various errors with regard to memory are all related to what Wittgenstein calls "a false picture of the processes called 'recognizing'; as if recognizing always consisted in comparing two impressions with one another." (PI 604.) Memory, he says, seems to be the agent for this "by allowing us to look into the past (as if down a spy glass)." We have a tendency, in other words, to want to give a memory that very "independence" which goes with a criterion or a justification, not realizing that a memory is not better off in this respect than what it is supposed to help us identify. No *comparison* is taking place in any case, for as Wittgenstein shrewdly puts it:

> It is not so much as if I were comparing the object with a
> picture set beside it, but as if the object *coincided* with the
> picture. So I see only one thing, not two. (PI 605.)

The point is illustrated by an example, which, however, of course, does
not apply to every case:

> What if someone were to say "In order to be able to sing a
> tune from memory one has to hear it in one's mind and sing
> from that"? (PI 333.)

What is sufficient for Wittgenstein's point is that we use the term
"memory" correctly when there is no comparison at all.

Summing up, Wittgenstein rejects the "inner spectator' (or "inner experiencer") conception of memory, as he rejects the "inner
spectator" (or "inner experiencer") conception of pain. In both cases
this is only a picture (or a picture of the application of a picture, for
the harm is not so much in the picture as in the way the picture is misused). Remembering is not an inner perception or an inner experience,
however much our ways of speaking may conjure up this picture as
somehow seemingly necessary.

> "But you surely cannot deny that, for example, in remember-
> ing an inner process takes place."—What gives the impression
> that we want to deny anything? When one says "Still an inner
> process does take place here"—one wants to go on: "After all,
> you *see* it." And it is this inner process that one means by the
> word "remembering."—The impression that we wanted to
> deny something arises from our setting our faces against the
> picture of the "inner process." What we deny is that the pic-
> ture of the inner process gives us the correct idea of the use
> of the word "to remember." We say that this picture with
> its ramifications stands in the way of our seeing the use of
> the word as it is. (PI 305.)

For Wittgenstein, to say that we are aware of our own memories is
no more than to say that the memories occur (although there might
be occasions in the flux of actual usage when we could say with sense,
things like "I am aware of having that memory"). In order to express a memory, however, we do not have to be "aware of the memory" and this "inner awareness" way of speaking (taken as a necessary picture) creates additional problems because it leads us to wonder
how we "recognize" our own memories, etc.

Wittgenstein wants to drop the "inner façade" in the case of memory, as in the case of pain, a proposal so new that it does not appear as even a possible alternative to many philosophers. We may on occasion say such things as: "My memory shows me," "The whole thing came back to me," or "I see the place all over again in my mind," but nothing requires us to take the pictures expressed by these words in the literal fashion of the Cartesian.

The picture of "remembering" as an "inner experience" leads to the notion that we can "inwardly examine" a memory and distinguish different features such as "a present datum" and "a past event which it refers to," or distinguish "a memory image which is occurring now" from "a feeling of pastness" and "the actual occurrence referred to." We imagine we *see* these different features in the *memory itself*. The distinctions can be made, but they are made in connection with the way we use the concept of memory. The memory itself comes to expression as pain comes to expression as *sui generis* and the ways of talking about it unfold from this. So Wittgenstein can say:

Man learns the concept of the past by remembering. (PI p. 231.)

Wittgenstein has a twofold task here (as in so many other places in his philosophy): to challenge the notion that we *experience* our memories, but to do it not as if this were a "factual" challenge or one depending on some further introspective inspection.

> Remembering has no experiential content.—Surely this can be seen by introspection? Doesn't *it* show precisely that there is nothing there, when I look about for a content?—But it could only show this in this case or that. And even so it cannot show me what the word "to remember" means, and hence *where* to look for a content!
> I get the *idea* of a memory-content only because I assimilate psychological concepts. It is like assimilating two *games*. (Football has *goals*, tennis not.) (PI p. 231.)

Remembering is not an experience, as pain is not an experience. But in each case to say this is to make a grammatical point, not one based on "inner observation." For the "inner observation" is the misleading picture, and this is the crux of the matter.

iv

The insistence that the felt experienced pain (so intense, so hor-

rible, so real!) must be *something*—that there must be *something* there
which leads me to cry out and which makes the all-important difference between pain-behavior with pain and pain-behavior without pain
leads to the following protest, which in turn elicits one of Wittgenstein's most illuminating, but least understood, metaphors in reply:

> "Yes, but there is *something* there all the same accompanying
> my cry of pain. And it is on account of that that I utter it.
> And this something is what is important—and frightful." Only
> whom are we informing of this? And on what occasion?"
> Of course, if water boils in the pot, steam comes out of the
> pot and also pictured steam comes out of the pictured pot.
> But what if one insisted on saying that there must also be
> something boiling in the picture of the pot? (PI 296-7.)

When we insist that pain is *something*, Wittgenstein suggests here, we
are trying to point to the actuality of pain, because it is the *actuality*
of pain which justifies the cry of pain (or so we would like to say).
But we cannot point to the actuality itself (the actual hurting pain);
we can only provide a picture of pain as an object (i.e. as something).
Then we say that, of course, the *reality* of pain is what counts. But
that isn't in the picture—though we act as if it were, for to accomplish
what we want, *actual pain itself would have to be in the picture*. We
would have to be able to call up the actual pain and give ourselves a
private exhibition of *that*, which we do not do. (There is, of course,
real water in the real kettle, but the picture does not show this, even
if the picture were to show water in the kettle, for the "realness" would
still not be there. In the case of pain the picture we call up is a picture
of pain-behavior and hence we do not even see the "inside" of the
kettle).

We have to ask ourselves where the urgent need to insist upon
the reality of pain *in this philosophical way* comes from. The answer
seems to be that it comes from the picture of pain as an object. The
picture creates, as it were, the very question which it answers by lay-
ing down what seems to be the necessity that "pain must be something." The denial of this is met by the reiteration of the picture, for
the very *frightfulness* of pain, its terrible force, seems to be at stake
then in its being an object. To say as Wittgenstein does of pain that

> It is not a *something*, but not a *nothing* either! (PI 304).

is for him only to reject a picture and a certain grammar. But for those

in the grip of the picture and the grammar it is like an attack on common sense itself in the form of a denial of the reality of hurt and suffering.

Some commentators have read the passage about the steam-kettle
and similar passages as meaning that Wittgenstein thought that pain
is indeed *something*, but that this *cannot be said*. In this interpretation
it is language which fails to express what is there, and an all-seeing
eye might be able to look inside the individual person and *see* the pain
there. But Wittgenstein's view is more sweeping than this. His view
is that there is *nothing to "see."* Pain is not something which "confronts
us" inwardly, or which we "look upon." It is *part of our manifesting*
in the circumstances of the world. So there is nothing that cannot be
done. As Wittgenstein puts it:

> The great difficulty here is not to represent the matter as if
> there were something one *couldn't* do. As if there really were
> an object, from which I derive its description, but I were un-
> able to show it to anyone. (PI 374.)

The *I* that cannot see itself here becomes the pain that cannot be seen,
but this is nothing that we cannot do, but rather *what we are*, so that I
cannot see my pain because I *am* my pain.

These are clumsy enough forms of expression, but they suggest,
as the metaphor of the steam-kettle does, that it is not the picture
of "I looking at my inner sensations" which does the harm, but
taking this picture as meaning that there *are* inner sensations (i.e. that
they are objects). Then it becomes easy enough to imagine all kinds
of "necessities" and to say things like: "There must be something
behind pain-behavior, something which accompanies or causes or is
caused by pain-behavior, but still *something*." The pain appears as a
mental fact, event, occurrence, or process which everyone is familiar
with from his own case, and which, whatever we say, *is* there in some
way or other. All this flows from the picture that "I experience my
pain," when we take it that way.

The fact that there are different kinds of pain, different intensities
of pain (for example, we tell the doctor that the pain is a "steady dull
ache" or an "intermittent sharp stabbing," etc.) seems to suggest that
I "read this off" from "inwardly observing." Is it not discriminating
and describing, as we discriminate and describe smells and tastes? And
then we say things like: "I alone know that I am in pain and what

kind of pain it is, when it starts and when it stops, and where in my body it is." Given the picture, all this looks like more and more convincing "proof" that the picture is a correct one. If we can really do all these things, how can it be said that we do not observe and know our own pains in a unique way?

The mistake in all this is that it takes as features or properties of pain what is either indistinguishable from pain (intensity) or what is not the same as pain and even involves a different grammar (location and duration). Thus we find Wittgenstein observing:

> I may know that he is in pain, but I never know the exact degree of his pain. So here is something that he knows and that his expression of pain does not tell me. Something purely private. He knows exactly how severe his pain is? (Isn't that much as if one were to say he always knows exactly where he is? Namely here.) Is the concept of the degree given with the pain? (Z 536.)

We cannot jump from experienced pain to any kind of a concept, any more than we can jump from experienced color to any kind of a concept in that case.

> Do not believe that you have the concept of color within you because you look at a colored object—however you look. (Z 332.)

There are different natural expressions of pain—moans, whimpers, shrieks, etc.—and words like *dull, throbbing, piercing*, etc., are analogous to these. The words are different pain-manifestations as the different kinds of cries are.[1] The intensity of a pain, in other words, is not something which belongs to a pain in the way that color belongs to a dress; we cannot imagine the same pain with a different intensity in the way that we can imagine the same dress with a different color.

With regard to my being able to locate my pain and say where in my body it is, Wittgenstein is clear that this is on the side of pain-behavior and not belonging to the pain as felt, even though we certainly have the temptation to say otherwise:

---

[1] It is well to call to mind here the enormous and subtle vocabulary of animal cries, as well as of animal markings and rituals. The complexity of the different ways in which pain manifests itself in language is no argument against these being understood as expressions and manifestations.

> Consider the following question: Can a pain be thought of, say with the quality of rheumatic pain, but *un*localized? Can one *imagine* this?
> If you begin to think this over, you see how much you would like to change the knowledge of the place of pain into a characteristic of *what is felt*, into a characteristic of a sense-datum, of the private object that I have before my mind. (Z 498.)

The statement that "Another cannot have my pains," in one respect (seeming to refer to the pain itself) is a grammatical statement about the way this word is used; and in another respect (if it refers to a place in my body) is false. In the second respect, Wittgenstein says it is quite possible that another person might be able to feel a pain in my body and I one in his. (When asked where it hurts, I might, if wired to someone else, point to a place in his body as the place and he to a place in mine. And if this has not yet been done, it may be very soon.) The difference is whether there is a criterion of identity for calling the pain mine, which there is if we take where we point to as the criterion, or whether there is no criterion of identity but merely the pain-expression. Wittgenstein sums this up:

> In so far as it makes *sense* to say that my pain is the same as his, it is also possible for us both to have the same pain. (And it would also be imaginable for two people to feel pain in the same—not just the corresponding—place. That might be the case with Siamese twins, for instance.) (PI 253.)

Being able to feel pain in another's body, we might be inclined to say, would not prevent it from being *my* pain; it would continue to be my pain if I felt it, no matter whose body it was in. Wittgenstein wishes to preserve this distinction by recognizing the two different kinds of language-games here—the one in which there is a criterion for calling two different pains the same, and the other in which there is no criterion. If I say this is the same pain because it is the same tooth, I am speaking in the first way. In the second way it will make no sense to say it is the same. This shows also why Wittgenstein is prepared to speak of *knowledge* in the first case and not in the second. Statements like "I know I am in pain" or "I alone know when I am in pain" are to him misleading because they conjure up the inner spectator picture and falsely suggest that there is something that I might know about myself in this way. But this is just a way of speaking and in saying "I know that I am in pain" I am saying no more than "I am in pain."[2] The distinction between the part of the body which hurts and the person who hurts is important and has to be preserved:

> Pain-behavior can point to a painful place—but the suffering person is the one who gives it expression. (PI 302.) (I have altered Miss Anscombe's translation here; she has for *die leidende Person* the translation *the subject of pain*.)

v

Why is the question of whether stones can have pains inserted into the middle of the private language discussion? What do stones with pains have to do with the impossibility of a private language? These questions are bound to occur to us as we read sections 281-8 and 390-7 in the *Investigations*.

A brief answer is that it is just these kinds of *futile imaginings* which tend to arise out of the picture of pains as private objects. If we think of pains in this way, it may indeed begin to seem that just about *anything* could conceivably have pains. All we have to do—we come to suppose—is to imagine anything at all having *just what we have when we have pain*. If pains and pain-behavior are thought of as two different "realities," to begin with, and pain is thought of as an "inner object," then it may seem quite possible to conceive of pain all by itself even in absurdly far-fetched cases. (When, on the other hand, we give up thinking of pains as private objects, then we will see that pain and pain-behavior go quite naturally together in the normal case which is that of living human beings.)

Wittgenstein gives a number of examples of how the private object picture of pain leads into weird imaginings.

First, it seems to be possible then to imagine that other people never actually have any pains at all, but may be walking around, showing pain-behavior on occasion, but never have *what I have* when I have pain because, after all, so this version goes, "I can never feel what

---

[2] This is the third place where Wittgenstein challenges the ascendency of the word *know*. He says it is better *not* to speak of *knowing* in connection with (1) mathematical propositions; (2) foundational propositions (of the kind G. E. Moore claimed to "know for certain") and (3) one's own inner sensations.

they feel." This "possibility"—that other people might just be automatons with no "insides" at all—may make me feel slightly dizzy (like certain theorems in set theory), but, given the private object picture, who can say that it is not "possible"?

As against such fantasies Wittgenstein observes:

> But just try to keep hold of this idea in the midst of your ordinary intercourse with others, in the street, say! (PI 420.)

What we are imagining is a kind of dream of our language, a "possibility" which is no more possible than, say, the multiplication table having pains or pains having children!

A converse "possibility" seems to be to imagine that inanimate things like stones might have pains or that even we ourselves might have frightful pains and turn to stone while they lasted (PI 283). Wittgenstein recognizes that we do say of certain inanimate things that they are in pain, as in fairy-tales or in playing with dolls, but he points out that these are "secondary" uses (PI 282), depending on looking at these things as human. He also asks: How would we know that we had turned to stone (if pain and pain-behavior are supposed to be *that* far apart)?

As against such "possibilities," Wittgenstein makes two important points: The first is to call attention to the temptation to suppose that meaningful expressions continue to make sense in different contexts if only the contexts *appear* to be similar (PI 350-1), and the second is to point out that not all images and imaginings make sense anyway.

In relation to the first point Wittgenstein imagines someone saying: "But if I suppose that someone has a pain, then I am simply supposing that he has just the same I have so often had" (PI 350). The trouble with this is that it gives us a certain picture of pain in two different places without supplying any notion of how this picture might function in concrete cases. Concepts do not keep their meanings when applied to just any old situations, just because the situations *appear* to be similar. (It is such deceptive similarities which lead us to imagine, for example, that it makes sense to say that "it is five o'clock on the sun" (PI 350-1) or that people must be hanging upside down on the other side of the earth.)

The picture of pain as a private object seems to give us just two alternatives: either the stone has that experience we are familiar with or it does not. The question we should rather ask is: How is the con-

cept of pain to be used in connection with stones? In what way can
the stone have a pain? In other words, what about the rest of the pain-
setting: the mouth which cries, the body which contorts, the people
consoling us, etc. (PI 283).

This example shows us that the whole question is tied up with
the broader question of *what we can imagine and cannot imagine*
and that this, in turn, is connected with the question of how even
imagining makes sense. Wittgenstein points out how mere word-play
may generate all kinds of images without these images having any use
at all (PI 351). We might, for example, imagine a mouse writing a
sonnet, or a number (numeral) having feelings (as in movie cartoons),
but from such "imaginings" nothing at all could be inferred about mice
or numbers if these words are to retain their usual meanings. (We
have here a counterpart to what the *Tractatus* called the "merely possible," as distinct from the determinate kinds of possibility which logic
is interested in (T 2.0121C). Similarly it is of no interest to the understanding of language or the world whether we can "merely imagine"
anything such as, for example, "green ideas sleeping furiously."

All this comes under the heading of what Wittgenstein calls
"image-mongery" (*Vorstellerei*).

> Could one imagine a stone's having consciousness? And if
> anyone can do so—why should that not merely prove that
> such image-mongery is of no interest to us? (PI 390.)

The distinction is suggested in these and other places between
imagination which phantasizes in almost any old way and imagination
which deals with what is conceptually understandable. A mere play
of images does not constitute a sense. Because in a movie cartoon two
"numbers" are shown hitting each other (animated Arabic numerals
wielding sticks), we are not going to modify our use of the word
"number" (or of the word "hitting"). It would be understandable not
to call what the movie cartoon shows a "possibility." For, as Wittgenstein would put it, What has hitting to do with numbers or numerals? And if such cartoon-numbers howl with pain, what has that
got to do with ordinary numbers or ordinary pain?[3]

In a similar vein Wittgenstein asks:

---

[3] These problems are discussed in an important article by Virgil C. Aldrich,
"Image-Mongering and Image-Management" in *Philosophy and Phenomenological
Research*, Vol. xxiii, No. 1 (Sept., 1962), pp. 51-61.

And can one say of the stone that it has a soul and *that* is what has the pain? What has a soul, or pain, to do with a stone? (PI 283.)

We might say that the concepts of soul and pain do not work with the concept of stone as these three concepts are used today. Hence if we try to give further content to the idea of a stone having pain, we do not know how to go about it. We are unable to answer such further questions as: Where does the stone have pain? Or, How do you console a stone? Or, How does the doctor prescribe for a stone?

Look at the stone and imagine it having sensations.—One says to oneself: How could one so much as get the idea of ascribing a *sensation* to a *thing*? (PI 284.)

What happens, of course, is that the attempt to give content to the idea of a stone having pain has to be done by trying to make the stone in imagination more and more resemble a human being. It would seem that we are not able to do it any other way, and this shows that the central case of pain is the one involving a living human being or what behaves like a human being. Hence Wittgenstein's assertion that the primary use of the word and indeed of all such words is in connection with human beings.

It should be noted that Wittgenstein does not say here "living organisms," but "living human beings." While we can more easily imagine a fly with pain than a stone or book, and a cat or dog than a fly, this is because their behavior more closely resembles that of human beings. There is a natural response to pain in other human beings which may extend to animals. (Z 540.) (The biologists' suggestion that an organism's possession of a nervous system is all that has to be taken into account in deciding whether organisms have pain or not is an interesting example of confusing language-games. The word *pain* must already have a meaning before the assumed connection between pain and nervous system can be made.)

While Wittgenstein rejected the view that "I know what pain is only from my own case," for there is no "knowing" here, he also rejects the view that the use of the word in my own case "depends upon" physiological happenings. There is a total situation of natural expressions and natural reactions among human beings where pain is concerned, and this is the matrix of the meaning of the word.

"But doesn't what you say come to this: that there is no pain without pain-behavior?"—It comes to this: only of a living human being and what resembles (behaves like) a living human being can one say: it has sensations; it sees; is blind; hears; is deaf; is conscious or unconscious. (PI 281.)

Once we put aside the inner object picture, then the problem of how body and soul go together disappears. We deal with a human being, and not a body that has a soul or a soul that has a body. (How can a body *have* a soul? Wittgenstein asks (PI 283).) It isn't the body we pity when someone is in pain, or the soul; but the person. And, as Wittgenstein adds, "We see emotions in the other person's face."

We do not see facial contortions and make inferences from them (like a doctor framing a diagnosis) to joy, grief, boredom. We describe a face immediately as sad, radiant, bored, even when we are unable to give any other description of the features.—Grief, one would like to say, is personified in the face. (Z 225.)

If we read it immediately after the preceding passage we can understand what Wittgenstein meant by saying:

The human body is the best picture of the human soul. (PI p. 178).[4]

---

[4]Philosophical phantasies about stones having pains may remind us of what the Roman poet Horace said about poetry in his *Art of Poetry* (1-13):
If a painter chose to join a human head to the neck of a horse, and to spread feathers of many a hue over limbs picked up now here, now there, so that what at the top is a lovely woman ends below in a black and ugly fish, could you, my friends, refrain from laughing? Believe me, dear Pisos, quite like such a picture would be a book, whose idle fancies shall be shaped like a sick man's dreams, so that neither head nor foot can be assigned to a single shape. "Painters and poets," you say, "have always had an equal right in hazarding anything." We know it: this license we poets claim and in our turn we grant the like; but not so far that savage should mate with tame, or serpents couple with birds, or lambs with tigers. (*Satires, Epistles, and Ars Poetica*, trans. H. R. Fairclough (N.Y.: Loeb Library, 1926), p. 451.)

Grammar—A New Beginning

Is possibility a sort of shadowy reality? Where is the shadow? There really is such a shadowy reality. It is your language.

WITTGENSTEIN (MN p. 33)

The word is mightier than he who speaks it.

HUGO VON HOFMANNSTHAL

The greater part of this world's troubles are due to questions of grammar.

MONTAIGNE

According to the traditional view a reverent study of grammar is an infallible source of spiritual illumination which culminates in securing the freedom of the soul.

GAURINETH SASTRI

CHAPTER 10

Grammar—A New Beginning

i

The most general term to describe what Wittgenstein himself is most concerned with and what he takes to be the central concern of philosophy is *grammar*. This word, which is perhaps the most important in his philosophy, has a vastly extended meaning for him, a meaning far wider than the ordinary one.[1]

Grammar (and this point has to be emphasized) is what replaces metaphysics and epistemology as the core of philosophy (PI 90). Traditional metaphysics finds its home in grammar. This is what Wittgenstein means when he says that

Essence is expressed by grammar. (PI 371.)

and even more sweepingly.

Like everything metaphysical the harmony between thought and reality is to be found in the grammar of the language. (Z 55.)

The purport of these statements is that what we have in the past expressed in metaphysical terms as the most general features of the world turn out to be from Wittgenstein's point of view features of language. Grammar is language in its possibilities, determining possibilities of sense. In the *Tractatus* these are the essences or structures held in common by language, thought and world, while in the *Investigations* they are the established linguistic practices and conventions.

Wittgenstein, in effect, locates the world within language (except for its residual unsayable "existence" and "immediacy"). In every

---

[1] Although Wittgenstein maintained that his use of the term *grammar* was not at variance with the ordinary use, G. E. Moore was not the first or the last to say that he could not understand the way in which Wittgenstein was using the word. (MLN p. 271.)

respect in which anything at all can be said about it, the world "be-longs to" language. From the one side, the side of the world, there is no world (about which anything can be said) which does not belong to some language activity. And from the other side, the side of lan-guage, there is no language which does not require established settings and applications without which it would not even be language. The important line is not, therefore, between world and language in the traditional sense, but between what can be said and what cannot be said.

Here we see how differently the world and language go together in Wittgenstein's philosophy from the ways they have gone together in previous philosophy. For Wittgenstein, on the one side is everything necessary for the functioning of language *including what language can refer to*, while on the other side are the single applications of language and what cannot be said. If we have in mind instead the traditional picture in which language and the world are imagined as separate from each other and each having a character of its own, then we forget that both sides of this picture are being spoken about and thus are subject to the conditions for making sense.

What has been most important in supporting the traditional view of the separation of the world and language is the notion of perception and sense impressions as *pre-linguistic* ways by which the world comes to be known as it is, independently of thought and language (knowl-edge of the world then either being "abstracted from" or "constructed out of" sense impressions). A critical step toward the Wittgenstein perspective is to recognize sense impressions as no more than an addi-tional kind of language, for we speak about "sense impressions," and whatever we say about them must meet conditions for making sense also. There is a "language of sense impressions" which we have to understand and which, like any other language activity, is founded on convention (PI 355).

The Wittgenstein point of view requires us to take meaning and sense as entirely immanent in language and to give up the idea that we have access *through* language to meaning and sense *independent of* language. (Language is not like a glass which one looks through, but like a measure which casts a certain shadow on the world.) Hence it is no longer possible to speak of a universal framework within which language functions and which has a reality independent of language. The actual functioning of language takes the place of any supposed framework. It appears then that the framework suggested by the "independent reality" of *world* and *mind* is a "way of talking," and the whole picture recedes into the "mythology of language." We had forgotten that such concepts as *world* and *mind* also rose out of language, for when they acquired the status of a universal picture, their home and source in language seemed to disappear from sight. Wittgenstein brings all such words back to their "original home." (PI 97, 108.)

What looks as though it *must* be so—that is what is *grammatical*. Or, as Wittgenstein puts it:

> What looks as though it *had* to exist is part of the language. (PI 50.)

Hence statements about what something *must* be in order to be what it is, even though they appear to be statements about the "way things are," are actually statements in which the functionings of language are shown. An example of such a grammatical statement is "Every rod has a length," which can be understood as "Every rod *must* have a length," and which, while it appears to say something very general about rods, actually expresses the way the concepts *rod* and *length* function and something about where their limits of sense are.

When we imagine the statement that "There is no rod which does not have some length" to be a statement about rods, we have a picture of a certainty in our knowledge of things, of which the opposite is inconceivable. But both these ways of putting it actually express the limits of sense of the concepts. We cannot with sense *say* the opposite. The arbitrariness of grammar is the only correlate which we can find for the intrinsic necessity of such statements. (PI 372.)

Wittgenstein sums up his conception of the grammatical character of necessity in this way:

> One is tempted to justify rules of grammar by sentences like "But there really are four primary colors." And the saying that the rules of grammar are arbitrary is directed against the possibility of this justification, which is constructed on the model of justifying a sentence by pointing to what verifies it. (Z 331.)

He then continues with the following defense of this view:

> Yet can't it after all be said that in some sense or other the grammar of color-words characterizes the world as it actually

is? One would like to say: May I not really look in vain for a fifth primary color? Doesn't one put the primary colors together because there is a similarity among them, or at least put *colors* together, contrasting them with e.g. shapes or notes, because there is a similarity among them? Or when I set this up as the right way of dividing up the world, have I a preconceived idea in my head as a paradigm? Of which in that case I can only say: "Yes, that is the kind of way we look at things" or "We just do want to form this sort of picture." For if I say "there is a particular similarity among the primary colors"–when do I derive the idea of this similarity? Just as the idea "primary color" is nothing else but "blue or red or green or yellow"–is not the idea of that similarity too given simply by the four colors? Indeed, aren't they the same?– "Then one might also take red, green, and circular together?" Why not?! (Z 331.)

This indicates that concepts establish similarity (for similarity is, otherwise, no more than the phenomena which are similar), and, therefore, we cannot appeal to similarity to justify concepts. We can certainly imagine concepts which would group phenomena quite differently (for example, a single concept for "red," "green" and "circular"), but then these other concepts would function according to different grammatical rules. Necessity does not attach to facts, nor to the "essence of the world," but to grammatical rules, whatever they happen to be, as the actually functioning conditions for making sense.

Statements like "Every rod has a length," Wittgenstein calls "grammatical propositions." Such statements he does not reject as senseless, as he did in the *Tractatus* (T 41.122-4.1274), but rather says "There is a language-game with this sentence too" (RFM 182). Other examples of such "grammatical propositions" are: "One plays patience by oneself" (PI 248), "My images are private" (PI 251), and "The class of lions is not a lion, but the class of classes is a class" (RFM 182).

It is clear from these and other examples that what Wittgenstein calls "grammatical propositions" are *a priori* (and hence necessarily true), but that some are analytic *a priori* and some are synthetic *a priori*. Of the latter he says:

It might perhaps be said that the synthetic character of the propositions of mathematics appears most obviously in the unpredictable occurrence of the prime numbers. But their being synthetic (in this sense) does not make them any the less *a priori*. They could be said, I want to say, not to be got out of their concepts by means of some kind of analysis, but really to determine a concept by synthesis. . . . (RFM 125.)

As an example of a grammatical proposition which is synthetic *a priori* he gives "White is lighter than black," and of this says:

Whence comes the feeling that "white is lighter than black" expresses something about the *essence* of the two colors?—But is this the right question to ask? For what do we mean by the "essence' of white or black? . . . Is it not like this: the picture of a black and a white patch serves us *simultaneously* as a paradigm of what we understand by "lighter" and "darker" and as a paradigm for "white" and "black." Now darkness "is part of" black *inasmuch as* they are *both* represented by this patch. It is dark *by* being black.—But to put it better: it is called "black" and hence in our language "dark" too. That connection, a connection of the paradigms and the names, is set up in our language. And our proposition is non-temporal because it only expresses the connection of the words "white," "black" and "lighter" with a paradigm. (RFM p. 30-1.)

In grammatical propositions, whether they are analytic or synthetic, what appear to be metaphysical statements are expressions of connections of paradigms and names "set up in our language." It is these internal relations (whether arising from the *meanings* of concepts or from the acceptance of the same paradigm for the relations between two sets of concepts, as in the above case) which give us the universality and necessity which are the marks of the *a priori*.

In the remaining sections of this chapter we examine three points about grammar as Wittgenstein understands it:

(1) its *presuppositional, autonomous* and *arbitrary* character; (2) its *normative* character; and (3) its *two-facedness* as, on the one hand, what deceives us and creates philosophical problems, and, on the other, what, when seen correctly, removes the deceptions.

ii

Wittgenstein speaks of grammar as a *description of the use of signs* (PI 496; cf. PG 23). In this innocent-sounding phrase it may be difficult to discern anything resembling the ontology of the *Tractatus*

–the *a priori* order of possibilities which is the structure of the world (T 6.13; PI 97). And yet when we recall that the *a priori* possibilities in the *Tractatus* are the possibilities of sense for both the world and language, the resemblance is easier to see. In the later philosophy the ontology is gone (for exact reference is no longer the essence of language), but the notion of language as the possibilities of making sense remains.

The principal similarity between the *ontology* of the early philosophy and the *grammar* of the later one is that both express a presuppositional way of looking at language. They are both answers to the question: What is the nature of language for language to be able to do what it does? The first answer, the structural one, is: Language must have a hidden core of exact structures mirroring the possible structures of the world. The second, the conventionalist one, is: Language consists of established patterns of human uses and activities.

While grammar in the later philosophy is still the essence of language (PI 92), it is at the same time only an aspect of language, the aspect which sees language and the phenomena connected with language in terms of their possibilities (PI 90, 129). This is the import of language-games and forms of life, as well as of the whole philosophical task of trying to get a clear view of the use of words.

Wittgenstein's way of looking at language throughout may be summed up in a formula: *Meaning comes before fact*. This central idea of his philosophy requires that *meaning does not in turn depend upon fact* and also that *meaning itself is not a fact*. So far it is the point of view of both the earlier and later philosophies. But the later philosophy takes a further step because it puts meaning not only before fact, but also before ontology or being. Even the mirror-image ontology of the *Tractatus* has been discarded in favor of what is now understood as an aspect of the phenomena of language, the aspect which Wittgenstein calls *grammar*. (PI 108.)

The principal point about grammar, however, is still that *grammar comes before facts*. Grammar is not dependent upon facts. It does not have the character which it has because the world has the character which it has, for there is no sense any longer in saying this if we no longer think of language as picturing the world. Grammar is *world-constituting*, not of the existence of the world (for existence as such for Wittgenstein is not sayable), but of the world having any character at all which can be said. Since it gives all the ways of speaking about the world, there is no further way by which we could say how the world itself is so that grammar might conform to it. The world as having an ultimate character in-itself—this picture has been given up. (Indeed it was all but given up in the *Tractatus*, since, in respect to everything that could be said, the world and language were identical there, except for the unsayable difference between existence and non-existence.) There is no world-in-itself which finally can adjudicate between different ways of speaking.

It is not "because of the facts" that we adopt a certain way of speaking, first of all, because there is nothing that we can call "the facts" without already having a certain way of speaking. The strong feeling we may have that there *is* no other way of speaking can be countered by imagining that certain very general facts were different. In a much quoted passage Wittgenstein says:

> if anyone believes that certain concepts are absolutely the correct ones, and that having different ones would mean not realizing something that we realize—then let him imagine certain very general facts of nature to be different from what we are used to, and the formation of concepts different from the usual ones will become intelligible to him. (PI p. 230.)

This, by no means, suggests that the concepts we do have "depend upon" the very general facts. It only suggests (as he puts it in the immediately preceding paragraph) that there is a "correspondence between concepts and very general facts of nature." The kind of very general facts of nature which he has in mind may be ones like these: that objects do not appear and disappear suddenly without reason, that colors and shapes go together in the visual world, and that we can usually remember something that happened a short time before. (In Wittgenstein's last book *On Certainty* such facts as these are taken as belonging to the common-sense framework of the world, which we take for granted and in terms of which we carry out all our investigating, knowing and speaking.)

The autonomous character of grammar means not only that grammar comes before facts and cannot be justified in terms of facts, but also that there is nothing which "connects" grammar to the world or enables us to apply it to the world. There is, for example, no "psychological" intermediary. Anything which is necessary to make it possible to apply language to the world already belongs to grammar. The actual application of language alone does not.

What Wittgenstein says about logic in the *Tractatus* applies to grammar here: first, that logic and the application of logic cannot overlap; they must be kept separate; and second, that nothing can come between logic and its application; they must be side by side (T 5.557.) In the case of grammar, the use of signs or the possible use of signs cannot, on the one hand, determine a single actual occurrence of language, but, on the other hand, nothing can mediate between grammar and its actual application, for this would either have to belong to grammar, as something more which is presupposed, or belong to the application.

All this suggests that Wittgenstein thinks of grammar as arbitrary and that he belongs in some way or other to the voluntarist tradition. The first is true, but the second is not. Grammar is arbitrary in the sense that it does not depend upon anything else, but it is not arbitrary in the sense of, therefore, depending upon the human will. It is open and subject to change, but not subject to willful change. Even in the case of concepts we cannot choose any ones we want.

> Compare a concept with a style of painting. For is even our style of painting arbitrary? Can we choose one at pleasure? (The Egyptian, for instance.) Is it a mere question of pleasing and ugly? (PI p. 230.)

While we may imagine different concepts and different language-games with different grammars (as Wittgenstein himself occasionally does), it would be virtually beyond our capacity to institute these. The number of changes in our activities and ways of living required would be prohibitive.

In what way grammar is arbitrary is suggested by the following:

> The rules of grammar may be called "arbitrary," if that is to mean that the *aim* of the grammar is nothing but that of the language.
> If someone says "If our language had not this grammar, it could not express these facts"—it should be asked what "*could*" means here. (PI 497.)

The second part of this passage may become clearer if we consider these questions: Do we know what the facts are independently of our grammar? Or does not our grammar establish just what it is possible to say (i.e. what makes sense)? If our grammar settles what it is possible to say, then we could not say what it is possible to say without it. Hence there is no way in which grammar itself can permit us to say something which *in some other sense* is possible. The point seems to be the same as the one Wittgenstein put in the Moore Lecture Notes this way:

> I can't say what reality would have to be like in order that what makes nonsense should make sense because in order to do so I should have to use this new grammar. (MLN p. 272.)

What Wittgenstein says about the arbitrariness of any notation in the *Tractatus* applies, *mutatis mutandis*, to grammar in the *Investigations*:

> Although there is something arbitrary in our notations, *this* much is not arbitrary—that *when* we have determined one thing arbitrarily, something else is necessarily the case. (This derives from the *essence* of notation.) (T 3.342.)

The next entry in the *Tractatus* explicates this as follows:

> A particular mode of signifying may be unimportant but it is always important that it is a *possible* mode of signifying. And this is generally so in philosophy: again and again the individual case turns out to be unimportant, but the possibility of each individual case discloses something about the essence of the world. (T 3.3421.)

To put this in the language of the later philosophy: when an arbitrary use has been established (as might happen in some areas of language), then certain further uses or possibilities of making sense necessarily go with it, and *these* are not arbitrary. Grammatical propositions express these necessary connections.[2]

The importance of grammar in Wittgenstein's philosophy is shown by the consideration that it is presuppositional, autonomous and, in the way we have discussed, arbitrary. It is also, what is of equal importance, *normative*. To this aspect we turn now.

---

[2] The best discussion of Wittgenstein's conception of grammar is to be found in Ernst Konrad Specht, *The Foundations of Wittgenstein's Late Philosophy* (Manchester: University Press, English translation, 1969), pp. 141-184.

iii

Grammar is implicit in language in the way that the rules of a game are implicit in the game, determining the structure and character of the game, but not in such a way that it or they cannot be changed in all kinds of different ways. And grammar is also the *description of* these implicit governing practices and conventions. As the rules of a game may be read off from the practice of the game "like a natural law governing the play" (PI 54), so grammar may be "read off" from the practices of language. And as the rules of the game permit us to distinguish between correct and incorrect playing of the game (and in this way are like a natural law), so grammar, or the rules of grammar, permit us to distinguish between correct and incorrect ways of using words (and so in this way also are *not* like a natural law).

It is very important that Wittgenstein's conception of grammar as a description of the use of signs (PI 496) does not mean a description of grammar as *fact* (in the way that a linguist might describe it), but rather means a description of grammar as *normative* or supplying the basis for the distinction between correct and incorrect. Grammar is not binding in the way that natural laws are binding; it is binding in the way that the rules of a game are binding, in *defining* mistakes, errors and violations. This is the way in which social conventions are binding. The members of a group who customarily do things the same way do so because of something more like a commitment than an external constraint.

In describing rules in their normative or rule-like character Wittgenstein first makes the point that rules *qua* rules are not facts—that is, they do not tell us that something is or is not the case, but rather require that something be done or not done. It may be true or false that such and such *is* a rule in a particular game, but the rule itself is not true or false, and to grasp the meaning of a rule is not to learn anything about how things are (or are not), but to learn what is expected to be done (or not done).

It is essential for Wittgenstein's view that a rule *cannot* be translated into a fact, a rule cannot *determine* a course of action. In each case a rule would lose its normative character if there were some way of equating it with a fact. Every interpretation may stand in need of another one, and still the jump to the act of obeying or disobeying the rule will have to take place. Furthermore whatever we do on some interpretation *could* be understood as obeying the rule. On this basis it would be impossible to say when a rule had been obeyed and when it hadn't. Wittgenstein sums this up so:

> This was our paradox: no course of action could be determined by a rule, because every course of action can be made out to accord with the rule. The answer was: if everything can be made out to accord with the rule, then it can also be made out to conflict with it. And so there would be neither accord nor conflict here. . . . What this shows is that there is a way of grasping a rule which is *not an interpretation*, but which is exhibited in what we call "obeying the rule" and "going against it" in actual cases. (PI 201.)

The force of this is to maintain the gap between a rule and any course of action whatsoever, so that no "correlation" can be established between a rule and a fact. If this distinction (which encompasses the distinction between grammar and facts) were to break down, it would pull Wittgenstein's philosophy down with it.

The acid test for Wittgenstein's conception of the absoluteness of the separation between a rule and any particular course of action which "follows" it, is the case of series in mathematics and the rules for forming such series. This subject is discussed at some length both in the *Philosophical Investigations* and in the *Remarks on the Foundations of Mathematics*. Wittgenstein wishes to show that *at no point* in the application of a rule does a rule *determine* what is to be done with it; there is always the *possibility* of doing something different with it.

If we consider, for example, a rule for forming a series like "Add 2," then it may seem as if this rule "contains" the series of numbers which is to be formed from it and "contains" the series, as it were, *in advance*. The idea of "logical necessity" suggests that there *is* only one right way of applying the rule, so that the "tracks" along which we must travel are laid out ahead of time, and anyone who "understands" the rule must "necessarily" form the series in just one way. Wittgenstein's point is that this "picture" is a myth and that it is always at least possible at any point whatever to apply the rule in some other way while maintaining that we are applying it in the same way. A person who began to form the series 2, 4, 6, 8 and then continued 12, 16, 20, 24 and was told that he had "switched" from "adding 2" to "adding 4" might, for example, maintain that when two-digit numbers were reached, then "adding 2" *meant* this and *this was now* (whatever anyone else said) what *he* called "doing the same thing."

Trying to argue with this, saying that if he continued the series in this way, he was "doing it wrong" since he should be able to "see" that he had changed the rule to "Add 4"—all this *could* be met by the insistence that it was other people who were "wrong" and *they* were the ones who were "changing the rule" when the series reached the two-digit numbers by proceeding "in a different way." To say that we all in fact tend to "continue the series in one certain way" is true enough. But to say that this is the *only possible* correct way of doing it shows a misunderstanding, for there is no necessity of this sort "contained in" the rule, and, more, even the word *same* is *always* open to another interpretation.

There is a custom of "obeying rules," and we learn to obey them in certain ways. But this is not because in the nature of the rules they *have* to be obeyed in these ways. The transition from the rule to what is done occurs "blindly." We have learned a certain response, but could have learned another one. The justifications we would give for obeying the rule in this way or that, would all be on the same footing.

In this Wittgenstein maintains an absolute distinction between a rule and any particular course of action (and hence between grammar and the application of grammar in any particular instance). While any particular grammatical rule is open to abandonment or change, whatever *is* a grammatical rule has this status—that it determines what is correct and incorrect, but does not determine any particular application. All the necessity belongs to the established uses of language (whatever these are) and all the contingency to the actual applications, and *there is no bridge between them.*

What is new about Wittgenstein's conception of rules is that it combines two points that are not usually thought to be able to go together: (1) the completely necessary and binding character of rules and (2) the idea that the rules, *nevertheless*, have to be accepted. Obeying rules is itself a custom, a form of life. That *something* plays such a role with us is a matter of the way we do things. Any particular rule then is accepted into that status for all sorts of contingent reasons. The model which Wittgenstein has in mind in thinking about necessity (whether it is mathematical, logical or grammatical) seems to be suggested by the following:

What I have to do is something like to describe the office of
a king; in doing that I must never fall into the error of explaining the kingly dignity by the king's usefulness. . . . (RFM
p. 160.)

Can we now distinguish: (1) having kings is a custom, (2) *nevertheless*
the absolute authority of the king and (3) contingent reasons why any
particular person becomes king.

iv

Grammar for Wittgenstein is two-faced in a very thorough-going
way. Indeed, it embodies the distinction between appearance and reality which used to belong to the world (and which marked the beginning of ontology in Greece). On the one hand, it is the authority of
language, what he calls "the account books of language," wherein we
see what actually works, "the actual transactions of language" (PG
p. 87). But, on the other hand, in its appearances, it is the source of
illusions and mystifications, creating the puzzles and seemingly inso-
luble problems of philosophy.

On its surface, grammar is full of similes which create false appearances (PI 112) and pictures which "force themselves on us" (PI
140, 397) and "hold us captive" (PI 115). It fascinates us with misleading analogies (BLB 49) and tempts us to misunderstand and invent
myths (PI 109, 345). We try to follow up the analogies which it suggests and we find that they conflict with each other and we get en-
tangled in our own rules (PI 125). Grammar is a snare and a delusion.

Yet these appearances of grammar can only be overcome by the
reality of grammar. We have to be able to see what is harder to see: the
actual workings of language. These are in a sense just as phenomenal
and just as "visible"; they are not to be arrived at by analysis. But they
require that we distrust the impressions provided by the first pictures
which language suggests. These pictures are the principal source of the
trouble.

To see how language really functions, Wittgenstein says, we need
an *overview* or a *survey-view*. But our grammar is lacking in this sort
of *surveyability* (*Übersichtlichkeit*). (The standard translation for this
is *perspicuity* with the adjective *perspicuous*.) If we had such an overview representation, he adds that we would have

just that understanding which consists in "seeing connections." Hence the importance of finding and inventing *intermediate cases*. (PI 122.)

At this point we need to ask ourselves: What does *surveyability*
mean and how does it relate to "seeing connections"? From the *Remarks on the Foundations of Mathematics* where Wittgenstein discusses the necessity of proofs being *surveyable* (RFM pp. 65-71) it
seems evident that *surveyability* means something like the property of
being able to be taken in at a glance. If something is surveyable, then
we can see the various parts of it in their inter-relations without being in the situation of having, in effect, forgotten the beginning before we get to the end. In saying that our grammar does not have this
kind of *surveyability* he is saying that if we look at what is ordinarily
called the grammar of our language, we cannot take it in at a glance
or see how the different parts of it go together.

To cite an example: Grammar in the case of statements like "I
have a pain" and "He has a pain" gives an impression of similarity. But
this is because we *cannot see at a glance* how the two sentences really
work. A whole nest of philosophical problems will be generated if we
try to push through the apparent similarity. On the other hand, if we
look more deeply, we will see how far apart the two statements actually are by filling in some of the missing intermediate cases.

This brings us to the question: What is the difference between the
grammar which misleads us (PI 187) by forcing itself on us (PI 304)
and creating illusions and superstititons (PI 110), and, on the other
hand, the grammar which, if we look more closely, becomes *surveyable*
and removes these illusions and superstitions (PI 90)? Wittgenstein
speaks of the differences in three main ways, as

1 — the difference between *surface grammar* and *depth grammar;*
In a passage reminiscent of the *Tractatus* comparing language to cloth-
ing, the outward form of which does not reveal the form of the body
(T 4.002) he says:

> We remain unconscious of the prodigious diversity of all
> everyday language-games because the clothing of our language
> makes everything alike. (PI p. 224.)

The way the appearance creates false expectations is spelled out in
the following:

What immediately impresses itself upon us about the use of
a word is the way it is used in the construction of the sentence, the part of its use—one might say—that can be taken in
by the ear.—And now compare the depth grammar, say of the
word "to mean," with what the surface grammar would lead
us to expect. No wonder we find it difficult to find our way
about. (PI 664.)

2 — the difference between *language idling* and *language working;*
If we do not look at language operating, but only look at its static
form, then we are also likely to be misled.

For philosophical problems arise when language *goes on holi-
day*. (PI 38.)
The confusions which occupy us arise when language is like
an engine idling, not when it is doing work. (PI 132.)

Just how looking at language in a static way creates illusions can be
seen from considering how pictures embedded in language then get
a grip on us. Such pictures as the contrast between *inner* and *outer*,
which seems to give us the way of understanding psychological concepts, but actually misleads us, or the picture of *exact reference for
names*, to which Wittgenstein himself succumbed, may force themselves on us and fix our thinking in moulds from which we then cannot escape. As he puts it:

A picture is conjured up which seems to fix the sense *unam-
biguously*. The actual use compared with that suggested by
the picture seems like something muddied. Here again we get
the same thing as in set theory; the form of expression we
use seems to have been designed for a god, who knows what
we cannot know; he sees the whole of each of those infinite
series and he sees into human consciousness. For us, of course,
these forms of expression are like pontificals, which we may
put on, but cannot do much with, since we lack the effective power that would give these vestments meaning and purpose. (PI 426.)

3 — the difference between *guessing* or *theorizing* and actually *looking* at the uses of words.
The admonition *not to think but to look* (PI 66) is directed against
the tendency to suppose that words *must* function in a certain way
because some theory prescribes this. As against *looking* this is more
like *guessing*, and Wittgenstein says of that:

One cannot guess how a word functions. One has to *look at*
its use and learn from that.
But the difficulty is to remove the prejudice which stands in
the way of doing this. It is not a *stupid* prejudice. (PI 340.)

Wittgenstein does not say what the prejudice is, but it may be that
referred to in the *Blue Book* as "the contemptuous attitude toward the
particular case" (BLB p. 18), which is connected there with the "crav-
ing for generality" and with being "misled by the example of science."

At every point Wittgenstein insists that the business of philosophy
is purely descriptive, and in no way to explain or theorize. In the
course of describing, the most the philosopher can do is to *assemble
reminders* (PI 127), *rearrange concepts* (PI 93), *find and invent intermediate cases* (PI 122) and *imagine fictitious natural history* for his
purposes (PI p. 230). These devices are used to break the hold of certain analogies and pictures so that we will be able to see and understand despite an urge not to.

What philosophy aims at is stated in this way:

1 – to command a clear overview of the aim and functioning of our
words (PI 5);
2 – to establish an order in our knowledge of the use of language (PI
5); an order with a particular end in view; one out of many possible
orders; not *the* order (PI 132);
3 – to look into the workings of our language and that in such a way
as to make us recognize those workings in spite of an urge to misunderstand them (PI 109).

Even though the operative words here are *overview, knowledge,* and
recognize there is no critical difference between the three formulations.
They all point to the *complete* clarity, which, Wittgenstein says,

simply means that the philosophical problems should *completely* disappear. (PI 133.)

Wittgenstein then adds the following cryptic but very important
comment:

The real discovery is the one that makes me capable of stopping doing philosophy when I want to.—The one that gives
philosophy peace, so that it is no longer tormented by questions which bring *itself* in question.—Instead we now dem-

onstrate a method, by examples; and the series of examples can be broken off.—Problems are solved (difficulties eliminated), not a *single* problem. (PI 133.)

What is the discovery which makes it possible to stop doing philosophy when we want and which gives philosophy itself peace? It is the giving up of the idea of *finality*—that is, the idea of philosophy closing itself out by setting up one solution (which is never satisfactory because it is never the solution to the right problem). Wittgenstein's discovery is of a kind of philosophy and philosophical activity which does not have this finality because it is not a "construction" but simply a point of view for getting rid of "constructions."

Wittgenstein's philosophy is at peace because it does not prove anything or establish anything, but leaves everything just as it is. In other words, it comes to rest in the ordinary, everyday world, the world which has never been good enough for philosophy, since philosophy has always tried to replace it with some other "more real" reality—scientific, metaphysical, materialist, idealist, etc. (And we must not forget, of course, that the everyday world itself is also shot through with illusions arising from just this notion of another superior "reality.")

It is a misunderstanding to imagine that Wittgenstein glorifies ordinary language in all of its aspects. How could he since it is also ordinary language which is full of the pictures, myths and metaphors which confuse and deceive us? What is important about ordinary language is what enables it to function, not the various theories and pictures which it suggests. In the Frazer Notes Wittgenstein said that a whole mythology is preserved in our language. It is certainly not this which is important to its actual grammar. The functionings of language proceed in despite of the mythology.

In thinking of Wittgenstein's conception of grammar, we are reminded of what a famous physiologist is reported to have said about his body at the end of his life—that "this body of mine knew a million times more than I did." We, of course, create another myth if we say that our language "knows" a million times more than we do, or even if we speak about language as a "vast intellectual repository" or as "the history of the human mind." Nor can we talk about grammar "revealing" the "structure of thought" without lapsing into the *Tractatus* point of view.

The temptation to formulate still another "myth of symbolism" remains strong. We cannot be sure that there are not such "mythical" elements left over in any description. But this is all the more reason for removing them if they can be recognized. The mythical ways of speaking do no harm if they are recognized as mythical.

Physiognomic Phenomenalism

A phenomenon isn't a symptom of something else; it is the reality.

WITTGENSTEIN (PR p. 283)

Do not look for anything behind the phenomena; they are themselves their own lesson.

GOETHE

What is there to explain? All things are just the realm that is before one's eyes.

Togan Koji (Noh play)

Description is revelation. It is not
The thing described, nor false facsimile.

WALLACE STEVENS

CHAPTER 11

Physiognomic Phenomenalism

i

No philosophy has put such a great emphasis on *description* as Wittgenstein's. In the *Tractatus* description is said to be not only the essence of language, but also the essence of the world (T 5.4711). The possibility of describing the world is taken as equivalent to the possibility of language itself, and, even more, to the possibility of the world itself. Description is the end-all and be-all.

When this conception was abandoned by Wittgenstein, and description came to have a variety of different meanings, then it was philosophy that was thought of as purely descriptive (PI 109, 124-8), explaining nothing, deducing nothing, adding nothing, subtracting nothing. Language and what went with language were taken as purely phenomenal, but seen in the *aspect* of their possibilities. Description, in a sense, even overcame structuralism.

It might be said that structuralism from the start was in the service of description, since it was as the *essence of description* that Wittgenstein was concerned with structure in the first place. When one or the other had to give way, it was the structuralism which was abandoned in the interests of a still greater commitment to description. Wittgenstein's descriptivism finally emerged as a full-blown, but very special kind of phenomenalism.

It was *description in opposition to explanation* which Wittgenstein consistently defended, particularly in reference to science. In the *Tractatus* this came out in his view that:

(1) There are no explanatory factors existing in nature; most important, there is no causal nexus (T 5.136).
(2) There are no hierarchies in nature; all facts are on the same level and all propositions of equal value (T 6.4).
(3) Science does not explain the world; it only describes it (T 6.341).

169

(4) Natural laws are not explanations; they are forms of description (T 6.271).

It was Wittgenstein's view that the principal modern illusion was the idea that the so-called laws of nature are the explanations of natural phenomena (T 6.271). This is part of what he called "our sickness," the desire to explain everything (VWC 134). This was also the gist of his criticism of Frazer: that Frazer tried to explain what cannot be explained and doesn't need to be explained. In one place Wittgenstein finally burst out:

Why don't we just leave explaining alone? (Z 615.)

It was, as Wittgenstein came to see, because the *Tractatus* itself ironically was in some way trying to *explain description*, instead of just staying with description, that the *Tractatus* failed. It was false to its own principles, and this is, indeed, what led to the self-contradiction expressed at the end of the book (that we cannot set up structural preconditions for description in language if language *can* only describe). From this point on Wittgenstein could only move toward an even more thorough-going commitment to description and an even more thorough attempt to purge out the explanatory elements.

Wittgenstein's initial point of view, what he started out from, has a great deal in common with the philosophy of Ernst Mach, a reigning figure in the Vienna of Wittgenstein's youth. It is free, however, from Mach's sensationistic and psychologistic framework. Wittgenstein's concern with logic and language and his Kantianism, inherited from Hertz and Boltzmann, as well as from Schopenhauer, preserved him from this. The idea of the role of "pictures" seems to have come from Hertz and that of "spaces of theoretical possibilities" from Boltzmann.[1]

Mach's general conception of science was that science does not describe a "real world" somehow underlying or causing the familiar world of phenomena, but rather that it is *a summary account of the phenomena themselves*. We find Mach, for example, saying:

Now one might be of the opinion, say, with respect to physics, that the portrayal of the sense-given *facts* is of less impor-

---

[1] These sources of Wittgenstein's ideas are discussed in Allan Janik and Stephen Toulmin, *Wittgenstein's Vienna* (N.Y.: Simon and Schuster, 1973), pp. 133-46.

tance than the atoms, forces and laws by which they are portrayed, and which form, so to speak, the *nucleus* of the sense-given facts. But unbiased reflection discloses that every *practical* and *intellectual* need is satisfied the moment our thoughts have acquired the power to represent the facts of the senses completely. Such representation, consequently, is the *end and aim* of physics; while atoms, forces and laws are merely *means* facilitating the representation. Their value extends as far, and as far only, as the help they afford. (*Analysis of the Sensations* (Chicago: Open Court, 1897), p. 154.)

For Mach, as for Wittgenstein, generality is always purchased at the price of leaving something out. Mach calls natural laws "abridged descriptions" and continues:

> In reality the law always contains less than the fact itself, because it does not reproduce the fact as a whole but only that aspect of it which is important to us, the rest being either intentionally or from necessity omitted. (*Popular Scientific Lectures* (Chicago: Open Court, 1894), p. 193.)

Wittgenstein similarly speaks of scientific theories as different kinds of nets which can only catch what is of approximately the proper size (T 6.341).

Finally Mach's conception of causality anticipates Wittgenstein's:

> . . . the law of causality is sufficiently characterized by saying that it is the presupposition of the mutual dependence of phenomena. (*History and Root of the Principle of the Conservation of Energy* (Chicago: Open Court, 1910) p. 61.)

Wittgenstein's formulation is

> The law of causality is not a law but the form of a law. T 6.32.)
> If there were a law of causality, it might be put in the following way: There are laws of nature. (T 6.36.)

Wittgenstein, it might be said, goes far beyond Mach in thinking not only of science as description, but indeed of all language as description and even the world itself as description. It would seem that the emphasis on description could go no further. But the *Tractatus* was couched in ontological terms, and these could not themselves be regarded as descriptive. Wittgenstein's structuralism and his conception of logical mapping, designed to vindicate description, in a sense turned it against itself. And this is what opened the way for the later philosophy.

ii

When we speak of the *phenomenalism* of Wittgenstein's later philosophy, we mean, first of all, that the term *phenomenon* replaces the term *fact* as the general word for what we deal with in the world.[2] *Phenomenon* is the word for what confronts us, even though what we say about it always takes place within a language-game since we cannot confront the world outside of language-games.

It should be evident that the term *phenomenon*, as used by Wittgenstein, does not mean what it has meant in previous philosophies, since for Wittgenstein it carries no ontological implications. It is not used, for example, in Kant's sense of *phenomenon* contrasted with *noumenon*. Nor does it mean what it meant for some varieties of logical empiricists—*sense data* or *sensibilia*. And it certainly does not have the meaning it has in phenomenology, since Wittgenstein's *phenomena* are not essences and have no essences.

As Wittgenstein uses the term, *phenomena* are not ontological realities, existing in themselves, nor appearances of such realities. They are neither objects of sense nor of intellectual intuition, nor are they presuppositions of sense or of thought. Instead they are the everyday things and occurrences which we recognize and identify—the phenomena of everyday life (PI 436).

What is most striking and important about Wittgenstein's phenomenalism is what we are calling its *physiognomic* character. This means that phenomena for him may be expressive in the way that the human face is expressive, and he refuses to separate the expressions from the phenomena and to imagine that we see the phenomena, as it were, without any expression, and then add on the expressions (as if we imagined that the face is there in some more basic way than its expressions). The phenomena for Wittgenstein tell us just what we can read off from them, and they are no more and no less than that.

---

[2] How the term *phenomenon* itself came into Wittgenstein's philosophy in his middle period and his various experiments with it should be a subject for further investigation. See, for example, Herbert Spiegelberg, "The Puzzle of Ludwig Wittgenstein's *Phänomenologie* (1929- ?)," *American Philosophical Quarterly*, Vol. 5, No. 4 (October 1968), pp. 244-256.

Wittgenstein's *physiognomic phenomenalism* is mainly characterized by this: that it does not regard "expressive" phenomena as any less "basic" or "primitive" than any other phenomena. This is the main import of the lengthy discussion of "seeing" and "seeing as" (or "seeing" and "aspect-seeing") which occupies almost forty pages in the second part of the *Philosophical Investigations*. There are two different concepts here, and neither is more "primitive" or more "basic" than the other. We cannot understand "seeing as" in terms of "seeing-plus-something-else"; nor can we understand "seeing" as always a case of "seeing as." (This subject is discussed more fully in section iv of this chapter.)

Phenomena for Wittgenstein are as expressive as they are taken to be or recognized as being. They are not, as in "sense data" views, "bare givens" along with something else which is subjectively added. (Here Wittgenstein's rejection of "private objects" is once more relevant.) The difference between phenomena and expressive phenomena (or, what is not the same difference, but is similar, between "seeing" and 'seeing as") is a conceptual and language-game difference, not an ontological one. There are no phenomena that are just primitively "given" outside of any language-game or in a way that is different from the way in which we are in the everyday world.

Wittgenstein's non-restrictive and non-reductive way of using the term *phenomenon* makes it possible for him to speak of all kinds of psychological phenomena. Some examples of these are:

the phenomenon of immediate realization (RFM p. 123);
the phenomenon of being able to continue a sentence (Z 38);
the phenomena of being struck by something (e.g. a face) (PI p. 211);
the phenomenon of guessing and that of guessing right (RFM p. 120);
the phenomena of seeing, believing, thinking, wishing (Z 471);
the phenomenon of hope (PI 583).

These examples show that for Wittgenstein anything we observe (along with its full content of "meaning" as observed) belongs to the phenomena. However subtle and however nuanced, what we see is "phenomenal" and no theories or psychological explanations are required. Such an extended use of the term *phenomenon*, as in the above examples, is likely to give the traditional philosopher a slightly dizzy feeling. He might recall the statement made by one of Wittgenstein's favorite authors Lichtenberg that "We can see nothing of the human mind if it is not present in the facial expressions" and a similar statement by Wittgenstein himself that "The human body is the best picture of the human soul" (PI p. 178).

What requires considerably more discussion is Wittgenstein's *phenomenalism without ontology*. The Wittgenstein world is, as has been several times observed, *flat*. Or, as he himself put it, it is all foreground and no background (PG p. 87). Or, as he also said, in it there is nothing hidden; everything lies open to view (PI 126). We might say that it is *all surface*.

This has to be understood, however, as not leaving anything out. And here there is an interesting analogy with contemporary painting and contemporary art theory. Wittgenstein's world is flat in the way that contemporary painting is flat because, as the painter now understands, this is the *wider* way of seeing since it is the way which *includes* the possibility of the third dimension. And similarly, phenomenalism, or just what appears, is the wider perspective in philosophy, since ontology also has to derive from that.

To pursue the analogy—what has been emphasized in contemporary painting is that, for the painter, *all* the possibilities lie in the flat canvas (as long as he sticks to that), and this includes even the possibility of the so-called "more real" three dimensions of "perspective." Breaking the "perspectival bonds" (developed in the Renaissance) is rediscovering the priority of the two-dimensional, in terms of which the third dimension *always* had to be stated.

And so with Wittgenstein's phenomenalism. All the possibilities of meaning and sense must lie in the phenomena, since they are always the source of the philosophical "third dimension" of ontology. The phenomena without ontology have this kind of a priority over ontology: any ontology must finally be accredited by the phenomena too. What is not phenomena must somehow reveal itself in or through phenomena. The phenomena do not then *require* ontology, or have to be understood in terms of ontology, any more than painting has to be three-dimensional or understood three-dimensionally.

This momentous change or reversal which is visible in Wittgenstein might be described as *appearance* and *reality* changing places, so that now "realities" are to be thought of as "contained in" the "appearances" rather than the "appearances" as "contained in" "realities."[3]

Respect for the appearances, which has a long history, has never quite reached the point before where it could challenge ontology without landing in scepticism and relativism. But many aspects of modern thought (including the emphasis on the analogical even in the sciences) have moved in this direction. And in Wittgenstein's later philosophy we have a complete statement of it, for in that philosophy, as he says, "everything lies open to view" and so "there is nothing to explain." (PI 126.)

iii

The most striking example of Wittgenstein's *physiognomic phenomenalism,* as might be expected, is his conception that we actually *see* (and do not merely *infer,* or *interpret* or *project*) states of mind and human emotions *in the human face.* (The human face is, of course, the prototypical or original case of physiognomic perception, from which, it might be said, we learn to look at other phenomena in that way and so to modify or extend the concept of *seeing,* though, in the Wittgenstein spirit, this must be regarded also as a grammatical and not a developmental point.) Wittgenstein, as usual, puts the matter most succinctly:

> Consciousness in another's face. Look into someone else's face, and see consciousness in it, and a particular *shade* of consciousness. You see on it, in it, joy, indifference, interest, excitement, torpor, and so on. The light in other people's faces.
> Do you look into *yourself* in order to recognize the fury in *his* face? It is there as clearly as in your own breast. (Z 220.)

He then continues by poking a little fun at those who think we can only know other people's states of mind from "our own case."

> (And what do we want to say now? That someone else's face stimulates me to want to imitate it, and that I therefore feel little movements and muscle-contractions in my own face and *mean* the sum of these? Nonsense. Nonsense,—because you

---

[3] The progenitor of this point of view in modern times was, of course, Goethe. Of him Paul Valery, the French poet, wrote: "Goethe is the great apologist of the world of appearances. He attributed to what is regarded as the surface of things an interest and a value in which I observe a frankness and a bias that seems to me of the utmost importance." *Collected Works of Paul Valery* (Princeton: University Press, 1968), Vol. 9, p. 161.

are making assumptions instead of simply describing. If your
head is haunted by explanations here, you are neglecting to
remind yourself of the most important facts.) (Z 220.)

Once again, the "sickness" of "wanting to explain" prevents us from
"just looking." The supposed "explanation" intrudes itself everywhere,
so much so that we cannot see what is manifestly in front of our eyes.
The same thing applies to emotions:

> "We *see* emotion."—As opposed to what?—We do not see
> facial contortions and make inferences from them (like a
> doctor framing a diagnosis) to joy, grief, boredom. We de-
> scribe a face immediately as sad, radiant, bored, even when we
> are unable to give any other description of the features.—
> Grief, one would like to say, is personified in the face.
> This belongs to the concept of emotion. (Z 225.)

What is the meaning of this last statement that it belongs to the concept of emotion that emotions are personified in the face? Presumably
that if we understand the concept of *emotion*, we also understand the
concept of *being personified in the face*. In other words, we cannot
use the word *emotion* successfully without accepting that human faces
show the emotions of persons. And presumably also this will be true
for those who would reject calling these, cases of *seeing*. Wittgenstein
recognizes that it is a certain *kind* of seeing, but still says that "naive
language" is right to use this word.

> "If you only shake free from your physiological prejudices,
> you will find nothing queer about the fact that the glance
> of the eye can be seen too." For I also say that I see the look
> that you cast at someone else. And if someone wanted to cor-
> rect me and say that I don't really *see* it, I should take that for
> pure stupidity.
> On the other hand, I have not *made any admissions* by using
> that manner of speaking, and I should contradict anyone who
> told me I saw the glance "just the way" I see the shape and
> color of the eye.
> For "naive language," that is to say our naive, normal way of
> expressing ourselves, does not contain any theory of seeing—
> does not show you a *theory* but only a *concept* of seeing.
> Z 223.)[4]

---

[4] Is the issue here between a *theory* and a *concept?* Or between two uses of
language? Or is it between two different world-views?

It is reflections like these which led Wittgenstein to recognize a conception of meaning quite different from the idea that the meaning of a word is its use. This is the idea that "meaning is a physiognomy" (PI 568). This must be added to the previous conceptions because (as we have just seen) it applies also to language itself since the physiognomy of a word may be thought of as part of its meaning (without coming into conflict with the other idea of meaning as the use of the word).

We should recall that Wittgenstein was always ready to consider other uses of the word *meaning*, for he said:

> For a *large* class of cases—though not for all—in which we employ the word "meaning" it can be defined thus: the meaning of a word is its use in the language. (PI 43.)

How important *meaning as physiognomy* is may be seen from Wittgenstein's "Notes on Frazer's *Golden Bough*," where it constitutes the essential difference between his understanding of magic and religion, and Frazer's. Frazer was under the impression that primitive magic was a kind of pre-science, a more or less unsuccessful attempt to *explain the world*. Wittgenstein, on the other hand, rejects this completely and says that magic and religion are *responses* to the *meanings of phenomena*, or interpretations of phenomena. They are *responses to the physiognomy of the world*.

From this point of view primitive peoples are not under the strange delusions about how nature works or how to control nature which Frazer (along with some other anthropologists) attributes to them. For, as Wittgenstein points out:

> Frazer so represents it as if these people had a wholly false (indeed lunatic) idea of the course of nature, while they have only a strange interpretation of phenomena. That is, their knowledge of nature, if they were to write it down, would not be distinguished from ours in any fundamental way. Only their magic is different. (NFGB p. 245.)

In Wittgenstein's view magic and religion are ways in which we are "gripped by" phenomena or respond to phenomena because we find phenomena in themselves meaningful. Primitive people, or people who are still able to respond to the world magically or religiously, do not have our mania for explanation, and they do not imagine that their magic *explains* anything. It is not a representation of the course of nature and an attempt to intervene to change that course, for this they know perfectly well they cannot do. (If they thought they could "make it rain" by the rain-dances they would certainly, as Wittgenstein points out, hold the rain-dances in the dry season, and quickly become disabused of the idea.) Rather it is a ritual reaction, like the ritualistic ways we continue to react to birth and death, New Year's Day, "anniversaries," etc.

Frazer's mistake is two-fold: first, to try to "explain" magic and religion, for as Wittgenstein points out, they cannot be "explained," but only "understood" through the same feelings and reactions in ourselves; and secondly, to regard magic and religion as themselves attempts to "explain" the world. Looked at in this way, primitive customs appear as *mistakes* and primitive people as lacking in sensitivity and intelligence, a view which simply shows our own inability to understand spiritual matters. This is why Wittgenstein says that "Frazer is much more savage than most of his savages" (NFGB p. 241).

It seems likely that in Wittgenstein's view the notion of science as an *explanation* of the world (instead of a description) is what he calls "our magic" (cf. T 6.371). This is the way *we* respond to phenomena, believing it to be the only correct response. We find this "meaning" in the phenomena themselves and take it to be the only possible "meaning." But this is a misunderstanding of science, which does not give us "meanings" in this sense at all, though Wittgenstein believed at the time of the *Tractatus* it gives us all that can be put into words.

> We feel that even when *all possible* scientific questions have been answered, the problems of life remain completely untouched. Of course, there are then no questions left, and this itself is the answer.
> The solution of the problem of life is seen in the vanishing of the problem. (T 6.52-6.521.)

In the later philosophy, as we will see in the next chapter, the way is open for other kinds of language, including the language of *belief*.[5]

---

[5] We should remind ourselves again here how strongly Wittgenstein believed that we do not understand the "language of things," the belief which was so eloquently expressed in Hofmannsthal's "Letter to Chandos" already referred to. This is a point also where Wittgenstein's philosophy coincides with the anti-Cartesianism of Giambattista Vico, who also maintained, *contra* Descartes, that we understand people better than we understand things.

The whole matter is summed up this way in the "Notes on Frazer":

> For no phenomenon is in itself particularly mysterious, but each one can become so to us, and that is just the characteristic of the awakening spirit of man, that a phenomenon means something to him. (NFGB p. 239.)

The kind of meaning we find in phenomena changes. What is peculiar about our time is that we take a particular kind of description of the course of nature as being the "meaning" of the phenomena and condemn those who do not share this as "superstitious."

In the course of his discussion of Frazer, Wittgenstein makes four principal methodological points:

(1) Frazer's "explanations" make it seem that magic and religious customs arise out of, or are based upon, opinions or views; whereas, on the contrary, Wittgenstein says, customs and the opinions or views connected with them arise together and "are both there together" (NFGB p. 235). Primitive man, he adds, does not act out of opinions (NFGB p. 243), and, in any case,

> the characteristic of ritual action is that it is not at all a view, an opinion, whether correct or false . . . (NFGB p. 240.)

(2) What Frazer's "explanations" aim at (the intellectual satisfaction to be derived from them) is already what the magical or religious custom itself, to the extent that it is understood, supplies. Magic and religious customs, in other words, are their own reasons for being, and explanations add nothing to this.

> In comparison with the impression which what is described makes the explanation is too uncertain. (NFGB p. 236.)

So-called "explanations," for example, of why we greet people, why we grieve in the ways that we do at the death of loved ones or why we "remember" certain days add nothing to these customs. We understand them because we share them, and the supposed "explanations" offer no more than this understanding does.

(3) To understand magic or religious customs which we do not share in we have to find something similar in our own practices or realize

the extent to which we ourselves are capable of inventing or imagining them.

> ... the principle according to which these customs are ordered is much more universal than Frazer considers it and is already there in our own soul, so that we ourselves can think out all the possibilities. (NFGB p. 238.)
> We could invent all these ceremonies ourselves. And the spirit which leads to our inventing them would be their spirit. (NFGB p. 251.)

As examples of understanding based upon our own reactions, Wittgenstein cites the meanings (the shudder, the fear, etc.) which people still find in the word *ghost*, or in such expressions as *fearing the vengeance of the gods* or in such actions as *kissing the picture of a loved one*. Any so-called "explanations" of our reactions in these cases would not be as important or "convincing" as the reactions themselves.

(4) Magic and religious customs are not done for any reasons other than their "intrinsic convincingness," and the phenomena that they respond to do not become any the less impressive through "explanations." Human reactions to death, for example, all over the world come to expression in rites and ceremonies. "We act so and feel satisfied." To attempt to "explain" these reactions would be trivial and irrelevant.

As a prime example of Frazer's misunderstanding of primitive magic Wittgenstein cites the case of rain ceremonies. The idea that these ceremonies are carried out *in order to make it rain* overlooks the point that they are arranged to take place when it usually does rain anyway. The ceremonies rather express the importance of rain; they are a reaction to the coming, or immanent coming of rain, and it is, after all, a wholly normal and natural reaction. Rain is greeted, is interpreted as a blessing, is hailed as a favor of the rain-god, etc.

It would be strange indeed, Wittgenstein points out, if primitive man actually did believe that the rain-king could *make* it rain, if he did not call on him to do it during the dry and arid season when rain would be even more welcome. And if he thinks the rain-king is responsible for the rain, it is even more remarkable that it does not occur to him to wonder how the rain occurs without the rain-king. We are asked, in other words, to imagine that primitive man is unbelievably obtuse in over-looking all this. (It is our own myth of *archaic stupidity*, which reflects rather our own stupidity.) Wittgenstein does

not, of course, deny that men do give up customs which rest upon
errors after they have perceived these errors, but he adds:

> But even this case only happens when it is sufficient to make
> the man mindful of his error in order to dissuade him from his
> way of acting. But that is still not the case with regard to the
> religious customs of a people, and when it is a matter involv-
> ing *no* error. (NFGB p. 235.)

Wittgenstein not only disagrees with Frazer, but in a sense turns
him upside down. For the way in which Frazer understands science is
in Wittgenstein's view an example of magic, particularly narrow because it permits a misunderstanding and a shutting-out of all other
"magic." In supposing that science *explains* phenomena, Frazer actually
takes science as an interpretation of phenomena, and not just one more
interpretation, but the only correct one. Beyond this, Wittgenstein
finds in his own earlier philosophy, quite striking similarities to primitive magic (NFGB p. 242). And was he not in the *Tractatus* engaged
in interpreting the world in order, in a sense, to show that it could
not be interpreted, but only described?

iv

The most far-reaching expression of Wittgenstein's phenomenalist
point of view is to be found in his discussion of "seeing" and "seeing as"
(PI pp. 193-214). This discussion brings out how "puzzling" the
business of *seeing* is (PI p. 212), how "tangled" the concept of it is
(PI p. 200), and how much it confuses us (PI p. 204) because we do
not see how it is "modified" from use to use (PI p. 209).

Wittgenstein begins by mentioning two uses of the word *see*:
(1) the case of "I see this" (followed by a description, drawing, copy),
and (2) the case of "I see a likeness between these two faces" (PI p.
193). The first of these he calls "seeing" and the second "seeing as"
or "seeing an aspect," and the following twenty pages in the *Investigations* charts the intricate relations between these two concepts.

What emerges (it is certainly Wittgenstein's point of view from
the start) is that there is no way of understanding "seeing as" in terms
of some standard simple case of "seeing" to which then is added something else to account for the "aspects." There is no use of the concept of *seeing* which would enable it to play this role. Consequently
"aspect-seeing" is as fundamental as any other "seeing" and we simply

have two different uses of the concept of "seeing." This is the point
of view of Wittgenstein's physiognomic phenomenalism. "Seeing an
aspect" is as much "seeing" as "seeing" anything else.

Wittgenstein repeatedly speaks of "seeing an aspect" as "perceiving," even though we cannot give a "report of the perception" in this
case as we can in the case of "seeing." Even when he would agree that
there is a great deal of imagination involved in the seeing or hearing
something, he still calls it a *perception*. For example, he says:

> Doesn't it take imagination to hear something as a variation
> on a particular theme? And yet one is perceiving something
> in so hearing it. (PI p. 213.)

We do, indeed, frequently have the impression that "seeing an aspect"
is, as it were, half-seeing and half-thinking (PI pp. 204, 212), but this
does not mean that we can "reduce" the concept of "seeing as" to two
separate concepts.

> Is being struck looking plus thinking? No. Many of our con-
> cepts *cross* here. (PI p. 211.)

There is a relation between "seeing" and "thought," but it does not im-
pair the "seeing."

> . . . what I perceive in the dawning of an aspect is not a prop-
> erty of the object, but an internal relation between it and other
> objects.
> It is almost as if "seeing the sign in this context" were an echo
> of a thought.
> "The echo of a thought in sight"—one would like to say. (PI
> p. 212.)

The presence of skill, imagination and thinking in "seeing an aspect"
does not mean that we do not have in it a perfectly legitimate case of
"seeing" (that this concept is not entirely correctly employed here).

> Might I not have a purely visual concept of a hesitant posture
> or a timid face?
> Such a concept would be comparable with "major" and
> "minor" which certainly have emotional value, but can also
> be used purely to describe a perceived structure. (PI p. 209.)

Wittgenstein considers these questions in great detail and from
many different points of view. We want to summarize here four main

things which he does: (1) he cites and examines a large variety of cases of "seeing as" or "seeing an aspect"; (2) he rejects a number of false explanations or false ways of thinking about these; (3) he mentions a number of differences between these cases and cases of "seeing," as revealed by differences in the concepts and (4) he makes some general remarks about the problem. These are the subjects we take up now.

A partial list of some of the examples of "seeing as" which are discussed will include the following:

1—dual changing-aspect figures (*noticing* . . .)
    duck-rabbit (PI p. 194)
    ascending-descending staircase (PI p. 196)
    black and white wheel (PI p. 207)
    puzzle pictures (PI p. 196)
2—multi-aspect figures (*taking as* . . .)
    schematic cube (PI p. 193)
    triangle (PI p. 200)
3—expressive figures (*regarding as* . . .)
    upside-down face (PI p. 198)
    backwards words (PI p. 198)
    galloping horse (PI p. 202)
    colored vowels (PI p. 202)
    interpenetrating hexagons (PI p. 203)
    animals stuck with arrows (PI p. 203)
4—familiar likenesses (*recognizing* . . .)
    rabbit flashing by (PI p. 197)
    friend in crowd (PI p. 197)
    hidden faces (PI p. 210)
5—phantasies of children (*pretending* . . .)
    chest seen as house (PI p. 206)

One of the most extreme cases is discussed at the very outset when Wittgenstein considers a drawing of a three-dimensional cube which is used as an illustration in a book, with different interpretations in each place.

> In the relevant text something different is in question every time: here a glass cube, there an inverted open box, there a wire frame of that shape, there three boards forming a solid angle. Each time the text supplies the interpretation of the illustration.

> But we can also *see* the illustration now as one thing, now as
> another.—So we interpret it, and *see* it as we *interpret* it. (PI
> p. 193.)

Now he considers the first false account: that the description of the
visual experience in each of these cases is an "indirect description," and
if we see the figure as a box, for example, what we mean is that we
are having the experience which we have when we look at a box. To
this Wittgenstein says succinctly:

> But if it meant this I ought to know it. I ought to be able to
> refer to the experience directly, and not only indirectly. (As
> I can speak of red without calling it the color of blood.) (PI
> p. 194.)

The "intermediary" which is supposed to be the basis for my "seeing
the figure as a box" is nowhere to be found. The "aspect" "box" is,
it seems, as "primitive" as the "cube drawing" itself.

A second mistaken way of thinking about the difference between
"seeing" and "seeing as" is that the experience of the aspect involves
an "inner picture" which can't be shown to anyone else. To this fancy
(for that is what it is) Wittgenstein replies:

> Of course it is not the drawing, but neither is it anything of
> the same category which I carry within myself.
> The concept of the "inner picture" is misleading, for this con-
> cept uses the "outer picture" as a model; and yet the uses of the
> words for these concepts are no more like one another than
> the uses of "numeral" and "number." (PI p. 196.)

A third mistaken approach follows quickly: this is thinking of an
aspect as an "organization" of the visual experience, and this in turn
as one more datum on a level with the color and shape. If you do this,
Wittgenstein says

> . . . you are proceeding from the idea of the visual impression
> as an inner object. Of course this makes this object into a
> chimera; a queerly shifting construction. For the similarity to
> a picture is now impaired. (PI p. 196.)

While we can point to or describe the colors and shapes, in the case
of the changing aspect (the rabbit or the duck in the duck-rabbit
drawing), there is nothing we can point to or describe as the "organization," and this shows the difference between the concepts. The

only thing we would be able to point to if we saw the aspect "rabbit" would be a picture of rabbits, which might or might not "make sense" to the person we show it to.

Finally various physiological explanations are of no use—first, because Wittgenstein is not interested in causes but in concepts (PI p. 193, 203); second, because "The psychological concept hangs out of reach of the explanation" (PI p. 212), and, thirdly, what also sometimes happens, the physiological only functions as a symbol of the logical (PI p. 210).

Wittgenstein sums up what goes wrong in attempts to formulate some such over-all difference between "seeing" and "seeing as" as follows:

> And now look at all that can be meant by "description of what is seen." . . . There is not *one genuine* proper case of such description—the rest being just vague, something which awaits clarification, or which must just be swept aside as rubbish.
> Here we are in enormous danger of wanting to make fine distinctions.—It is the same when one tries to define the concept of a material object in terms of "what is really seen."—What we have rather to do is to *accept* the everyday language-game, and to note *false* accounts of the matter *as* false. The primitive language-game which children are taught needs no justification; attempts at justification need to be rejected. (PI p. 200.)

What happens is that a concept *forces* itself on us (PI p. 204) and then we find it difficult *not* to look in that one way.

We have been discussing false accounts which must be "noted as false." Wittgenstein, however, also brings out a number of differences between "seeing" and "seeing as" which arise from the different ways these concepts function, differences of use. Unlike "seeing" he says, "seeing an aspect"

1—is not seeing something which can be specified by a description, a drawing, a copy (PI p. 193);
2—is perceiving, but is not reporting a perception (PI p. 193);
3—is, like imagining, subject to the will (PI p. 193);
4—requires the mastery of a technique (PI p. 208).

If the last point puzzles us because we do not see how "experience" and "seeing" could depend upon having learned a technique, this simply means that the concepts of "experience" and "seeing" are being modified here (PI p. 208).

The best summary of Wittgenstein's conception of "seeing as" is perhaps the following:

> But how is it possible to *see* an object according to an *interpretation?*—The question represents it as a queer fact; as if something were being forced into a form it did not really fit. But no squeezing, no forcing took place here.
> When it looks as if there were no room for such a form between other ones you have to look for it in another dimension. If there is no room here, there *is* room in another dimension. (PI p. 200.)

He then goes on to compare this case with the concept of imaginary numbers which cannot be fitted into the continuum of real numbers, but, nevertheless, when we get down to the application

> . . . the concept finds a different place, one which, so to speak, one never dreamed of. (PI p. 202.)

What is the "other dimension"? Following the analogy with the imaginary numbers, we might call it a *different kind of seeing*, though this would mean no more than a *different way of using the concept of seeing*. "Physiognomical seeing" or "aspect seeing" might not find a place in the continuum of previous "seeing," but it would open a new dimension. The new dimension would not be "metaphysical" but, equally important and strange, grammatical.

Wittgenstein now turns to the important topic of the connection between "seeing an aspect" and "experiencing the meaning of a word" (PI p. 214). Experiencing the meaning of a word as a particular way of hearing it or saying it (feeling or understanding it) may be thought of as seeing or hearing an aspect of the word. There is something like the *feel* of a word, what it *sounds* like, the way we *mean* it, and these Wittgenstein wishes to compare to aspects.

> But if a sentence can strike me as like a painting in words, and the very individual word in the sentence as like a picture, then it is no such marvel that a word uttered in isolation and without purpose can seem to carry a particular meaning in itself. (PI p. 215.)

He gives as an example saying *March!* at one time as an imperative and at another time as the name of the month and then asks:

> Does the *same* experience accompany the word both times—are you sure? (PI p. 215.)

There is certainly no criterion of *sameness* here, and perhaps some might answer one way and some another.

Our attachment to words (shown, for example, by our resistance to changes in spelling, feeling that names of well-known people "fit" them, etc.) is not "explained" by referring to words as "familiar faces," but the comparison is helpful:

> The familiar face of a word, the feeling that it has taken up its meaning into itself, that it is an actual likeness of its meaning—there could be human beings to whom all this was alien. (They would not have an attachment to their words.)—And how are these feelings manifested among us?—By the way we choose and value words. (PI p. 218.)

Once again the pull toward trying to deal with meaning in terms of psychological states arises here. The last ten pages of this part of the *Investigations* (II-xi) deal with psychological concepts discussed more fully elsewhere ("saying inwardly," "thinking," "guessing thoughts," "certainty," "cause and motive," "intention" and "meaning").

Wittgenstein's position is summed up here when he says that the "hiddenness" of other minds is either a picture, or part of a concept.

> "I cannot know what is going on in him" is above all a *picture*. It is the convincing expression of a conviction. It does not give the reasons for the conviction. *They* are not readily accesible. (PI p. 223.)
> That what someone else says to himself is hidden from me is part of the *concept* "saying inwardly." Only "hidden" is the wrong word here; for if it is hidden from me, it ought to be apparent to him, *he* would have to *know* it. But he does not "know" it; only the doubt which exists for me does not exist for him. (PI p. 221.)

The temptation is to treat the "hiddenness" of other people's thoughts and feelings as a factual matter, as if *there were something* that is seen or known or experienced by the person who has the thoughts and feelings, but by no one else. It does not occur to us to question this starting point. But once it is realized that I do not see or experience or know my own thoughts and feelings (being in no such contortionist relation to myself), then the picture loses its force.

v

Looking back over Wittgenstein's entire philosophy, we can see that one of its leading principles from beginning to end was a kind of Machian (not to say Goethean) respect for appearances. This meant not to go beyond the phenomena, not to attribute to the phenomena *more* than we actually see there. But it also meant not to attribute to the phenomena *less* than we actually see there. If the former emphasis predominated in the *Tractatus*, the latter predominated in the *Investigations*.

Not to attribute to the world *more than we see there* meant not to attribute to it *more than we can say we see there*. But in exploring this Wittgenstein was led into hypostatizing an entire realm of possibilities which, paradoxically, were more real than the actualities which they were supposed to account for. The failure of this attempt to vindicate the phenomena in structural terms led finally to the realization that the phenomena have to justify themselves—that is, that the justifications have to be found in the phenomena too. (And this helps us to understand such concepts as *criteria* and *family resemblances*.)

Even the essence of language must be understood now in phenomenal terms (PI 90, 92), to be seen by a rearrangement of the phenomena rather than by an analysis of them. As Wittgenstein put it:

> We are talking about the spatial and temporal phenomenon of language, not about some non-spatial, non-temporal phantasm. [Note in margin: Only it is possible to be interested in a phenomenon in a variety of ways.] (PI 108.)

What happened was that the word *essence* too changed its meaning; it too acquired a phenomenal meaning (or use with reference to phenomena):

> If we too in these investigations are trying to understand the essence of language—its function, its structure,—yet *this* is not what those questions [the questions asked and answered in the *Tractatus*] have in view. For they see in the essence, not something that already lies open to view and that becomes surveyable by a rearrangement, but something that lies *beneath* the surface. Something that lies within, which we see when

we look *into* the thing and which an analysis digs out. (PI
92; bracketed words added.)

Essence lies open to view—here *Wittgenstein's essentialism finally
reaches the phenomena* by way of the concept of *rearrangement*. And
here we see, stripped of its last metaphysical trappings, the full extent
of Wittgenstein's commitment to the phenomena. Coming to rest in
the phenomena is coming to rest in language as phenomena as well as
in the world as phenomena. Philosophy insures its future because language as phenomena cannot be "solved" once and for all, but simply
goes on and on. Not subject any longer to harassment by science or
religion, philosophy goes on dealing with the illusions generated by
language as phenomenon, without itself leaving the phenomena.

This is the problem which presented itself to Wittgenstein in the
1930's: how to do justice to the paradigmatic character of language
(and of mathematics) without again leaving the phenomena. The answer lay in the different *aspects* of the phenomena (different ways of
being interested in them), combined with the idea of a rearrangement
to make an aspect clearly visible. What we need is already in one way
in full view though it will take some investigating to make it *surveyable*. The rearrangement is at the same time a rearrangement of the
"possibilities of phenomena," for these are located in language, when
language is looked at in that aspect. Being able to "find our way about"
among the phenomena is equivalent to "seeing" the grammar of the
world, but this time not as a hidden ontological dimension, but as the
phenomena seen in a different way.

Language itself has to be treated as a phenomenon in the later
philosophy, not only because treating it as a super-phenomenon in the
early one generated a self-defeating metaphysics (T 6.54), but also because we have no other language in which to talk about language except the same language which we use to talk about everything else.

> When I talk about language (words, sentences, etc.) I must
> speak the language of every day. Is this language somehow too
> coarse and material for what we want to say? *Then how is
> another one to be constructed?*—And how strange that we
> should be able to do anything at all with the one we have!
> In giving explanations I already have to use language full-
> blown (not some sort of preparatory, provisional one); this
> by itself shows that I can adduce only exterior facts about lan-
> guage. (PI 120.)

A striking number of Wittgenstein's illustrations of how we find essence in language *by looking at it differently* are drawn from the realm of *meaningful visual experience*: the jigsaw puzzle pieces that cannot be fitted together until we think of turning them over (RFM p. 18); the arrows which show the different ways to read tables and also that there is no one right way (PI 86); the logical proofs which have to be able to be taken in as a geometrical vision if they are to function logically (RFM p. 83); the picture of the machine's connecting rods and the various handles in the engineer's cabin (RFM p. 120; PI 12)—all show the importance of the "surveyable seeing" which is the essential aspect.

The question remains: What is the criterion for seeing phenomena rightly or for having arranged them in such a way that they show their essential aspect? There are countless ways in which we can talk about phenomena; why should one way be preferable to others?

Wittgenstein's answer is that we do not need some absolutely correct way of looking (a meaningless idea in any case). We are looking for *an* order which removes our problems and enables us to find our way about. We know that we are seeing things rightly in this way when a particular philosophic problem altogether disappears (PI 132-3). Then we "know where we are" when we have seen the grammar correctly. But there is no reason to suppose that we will ever reach this for *all* problems or that new problems are not perhaps being generated all the time.

To sum up this side of Wittgenstein's philosophy: in the end the world for him is an *expressive phenomenon* (rather than for example a causal one, logical one, an organic one or an evolutionary one, etc.). And *objectivity* finally comes to mean the *acceptance of appearances*, rather than the demand for absolute objects. This "physiognomical" way is the new way in which Wittgenstein looks at the world.

The remarkable thing is that this point of view—this seeing of the world as something like a face[6]—is combined with the equally

---

[6]A the end of her *An Introduction to Wittgenstein's* Tractatus (London: Hutchinson University Library, 1959) p. 172, G. E. M. Anscombe wrote: "There is a strong impression made by the end of the *Tractatus*, as if Wittgenstein saw the world looking at him with a face . . ." His final "acceptance of the appearances" expresses just this point of view.

strong principle that *the phenomena have no character of their own at all*, but all meaning lies in the language and human activities with which we respond to the phenomena. We turn now to this other side of Wittgenstein's philosophy where are the human activities which give the phenomena all their meanings.

The Groundlessness of Action

As if giving grounds did not come to an end sometime. But the end is not an ungrounded presupposition, it is an ungrounded way of acting.

WITTGENSTEIN (OC 110)

... the power of eternal, self-evident truths over man, although it seems to lie at the very basis of existence and therefore to be insuperable, is nevertheless an illusory power.

LEV SHESTOV

Nothing practical should ever be allowed to overtake pure doing.

ERIC GUTKIND

The notion that "I am the agent" is fallacious equally from Islamic, Vedantic and Buddhist points of view. . . . This by no means relieves the "individual" of full responsibility for his actions.

ANANDA COOMARASWAMY

CHAPTER 12

The Groundlessness of Action

i

However meaningful phenomena may appear to be "in themselves," and however many aspects they may have, in Wittgenstein's philosophy they have no meaning "in themselves" and no aspects "in themselves" at all. They remain *all surface*. There are no features or characteristics which belong to them. They do not even appear without appearing in some form, and this is what human language and activities provide. Without language and forms of life the phenomena are of no kind at all.

While Wittgenstein's philosophy therefore culminates on one side in what may be called *altogether meaningful phenomena*, it culminates on the other side in the language and forms of life without which the phenomena are not meaningful at all. For, except in terms of what we say about them (or how we respond to them) the phenomena *have* no character or "reality." Language and human activities constitute them in every meaningful respect. (Their sheer existence as such is for Wittgenstein, of course, not meaningful.)

Even the philosopher who is interested in language itself as a *phenomenon* is interested in it only in that aspect in which it is the precondition for phenomena (including itself) having any meaning (the aspect in which we see language in terms of its possibilities).[1]

All this means that *we cannot appeal to the phenomena in themselves to justify what we say about the phenomena*. Nor can we appeal to something which lies *within* the phenomena or *behind* the phenomena, since the phenomena are just what they seem to be, and no

---

[1] In the history of philosophy Wittgenstein's phenomenalism may seem the discovery of a *new way of seeing*, but it is this only because it is also an investigation and understanding of *an ordinary way of speaking*. If Wittgenstein was looking at the world in a new way, he was doing it not by inventing new theories or expressing new opinions, but by vindicating a familiar use of the word *seeing*.

more and no less. To put the matter briefly: it is not the phenomena
which justify us in applying certain concepts to the phenomena because all we know about the phenomena is already given just in terms
of the application of these concepts. Hence the correctness of what
we say about the phenomena cannot be decided by the phenomena
since we have no other ways of dealing with them except just the ways
in which we do deal with them. Therefore we must look elsewhere
for the justification for using the concepts which we do. Where else
would this be? Clearly only in language itself and whatever it is which
underlies language.

Questions of this sort occupy an important place in the *Philosophical Investigations*: What establishes correctness in the way we
speak about the world? How do we know we speak about it rightly?
How do we know that we see things rightly, use the right concepts
and understand things rightly? What preserves us from whim and
phantasy disguised as truth?

The very form of these questions suggests the ontological answer
—the appeal to *the way the world is* independent of us. But it must be
understood that while such questions were traditionally answered ontologically (as they were in the *Tractatus*), this is just the way in which
Wittgenstein in his later philosophy *does not* answer them.[2]

The traditional answers appealed to "the way things are in themselves" as this was supposed to be known, principally either through
experience or *reason* (though sometimes through *inspiration*, or *common sense* or *pragmatic outcomes*). Even when, for example, philosophers defended common sense, they did it in the traditional ontological terms that common sense gives us the world *as it really is*. The
conception of the independent reality of the world (in some sense
other than its sheer existence) was accepted by all. (One of the main
reasons why it was accepted, of course, was that the alternative always
appeared to be skepticism and relativism, undercutting the possibility
of any knowledge at all, the point escaping notice that the skepticism
and relativism themselves depended upon the very same picture of the
way things really are, which they simply denied we were able to
know.)

---

[2] The much-heralded "end of ontology," proclaimed as immanent by Heidegger and other philosophers, actually takes place in Wittgenstein, who finally
for the first time in Western thought provides a philosophy without subject or
object.

To drop the picture of "the way things really are" (in some sense other than the way they seem to be or are ordinarily said to be) does not dispose of the question of what justifies the way we speak about them but simply shifts its locus. If there is no sense in talking about how the world is, entirely apart from the ways we make sense of it, then we still have the problem of what constitutes sense, even if this will no longer be decided in the old way.

Wittgenstein is interested in the traditional ways by which philosophers have thought to transcend language—such as experience, mathematical and logical inference, thinking, inspiration—as *themselves phenomena* and consequently also as concepts which have to be used correctly and therefore have to be justified in the way that all language is justified. How do we know that we are using words like *experience* and *thinking* correctly? For even such philosophically loaded words as these have uses quite apart from any super-conceptual status which philosophers may have bestowed on them.

For Wittgenstein, then, neither "experience," nor "logic," nor "inspiration," nor "common sense" transcend phenomena or language in such a way as to provide a basis for the correct use of words. They do not give us access to a "reality" which would enable us to say that our concepts were correct and used correctly. Instead these words themselves must be used correctly and the activities connected with them carried out correctly (that is in a way which is justified). To put this somewhat differently: we identify and describe phenomena, using such words as *experience, logical inference, inspiration,* etc., and then we also need a justification for using these words since the phenomena do not provide *this*.

Before we examine how language is justified in Wittgenstein's philosophy, we want to look briefly at what he says about justification itself. There are three main points about this. The first is that justification must appeal to something independent (PI 265), and for this reason an imaginary justification is not a justification, and in addition

> if I need a justification for using a word, it must also be one for someone else. (PI 378.)

Secondly, certain language activities and certain uses of words need no justification. This is true of the primitive language-games which children are taught (PI p. 200) and also of our practice of accepting proofs in mathematics (RFM p. 98). And Wittgenstein also adds, referring to a statement like "I am in pain"

> To use a word without justification does not mean to use it without right. (PI 289.)

Thirdly, as we will see, justifications come to an end, and with regard to justification by experience, he says that if it did not come to an end, it would not be justification.

In the rest of this chapter we consider first the justification of language and then turn to the topic of *grounds* and giving grounds and where this too comes to an end in forms of life and rites and ceremonies. And finally we take up the question of the groundlessness of belief and thought.

ii

Grammar itself may be said to be the justification for the way we speak since grammar is normative, and it is norms which justify. But grammar is not something which hangs in the void; it is the practice of language, what we do, as this embodies the patterns and rules of correctness.

There is a compact statement of this which brings together several of the basic themes of Wittgenstein's philosophy in the *Remarks on the Foundations of Mathematics*:

> You cannot survey the justification of an expression unless you survey its employment; which you cannot do by looking at some facet of its employment, say a picture attaching to it. (RFM p. 63.)

Here is the idea of "surveyability" applied to both the justification and the use of an expression, and both of them distinguished from the pictures which mislead us. Justification too has to be "surveyable," and this is done by "surveying" the use of expressions. If we get a bird's-eye view of the functioning of a word, we will at the same time get a bird's-eye view of what is correct. In this case how a word *is used* is the justification for *using it* that way.

When we look into it, we find that the justification for using a word in a particular way amounts to an implicit rule of grammar, and it is these rules which justify us and which determine correctness in the various things which we do with words. Typically, Wittgenstein begins by describing the physiognomy of the phenomenon of "obeying a rule," at least indirectly.

> Would it not be possible for us, however, to calculate as we actually do (all agreeing, and so on), and still at every step to have a feeling of being guided by the rules as by a spell, feeling astonishment at the fact that we agreed? (We might give thanks to the Deity for our agreement.)
> This merely shows what belongs to the physiognomy of what we call "obeying a rule" in everyday life. (PI 234-5.)

In Wittgenstein's description of "obeying a rule" both in the *Philosophical Investigations* and in the *Remarks on the Foundations of Mathematics* two points stand out:

1—there is no necessity about obeying a rule in any particular way; we could always *at every point* do it differently and still call it obeying that rule; but, nevertheless,
2—obeying a rule, however we obey it, is something that is done blindly (PI 219) and as a "matter of course" (PI 238) and is different from any interpretations (PI 201).

These two points are not in conflict, since the first concerns what is done in obeying a particular rule and the second the manner in which it is done. But they both leave out the most important point, which is the real crux of Wittgenstein's attitude toward logical necessity. This is that a rule compels only if we go along with it, or in a sense *agree to be compelled.*

> Why do I always speak of being compelled by a rule; why not of the fact that I can *choose* to follow it? For that is equally important.
> But I don't want to say, either, that the rule compels me to act like this; but that it makes it possible for me to hold by it and make it compel me. (RFM p. 193.)

Something similar holds in mathematics and logic:

> it is not our finding the proposition self-evidently true, but our making the self-evidence count, that makes it into a mathematical proposition. (RFM p. 114.)

This is an expression of Wittgenstein's antinomianism with regard to logical and mathematical necessity. Without weakening the necessity, he nevertheless makes it dependent upon our choice to accept the necessity. (We do not have something like a "logical nexus" whereby logical necessity compels us, as it were, in something like a causal fashion.) And the same thing holds true with regard to grammatical rules. Wittgenstein speaks of our "committing" ourselves to them and of its being possible for us to "be led by a language." (MLN p. 254.) Grammatical rules do not operate in a causal way on our actual behavior, for if they did, they would lose their rule-like status. It has to remain possible, not only to disobey them, but to understand them differently, follow them differently and even not choose to follow them at all.

If now we require a justification for what we do in "obeying a rule," what will it be? Or, Wittgenstein asks the questions:

> Following a rule is analogous to obeying an order. We are trained to do so; we react to an order in a particular way. But what if one person reacts in one way and another in another to the order and the training? Which one is right? (PI 206.)
> "How am I able to obey a rule?"—if this is not a question about causes, then it is about the justification for my following the rule in the way I do. (PI 217.)

The answers to these questions are: that rules are what justify, and there is no way of justifying a rule itself except by more rules, and all rules together will not do better in this regard than one rule.

> However many rules you give me—I give you a rule which justifies my employment of your rule. (RFM p. 34.)

Grammatical rules are in Wittgenstein's philosophy the last court of appeal for the correctness of language. There are no reasons we can give for following them in the particular ways we do, nothing to which we can appeal to show that the rules themselves are "correct."

This is the point, of course, at which we would like to appeal to the "way things are in reality" to justify the rules being the way they are. We would like to find some further ground "in the nature of things" which the rules might "correspond" to. But for Wittgenstein this road is closed since it is supplied only by pictures which themselves would have to be applied and *could* be applied differently. The lesson of the *Tractatus* is again at hand—that even the picture of an absolutely final isomorphism between language and the world *could* be applied or understood in some other way.

In the Moore "Lecture Notes" we see Wittgenstein closing the door between grammatical rules and the world. Moore describes what he said thus:

> He (Wittgenstein) first tried to express his view by saying that it is impossible to "justify" any grammatical rule . . . but he also expressed it by saying that we can't give reasons for *following* any particular rule rather than a different one. And in trying to explain why we can't give reasons for following any particular rule, he laid very great stress on an argument, which he put differently in different places and which I must confess I do not clearly understand. Two of the premisses of this argument are, I think, clear enough. One was (1) that any reason "would have to be a description of reality": this he asserted in precisely these words. And the second was (2) that any description of reality must be capable of truth and false-hood." . . . (MLN p. 272.)

The "two premises of the argument" at the end are, of course, still couched in the language of the *Tractatus* and would not have been put in this way later. The same point, however, would have been made by speaking about the impossibility of appealing to the phenomena out-side of all language-games and all concepts, i.e. to the phenomena "in themselves."

The final justification, or final basis, for our language and language activities (and hence for our way of looking at and understanding the world), Wittgenstein says, is simply that *that is what we do*. In other words, it is a doing which has no further ground; *ungrounded* or *groundless* action. It is most vividly expressed as follows:

> If I have exhausted the justifications, I have reached bedrock, and my spade is turned. Then I am inclined to say: "This is simply what I do." (PI 217.)
> The danger here, I believe, is one of giving a justification of our procedure where there is no such thing as a justification and we ought simply to have said: *that's how we do it*. (RFM p. 98.)

At bottom, language is a doing; and this doing cannot be further jus-tified or accounted for. It is what one commentator has called *a full stop*.

iii

We turn now to the question of giving grounds (or reasons) for *beliefs*, especially ones about the future. This is Wittgenstein's discussion of the *justification for induction*. (PI 471-490.)[3] Here we are discussing ordinary and scientific beliefs.

The topics discussed are: (1) beliefs accepted as certain; (2) beliefs based on calculation; (3) "good grounds" for beliefs; (4) inferences from sense-impressions to objects and (5) ideal certainty.

1—For a great many beliefs about the future we have *certainty* that does not need reasons or grounds. In fact these beliefs illustrate what is meant by *certainty*. A good example is the belief that "I shall get burnt if I put my hand in the fire." Here we have expectation, coupled with fear, that is so strong that I am prepared to act on it with total certainty, and *this is what the meaning of certainty amounts to* (PI 474). In the case of such beliefs the problem is not that there are no reasons, but there are too many reasons. For example, for believing that "my finger will feel resistance when it touches the table" or that "it will hurt if this pencil pierces my hand," Wittgenstein says that "a hundred reasons present themselves" (PI 478).[4] Beliefs of this kind which, in so far as they are expressed in our acting-with-surety, are what we mean by certainty. There are no grounds for such beliefs, but as Wittgenstein says:

> The difficulty is to realize the groundlessness of our believing. (OC 166.)
> At the foundation of well-founded belief lies belief that is not founded. (OC 253.)

2—In a second case grounds for a belief or opinion may be a *calculation* which is actually carried out before arriving at the opinion. In this case we take grounds for an opinion "to mean only what a man has said to himself before he arrived at the opinion." Wittgenstein says of this that *we play that game too*, the game in which a certain kind of statement about the past is

---

[3] For a thorough discussion of this and related subjects see Ilham Dilman, *Induction and Deduction—A Study in Wittgenstein* (Oxford: Blackwell, 1973).

[4] Such facts as these which we take for granted in all our knowing and acting are discussed more fully in *On Certainty*, and in the next chapter.

what we call a ground for assuming that this will happen in the future.

To this he adds

And if you are surprised at our playing such a game I refer you to the *effect* of a past experience (to the fact that a burnt child fears the fire). (PI 480.)

Although Wittgenstein stops short of saying that referring to the causal relation here becomes part of the "reason," this may be, in effect, what it is.

3—In some cases there arises the question of whether something is a "good" ground, and then we may be misled into supposing that a reference to the "way things really are" is being introduced which *justifies the ground*. We are likely to be misled this way by an expression which says that a good ground "makes the occurrence of an event probable," which may lead to the false idea that the ground actually *influences events*. All the expression a "good" ground means is that

this ground comes up to a particular standard of good grounds—but the standard has no grounds! (PI 482.)

Grounds, no matter how good, do not themselves effect what will happen (as if experience piling up must have some weight!) But grounds support (justify) beliefs and opinions and add nothing to the course of events.

4—There is the case of the relation between sense impressions and objects—do we infer from one to the other? Wittgenstein's answer is *No*, not even if we say that we are inferring from statements about sense impressions to statements about objects. There are cases where we do make such inferences; I see a photograph, for example, and say "There must have been a chair over there." But the normal situation is not this. Nor when we see a glowing stove, or a steaming radiator do we *infer* that they are hot.

5—Finally what do we do with those people who say that there are no grounds good enough to convince them that what has happened in the past will happen in the future? Of such people Wittgenstein asks: What could possibly convince them? And what would they call "being convinced"?

If anyone said that information about the past could not convince him that something would happen in the future, I
should not understand him. . . . In what kind of way do you
expect to be convinced?—If *these* are not grounds, then what
are grounds?—If you say these are not grounds, then you
must surely be able to state what must be the case for us to
have the right to say that there are grounds for our assumption. (PI 481.)

Though Wittgenstein does not make the comparisons here, the notion
of *ideal certainty* is as unsatisfactory (and for very much the same
reasons) as the notions of an *ideal language* (PI 81), *ideal exactness*
(PI 88) and an *ideal game* (PI 100). The ideal is a chimera generated
by a picture. It represents a certain kind of finality, and it is characteristic of Wittgenstein's later philosophy that at every point it gives
way to the *norm*.

iv

In the texts presently available to us religion is discussed by Wittgenstein in connection with *religious beliefs* in the Notes compiled by
his students on his "Lectures on Religious Belief" and in connection
with rituals and ceremonies in his own "Notes on Frazer's *Golden
Bough*." Both *religious beliefs* and *rituals* are regarded by Wittgenstein
as *sui generis*, which means autonomous human activities having no
grounds beyond themselves. We examine what he says about religious
beliefs in this section and then about rituals in the next.

Wittgenstein is concerned with religious belief as a phenomenon,
with describing its physiognomy, and also with its grammar, that is,
with describing how that particular concept operates. He is not concerned with the truth or falsity of beliefs, since these do not belong
to the concept of religious belief as he understands it.

The main point about religious beliefs which Wittgenstein emphasizes is that they occupy a place apart from *facts, knowledge*, or
reason, none of which can either substantiate or refute them. Religious
beliefs have no grounds, and in this they are different from many ordinary beliefs. Three basic points are made about religious beliefs (separating them from facts, knowledge and reason). For them

1—what we normally call *evidence* is irrelevant, and "if there were
evidence this would in fact destroy the whole business" (NLRB p.

56); for to treat a religious belief as a matter of fact completely alters its meaning. (NLRB p. 51).

2—there is no question of *hypotheses, probability* or *knowing,* or of *possibility* or *indubitability;* all these modalities have no application, for none of them "would be enough to make me change my whole life" (NLRB p. 57); and

3—reason doesn't enter because religious beliefs are not only *not reasonable,* but don't even pretend to be (NLRB p. 58); Wittgenstein feels himself that it is "ludicrous" to try to make religion appear to be "reasonable" and that this trying to make religion appear to be "reasonable" is itself "unreasonable" (NLRB p. 59).

To bring out the difference between ordinary beliefs and religious beliefs Wittgenstein points out that people *do not risk their lives for facts, knowledge* or *reason,* while they do, on occasion, risk their lives for religious beliefs. A different principle must, therefore, be at work. A religious belief is more like an icon or compass that we live by, allowing it to regulate everything in our lives, giving up things for it and sometimes risking everything for it.

> This is a very much stronger fact—foregoing pleasures, always appealing to this picture. This in one sense must be called the firmest of all beliefs, because the man risks things on account of it which he would not do on things which are by far better established for him. (NLRB p. 54).

The unshakableness of religious beliefs is not shown by reasoning or appeal to ordinary grounds, as in the case of ordinary beliefs, but rather by "regulating for all in life" (NLRB p. 54). Hence there are two entirely different ways of comparing beliefs: one way, which we use with ordinary beliefs, is "seeing what sort of grounds will be given" and the other way, which we use with religious beliefs, is comparing the *strengths* of the beliefs. The kind of measure which we might use for the latter would be comparing what *risks* would be taken for the beliefs (NLRB p. 54).

What is most important for Wittgenstein about religious beliefs (the way he sees them and understands them) is that they are the *expression of what people think of constantly* and of what pictures come before their minds when they have to do something or something happens to them. Religious beliefs, in other words, are not assertions that something is so, or that something will or will not happen, but they are *ways of expressing what we constantly think about and live by*. This is why, in Wittgenstein's sense of the term, it is impossible to contradict a religious belief; all we can say is that we do not have those thoughts all the time as the other person does, and this is not contradicting his thoughts. This is why also the *expression* of beliefs is not of primary concern, since people may have such admonishing and guiding thoughts without ever bothering to express them at all. Different ways of thinking and living need not be expressed in terms of "belief." For example, in Wittgenstein's sense, a person might have thoughts and pictures of a certain kind guiding him constantly without ever voicing them or voicing them in any particular way.[5]

Not to have the same dominating and guiding thoughts as another person is not to contradict that other person (or to "believe the opposite" from what that other person believes); and this non-contradicting is the form which differences of religious belief take for Wittgenstein. The matter is more complicated, however, because if, for example, we express certain guiding thoughts and pictures by saying that we believe that "There will be a Last Judgment," this form of expression in such a case does not by itself make such a statement into a factual assertion. If the believer chooses to say that he believes the Last Judgment will happen, this may still be his way of expressing his dominant pictures, and so for all that way of putting it, it does not thereby become a "factual prediction."

The constant thought of the Last Judgment (that icon) is important not because it "corresponds" to some happening or cosmic event which we think "will happen," but because we live by it, steer by it, regulate by it. Whether there will or will not be a certain factual occurrence is not the basis on which we are attached to such a steering principle, and in fact there *is* no basis for these attachments. As the history of religions attests, facts never add up to a faith and faiths are never refuted by facts.

The grammar of religious beliefs (as of theology (PI 373)) is clearly of a special kind, and this is shown, not only by the ways in

---

[5] This sheds light on the case of a primitive people who do not have a word for "belief" but nevertheless appear to have "beliefs," as discussed by Rodney Needham in his book about the Nuer people of the Sudan called *Belief Language and Experience* (Oxford: Blackwell, 1972). They may certainly have beliefs in Wittgenstein's sense without ever expressing them in that way or without having the concept of "belief."

which we compare and talk about religious beliefs (in contrast with the ways in which we compare and talk about ordinary beliefs), but by the fact that in religion we encounter such terms as *dogma* and *faith*, rather than such terms as *opinion* and *hypothesis*.

The way Wittgenstein thinks about religious beliefs comes out vividly in the following:

> If you ask me whether or not I believe in a Judgment Day, in the sense in which religious people have belief in it, I wouldn't say: "No. I don't believe there will be such a thing." It would seem to me utterly crazy to say this. (NLRB p. 55.)

Why would it seem to Wittgenstein "utterly crazy to say this"? The answer is because the important question is what we think of all the time, what pictures we have before us when we have to make a decision, and *not* whether there will be such a happening or not. The religious belief is the expression of having certain thoughts, and if somebody says "This is what I think of all the time and steer my life by," how can we contradict him? Not by saying "I don't think of it."

The misunderstanding of religious belief would appear to be in imagining that there is some common subject matter about which statements are being made (such as in "There will be a Judgment Day" or "There will not be a Judgment Day"), rather than realizing that whether people are making such assertions in expressing their beliefs is incidental and altogether subordinate to the belief-character.

To dramatize the difference between ordinary beliefs and religious beliefs Wittgenstein imagines the following:

> Suppose we knew people who foresaw the future; make forecasts for years and years ahead; and they described some sort of a Judgment Day. Queerly enough, even if there were such a thing, and even if it were more convincing than I have described, belief in this happening wouldn't be at all a religious belief.
> Suppose that I would have to forego all pleasures because of such a forecast. If I do so and so, someone will put me in fires in a thousand years, etc., I wouldn't budge. The best scientific evidence is just nothing. (NLRB p. 56.)

I will not be convinced to change my whole life by scientific fore-
casts, no matter how well backed up by evidence, whereas with a
religious belief

> A man would fight for his life not to be dragged into the fire.
> No induction. Terror. That is, as it were, part of the sub-
> stance of the belief. (NLRB p. 56.)

As Wittgenstein says, we are on an "entirely different plane" here, for
the scientific evidence does not have the same consequences as the religious belief and moves in an entirely different dimension.

Even in the case of Christianity which, Wittgenstein points out,
it has been said, rests on an historic basis

> It doesn't rest on an historic basis in the sense that the or-
> dinary belief in historic facts could serve as a foundation.
> Here we have a belief in historic facts different from a belief
> in ordinary historic facts. (NLRB p. 57.)

For example, the people who had faith "didn't apply the doubt which
would ordinarily apply to *any* historical proposition," and were willing to base "enormous things" on evidence that "would seem exceed-
ingly flimsy," in a different context. They were not concerned with
being "reasonable."

Wittgenstein's position is summed up by this:

> Why shouldn't one form of life culminate in an utterance of
> belief in a Last Judgment? But I couldn't either say "Yes"
> or "No" to the statement that there will be such a thing. Nor
> "Perhaps," nor "I'm not sure." (NLRB p. 58.)

The reason Wittgenstein could not say either "Yes" or "No" to the
statement that there will be a Last Judgment is because this statement
*does not contain the substance of the belief which it attempts to ex-
press.* For the substance is not whether something will happen or not.
It is whether we constantly have the thought of the Last Judgment
(or something along those lines) in our minds and keep living by that.
And it is then a secondary matter (and not one that can be decided
on the basis of what people say) whether a "happening" is or is not
part of the expression of the belief. Wittgenstein himself may believe
in the Last Judgment in the sense that he has such thoughts and they
constantly admonish him, but still he would not be able to say whether
there will or will not be such a thing. And, more than this, it might

even be that he would not express these "guiding thoughts" in terms of this belief or even in any words at all.

In the second section of the "Notes on 'Lectures on Religious Belief' " Wittgenstein takes up the question of under what circumstances he is inclined to leave aside ordinary ideas of evidence and consider something as a matter of religious belief (and perhaps as "miraculous"). He gives the following example:

> Suppose there is a feast on Mid-Summer Common. A lot of people stand in a ring. Suppose this is done every year and then everyone says he has seen one of his dead relatives on the other side of the ring. In this case we could ask everyone in the ring: "Who did you hold by the hand?" Nevertheless we'd all say that on that day we see our dead relatives. You could in this case say: "I had an extraordinary experience. I had the experience I can express by saying: 'I saw my dead cousin.' " Would we say you are saying this on insufficient evidence? Under certain circumstances I would say this, under other circumstances I wouldn't. Where what is said sounds a bit absurd I would say: "Yes, in this case insufficient evidence." If altogether absurd, then I wouldn't. (NLRB p. 60.)

What are the differences of "circumstances" which would decide for us how we would understand this ceremony? They would be, for example, whether the people involved tried to get in touch with their dead relatives again after they had gone home, whether they went to other places to look for them, consulted special people about it, etc. These might come under the heading of "circumstances." But also under this heading would be how the people in the group were connected with each other, what other ceremonies they had, whether some years the relatives might not show up and what they would do then, etc.

There might be a tendency to try to separate scientific cases from religious cases along these lines: by a person involved saying that in the religious cases "he didn't mean it literally." Wittgenstein's reply to this is: "I want to say this is not so." And then he continues:

> And I would say: "I would disencourage this kind of reasoning" and Moore would say: "I wouldn't disencourage it." That is, one would *do* something. We would take sides, and that goes so far that there would really be great differences between us, which might come out in Mr. Lewy saying: "Wittgenstein is

trying to undermine reason," and this wouldn't be false. This
is actually where such questions rise. (NLRB p. 64-5.)

This passage makes a number of very important points: (1) that
Wittgenstein rejects making the difference between the scientific and
the religious that the former takes literally what the latter does not
take literally (i.e. religion for Wittgenstein is not "symbolic" in the
special fashionable sense of recent years); (2) taking this position is
"disencouraging" a kind of reasoning which, he says, Moore, for example, would not "disencourage"; (3) this is *doing* something, taking
sides, and "there would really be great differences between us;" and
(4) it would not be false to say that in doing this Wittgenstein was
"trying to undermine reason."

The suggestion here is that the difference between Wittgenstein
and Moore is a very fundamental one, perhaps indeed a "religious" one.
On this issue, in other words, *where the character or place of reason
itself is at stake* there is no further common ground to appeal to. Do
we not have then a religious belief on the parts of both Wittgenstein
and Moore (even if Moore might not speak of it in that way)?

Since the question is frequently raised as to Wittgenstein's own
religious views in his later philosophy, it is important that they come
out here as the great differences between him and Moore over the character of religion itself as well as over the character of reason.

The final section of the "Notes on 'Lectures on Religious Belief' " deals with the question of

What is it, to have different ideas of death? (NLRB p. 65.)

as, for example, in the case where someone says:

"I have two different ideas, one of ceasing to exist after death,
the other of being a disembodied spirit." (NLRB p. 65.)

First of all, Wittgenstein warns us against thinking of "an idea
of death" as a "super-picture" which we understand while we are thinking of it. He reminds us that "death" is a public word, "an instrument
functioning in a certain way," and therefore there is something "queer"
about using the word in the expression "an idea of death." And, similarly, what is meant by "having an idea"? This too must be an expression which involves a certain technique and use of words. And so too
with the expression "idea of death" as meaning some kind of a picture.

If what he calls his "idea of death" is to become relevant, it must become part of our game. (NLRB p. 69.)

Wittgenstein then considers a number of possible pictures which some might take to be "part of our game," examining how these pictures function or what their consequences are. The first one he considers is "the separation of soul from body." About what the consequences of saying this are he says

I am not, at least, at present at all clear. (NLRB p. 69.)

And when it is suggested that this be contrasted with being "extinguished" he says:

If you say to me—"Do you cease to exist?"—I should be bewildered, and would not know what exactly this is to mean. (NLRB p. 69.)

Wittgenstein himself cannot use either the picture of "separation of soul from body" or the picture of "ceasing to exist," because he does not know what consequences to draw from them.

Suppose someone said: "What do you believe, Wittgenstein? Are you a skeptic? Do you know whether you will survive death?" I would really, this is a fact, say "I can't say. I don't know," because I haven't any clear idea what I'm saying when I'm saying "I don't cease to exist," etc. (NLRB p. 70.)

Despite the fact that he would not have a clear idea of what he himself was saying if he were to say this, Wittgenstein nevertheless goes on to make the point that he might "*understand* entirely" if someone else expressed a belief in life after death, at least in this form:

Suppose someone, before going to China, when he might never see me again, said to me: "We might see one another after death"—would I necessarily say that I don't understand him? I might say (want to say) simply, "Yes, I understand him entirely." (NLRB pp. 70-1.)

Wittgenstein then says that this would *not* mean that he approved of the man's attitude or anything of that sort. The entire *weight* might be in the picture itself. It is as if on this kind of occasion a man holds up a picture, an icon, which is one of the great pictures available for such times. And then, of course, one understands if one understands that use of that picture.

What has to be assumed is that "we associate a particular use with a picture" (NLRB p. 71), and then a person may or may not be using it that way. There is a particular technique of usage which may or may not be the one expected. The only question is what he wanted to do with the picture, what consequences or conventions he wanted to draw from it. The picture says it all; very likely there is no other picture which could be substituted, and there is nothing "psychological" which will take the place of the picture or in any way "explain" the picture. Wittgenstein sums it up thus:

> When I say he's using a picture I'm merely making a *grammatical* remark: (What I say) can only be verified by the consequences he does or does not draw. . . .
> If I wished to say anything more I was merely being philosophically arrogant. (NLRB p. 72.)

v

In an interview with Friedrich Waismann which took place in 1930 Wittgenstein expressed the view that speech is not essential to religion. He told Waismann:

> Is speech essential for religion? I can quite well imagine a religion in which there are no doctrines, and hence nothing is said. Obviously the essence of religion can have nothing to do with the fact that speech occurs—or rather: if speech does occur, this itself is a component of religious behavior and not a theory. Therefore nothing turns on whether the words are true, false or nonsensical. (LE p. 16.)

We have already seen Wittgenstein pointing out how relatively unimportant expression of a religious belief may be (compared to the thoughts which dominate and guide our lives). In the "Notes on Frazer's *Golden Bough*" it becomes clear how relatively unimportant speech is by contrast with the rituals and ceremonies of magic and religion. Speech, it would appear, is subordinate to the ritual actions which are the prime language of magic and religion. In one place Wittgenstein says, for example, that

> In the old rites we have the use of an utterly complex gesture-language. . . . (NFGB p. 242.)

How does Wittgenstein understand ritual action as we find it in primitive societies as well as in our own? First of all, it is something like an "instinctive action" (NFGB p. 244), but it is not mere physiological behavior (NFGB p. 239). Such actions express the meaningfulness of phenomena to us and our reactions to the phenomena at a more primitive level than spoken language.

> It is just the characteristic of the awakening spirit of man that a phenomenon means something to him. We could almost say man is a ceremonial animal. (NFGB p. 239.)

We are "grasped by the phenomena" (sun, fire, rain, birth, death, etc.) and we "let our feelings out" in various ways (striking the earth, greeting the sun, enthroning the rain-king, welcoming the new year, etc.). The vast language of the ritual is the result. (NFGB pp. 236, 244.)

> How could fire or the similarity of fire to the sun fail to make an impression on the awakening spirit of man? But not "because he cannot explain it" (the dumb superstition of our time)—for does it become any the less impressive through an "explanation"? (NFGB p. 239.)

Ritual action is, in a certain sense, *pure action—ungrounded action* —because it has no purpose beyond itself and no further basis or explanation.

> When I am furious about something, I strike many times with my stick on the earth, or on a tree, etc. But I still do not believe that the earth is guilty or that the blows can help something. "I let my anger out." And all rites are of this kind. Such actions one can call instinctive actions. And an historical explanation that perhaps I earlier or my ancestors believed that the blows on the earth would help something, are delusions, for they are shallow assumptions which explain *nothing*. The similarity of the act to an act of punishment is important, but more than this similarity cannot be said for sure. (NFGB p. 244.)

Wittgenstein says that the only "explanation" we can find of such actions is the understanding based upon connecting them up with some instinct or expression which is already familiar to us.

An anthropologist who believes that primitive rituals are aimed at practical results may be compared to a person who imagines that a funeral is an attempt to bring a dead person back to life, or a New

Year's celebration a way of making sure that the New Year "comes in." Or (in a striking example of Wittgenstein's) like someone who imagines that the phrase "the majesty of death" itself might serve to prolong life. For Wittgenstein this phrase, and others like it which might still come to mind, is as much of a ceremonial expression as the most elaborate death rituals.

> When we put together this story of the priest-king of Nemi with the words "the majesty of death," we see that they are both one. The life of the priest-king represents what is meant by those words.
> Whoever is grasped by the majesty of death can bring it to expression through such a life.– This is naturally also no explanation, but simply puts one symbol in place of another. Or: one ceremony for another. (NFGB p. 236.)

As with any language, in Wittgenstein's view, we understand rituals because we share in them or because we find similarities between them and those which we do share in. He suggests that there is much more universality here than we usually imagine. In the common spirit lies the matrix of ritual. But this, of course, is not an explanation or a ground of ritual. It is another ritual expression. And when Wittgenstein says that "man is a ceremonial animal," he adds

> That is indeed partly false, partly without sense, but there is also something correct in it. (NFGB p. 239.)

vi

A final example of groundless action is to be found in the case of *thinking*, which is a concept which gave Wittgenstein a great deal of difficulty (especially in trying to express its relation to speaking).

Wittgenstein asks two kinds of questions here: first, "What does one include in 'thinking?' What has one learnt to use this word for?" (PI 328) and second, "What does a man think for? What use is it? . . . What would show why he thinks?" (PI 466, 468).

To begin with the first set of questions. Thinking, Wittgenstein says, is a "widely ramified concept" because "the phenomena of thinking are widely scattered" (Z 110). The use of the word is "confused," as is to be expected (Z 113), for we are not prepared for the task of describing the use of it (Z 111).

Wittgenstein is quite clear about what thinking is *not*. Thus in

various places he attacks and rejects various pictures of what thinking
is because they do not give us a clear idea of what the use of the
word is. He says that thinking is *not a play of images* (Z 94), *not an
incorporeal process* (PI 339), *not talking out loud or silently* (PI p.
217; Z 98), *not a mental process accompanying talking* (PI 330-2; Z
93), *not an accompaniment of any activity* (Z 101), and *not a concept
of experience* (Z 96).

In all these cases the word *thinking* itself functions in a way which
shows us, if we look closely enough at it, that these pictures are inadequate. Behind them all are the dangers of taking thinking as a
"mental" activity, something which goes on "in our heads" (Z 605-6),
which we can "observe" happening in our own case (PI 316) and
which is somehow the real "life" of what we write and speak (Z 140).
A picture of some kind of a process in an "ethereal medium" is conjured up. (Z 20; PI 36, 109.)

All these, of course, are "grammatical" points, for Wittgenstein
is careful to follow his constant admonition not to imagine that one
is "looking at one's own case."

What emerges is that thinking is a doing or an activity (PI p.
212), but one which has this peculiarity that, though the concept of
thinking is "formed on the model of a kind of imaginary auxiliary activity" (Z 106), still it should not be thought of as an "accompaniment" of other things, for it cannot be separated from the activities
which we carry on "with it."

> Of course we cannot separate his "thinking" from his activity.
> For the thinking is not an accompaniment of the work, any
> more than of thoughtful speech. (Z 101.)

This is particularly the case with regard to speaking. The connection between thought and language is so close that Wittgenstein regarded them as virtually isomorphic in the *Tractatus*, and even in
Zettel he asks

> Indeed, where no language is used, why should one speak of
> "thinking?" (Z 109.)

Thinking is not talking, however, and not even "inward speech" for,
however close the two concepts are, they are different. This is clearly
stated in the following:

"Talking" (whether out loud or silently) and "thinking" are not concepts of the same kind, even though they are in closest connection. (PI p. 217.)

An important addendum to this appears to be contained in an earlier parenthetical remark:

("Thinking" and "inward speech"—I do not say "to oneself"—are different concepts.) (PI p. 211.)

While another interpretation is possible, the most plausible way of taking this would appear to be *not* to recognize "inward speech" and "inward speech to oneself" as different concepts (the latter perhaps the same as "thinking"), but rather to take "inward speech to oneself" as a *picture* attached to the concept of "inward speech" and not adding anything to it. Looked at in this way, "thinking" and "inward speech" *are* different, and "to oneself" does not alter this.[6]

What we must *not* imagine is that thinking is an *accompaniment* either of speech or of inward speech, for

While we sometimes call it "thinking" to accompany a sentence by a mental process, that accompaniment is not what we mean by a "thought." (PI 332.)

As he had stated earlier:

Suppose we think while we talk or write . . . the thought seems not to be separate from the expression. (PI 318.)

Just as the facial expression cannot be separated from the face, or the expressiveness of the music from the music (two of Wittgenstein's favorite examples) so thought may not be regarded as separable from its vehicle.

While these considerations suggest that it may be helpful to think of the concept of thinking *adverbially* sometimes ("He carried out the activity thinkingly"), we also have to bear in mind that sometimes

---

6 This may help to explain a footnote added to section 32 of the *Investigations* by the translator in the first American edition (though later removed). In section 32 Wittgenstein speaks of St. Augustine's conception of how children learn language and says it is "as if the child could already *think*, only not yet speak. And 'think' would here mean something like 'talk to itself'." Miss Anscombe's footnote read: "Wittgenstein later rejected this. See e.g. p. 217. He asked me to make such a note." Wittgenstein appears to have rejected this as his own conception of "thinking." But did he reject it as implied in St. Augustine's conception? The wording of section 32 is ambiguous as to which of these ways we are to take it.

the thinking *is* the activity ("What is he doing? He is thinking"), and
even in this case, if there are accompanying movements of the larynx,
the concept still has a different use.

Wittgenstein's position is that thinking is an ungrounded activity,
in the sense that it cannot be identified with anything else, but also ungrounded in the sense that it is not necessarily done for any other reason than that it is done. It does not have to have a purpose beyond
itself.

> Does man think, then, because he has found that thinking
> pays?—Because he thinks it advantageous to think?
> (Does he bring his children up because he has found it pays?)
> (PI 467.)

Wittgenstein admits that *sometimes* we think "because it has been
found to pay" (PI 470), but this is far from being the case always.

Although he says that he is not interested in causes, with regard
to *thinking* the question of cause becomes part of the way we think
about thinking, and the problem of the relation between thinking and
brain-processes cannot be handled merely as a matter of differences
of concepts and language-games. At least this would appear to be the
conclusion to be drawn from the speculations toward the end of
Zettel pointing toward a rejection of psycho-physical parallelism. It
is worth quoting an intriguing passage here in full:

> No supposition seems to me more natural than that there is
> no process in the brain correlated with association or with
> thinking; so that it would be impossible to read off thought-
> processes from brain-processes. I mean this: if I talk or write
> there is, I assume, a system of impulses going out from my
> brain and correlated with my spoken or written thoughts.
> But why should the *system* continue further in the direction
> of the center? Why should this order not proceed, so to
> speak, out of chaos? The case would be like the following—
> certain kinds of plants multiply by seeds, so that a seed always
> produces a plant of the same kind as that from which it was
> produced—but *nothing* in the seed corresponds to the plant
> which comes from it, so that it is impossible to infer the prop-
> erties or structure of the plant which comes out of it from those
> of the seed; this can only be done from the *history* of the seed.
> So an organism might come into being even out of something
> quite amorphous, as it were causelessly; and there is no reason

why this should not really hold for our thoughts and hence
for our talking and writing.
It is thus perfectly possible that certain psychological phenomena *cannot* be investigated physiologically, because physiologically nothing corresponds to them. (Z 608-9.)

This says that thinking is an *uncaused, self-originating activity, which
develops out of "chaos"* and which has nothing corresponding to it in
the brain up to the point where talking or writing occurs. The very
idea of this goes against so many ingrained philosophic predilections
that the matter cannot be left there. Wittgenstein goes on to suggest
that not only may thinking be uncaused, but there may be a psychological causality not accompanied by a physiological one. It may be
time to discard the whole picture of memories, for example, being
stored up in the brain and *traces* left in the nervous system.

Why must something or other, whatever it may be, be stored
up there *in any form?* Why *must* a trace have been left behind? Why should there not be a psychological regularity to
which *no* physiological regularity corresponds? If this upsets
our concept of causality then it is high time it was upset.
The prejudice in favor of psychophysical parallelism is a fruit
of primitive interpretations of our concepts. For if one allows
a causality between psychological phenomena which is not
mediated physiologically, one thinks one is professing belief
in a gaseous mental entity. (Z 610-11.)

Since no one attacked "gaseous mental entities" more seriously and
more consistently than Wittgenstein, we do not have to fear that when
he speaks of strictly psychological causality, he is thinking of it in that
way. In no sense does it have to be a causality between objects, but
only between actions, which may still develop and grow *according to
self-actualizing laws.*

These passages challenging psychophysical parallelism are not a
footnote to Wittgenstein's philosophy. They are an essential part of it
because they carry forward the idea of the autonomy of action, and
of language and forms of life as action. If, for example, causality is a
form of description, there is no reason it would have to be applied in
the same way to the realm of action as to the realm of phenomena.
Nor would causal chains have to stop where they have traditionally
stopped.

The notion of thinking as *uncaused, self-creating activity* gives to thinking a primacy and freedom which we may say it has seldom, if ever, had before in the history of philosophic thought. In such terms thinking is a free coming-to-be, an active potency, ever new and ever renewed, an act not tied to any form but which creates forms.

Language and thought may both be seen in Wittgenstein's later philosophy as expressions of primal activity, spontaneous and new, self-originating and self-developing. This is the way he things of language-games when he speaks of them as Ur-phenomena (PI 654) and as what is spontaneous and new (PI p. 224). And it is the way he imagines thinking when in the passages just quoted he speaks of it as uncaused and originating from chaos (Z 608).

vii

One of the most serious objections sometimes made to Wittgenstein's later philosophy is that it "leaves no room for values." The *Philosophical Investigations*, it is said, shows a world flattened out to the point where all that has meaning is phenomena and the description of phenomena. Where in such a world is there a place for ethics and ethical valuation?

In considering this, what needs to be remembered, first of all, is that Wittgenstein thought of his own philosophy as an ethical act, a "taking of sides," as he put it in the "Lectures on Religious Belief." He said on many occasions that he was trying to encourage a certain way of thinking, a way of thinking which he believed to be of great importance. This way of thinking could not be demonstrated to be "right"; at some point it simply required a choice, and this choice is certainly an ethical one.

But, more than this, the nature of his way of thinking (i.e. the content of Wittgenstein's philosophy) is intrinsically of ethical significance, and this is the main point which is overlooked. The ethics is there indeed in Wittgenstein's later philosophy, but it is completely immanent in the philosophy (or in the human situation seen from that point of view) and, therefore, does not have to be given a special place. Even Wittgenstein's phenomenalism has an ethical significance, though this may be one which is unfamiliar to us.[7]

---

[7] A Buddhist scholar once told the present writer that a fundamental principle of Buddhist ethics is "the perfect assurance of relying completely on what we see." This beautifully expresses one side of Wittgenstein's philosophy.

We can see the ethical significance best of all, however, in the place which Wittgenstein's philosophy gives to *action*. It is in our capacity for action, when this is freed from extraneous interference, that ethical value lies. And no philosophy is more aware of this primal source of action and makes a larger place for it than Wittgenstein's. (The implicit conception of freedom as an *openness to the new* is, for example, far more ethically significant—not to say also revolutionary—than the rationalistically circumscribed freedom of Kant, which is still, after all, "playing it safe" with universal moral laws.) For Wittgenstein action in the end is ungrounded. And it must be said that *all action arising out of this ungroundedness has intrinsic value*, and this is the fundamental point of Wittgenstein's ethics.

We have in Wittgenstein's philosophy (unnamed but presupposed) a primal freedom underlying language, forms of life, rites and ceremonies, religious beliefs and thinking, all of which have their source in this primal groundlessness.[8] The term *free will* is misleading because it suggests that we control and dispose of this freedom (a Cartesian way of thinking, but not Wittgenstein's), while actually we allow something to happen or do not allow it to happen. The freedom, in other words, which is pointed to here is not the freedom of an ego to control and dominate, but of a certain kind of response to the sources of action.

Wittgenstein's philosophy has an unmistakable ethical import because it rejects in principle the notion of any ultimate control over human action by ideas (or ideologies), nature, causality, reason, will, or, indeed, any authority or external standard understood as a determinant of value. Instead his philosophy tells us (or rather leaves us to find out for ourselves by closing off all other avenues) that all action is of value to the extent that it arises selflessly out of the primal groundlessness. It is hard to imagine a more important ethical point, a stronger affirmation of the autonomy of action and hence of freedom and the ethical.

---

[8] We are much more likely to think of writers like Boehme, Dostoievsky, Berdyev and Shestov in connection with Wittgenstein than of the general run of modern rationalists, though this must not be understood as saying that Wittgenstein is an "irrationalist."

PART IV

CONCLUSION

Ordinary Certainty

We went sleepwalking along a road between abysses.—But even if we now say: "Now we are awake,"—can we be certain that we shall not wake up one day? (And then say—so we were asleep again.)

WITTGENSTEIN (RFM p. 101)

Rational thought is interpretation in accordance with a scheme that we cannot throw off.

NIETZSCHE

We may perhaps have to admit that . . . certainty has absolutely nothing to do with truth.

LEV SHESTOV

One must know when to stop—
Knowing when to stop averts trouble.

LAOTZU

CHAPTER 13

Ordinary Certainty

i

One of the most striking things about the *Philosophical Investigations* is the number of seemingly factual observations which it contains. We might suppose in many places that Wittgenstein had adopted a more empirical orientation after the formalism of his early philosophy. Then we come upon sentences which appear to draw conclusions so strange that we do not know what to make of them. Suddenly what looked like a familiar landscape disappears from sight, and nothing looks recognizable any more.

This illustrates the ever-present difficulty which Wittgenstein faced—that of trying to express something new in old terms. And the *Philosophical Investigations is* something new. It is not anthropology or linguistics or theories or generalizations about the social character of language or how children learn. There is in it no theory of meaning, or theory of language, or theory of anything else. What we have instead is a new point of view, which if accepted, would *change our way of looking*, including our way of looking at anthropology, linguistics, and "theories."

One aspect of this new way of looking is a new role for certain empirical statements: they may be used to convey a philosophical perspective. How do such statements then differ from ordinary factual statements? What kind of certainty do they have? What is the basis of it? It is these kinds of questions with which Wittgenstein's last book *On Certainty* deals.

On Certainty concerns the role of facts which serve as frameworks for world views. They might be called *framework facts* because in some ways they are like other facts, though in other ways they are not like other facts at all. They are the facts which, Wittgenstein says, are the basis for our thoughts, our language, our judgments, and our actions. Such *world view facts* (to give them still another name) include also the various strata of what we call common sense. They include the

221

vast numbers of things which we take for granted and which provide
the settings for all our questions and investigations, as well as for our
language activities. They are the facts which we do not doubt because,
among other things, they define what *doubting* is or *what it makes
sense to doubt*. They establish what is accepted or agreed-upon in ways
of talking and acting.

In *On Certainty* Wittgenstein approaches the study of these peculiar facts in terms of an analysis of the concepts of *doubt* and *knowing*. The book's fundamental thesis, if we may call it that, is that what
we find it impossible to doubt is not what we *know* for certain, but
rather what we *take* as certain or *treat* as certain—in other words, what
plays that role for us. As Wittgenstein sees it, there is no question of
knowing involved, but rather a certain logical status given to certain
kinds of facts. It is suggested that there is something like a factual
a priori because we cannot proceed without these defining and method-
determining facts, but in their foundational role they are not a matter
of knowledge.

We can get an idea of what Wittgenstein thinks of these *framework facts* by looking at them as what replace the *atomic facts*, or
absolutely simple facts, of the *Tractatus*, which in that book were the
ultimate ground of thinking, language, and the world. What, however,
confers on ordinary facts, in Wittgenstein's later view, a preeminent
character is their functioning as immune from doubt, not some presump-
tive ultimate simplicity or absoluteness. They are, as he puts it, the
axis (OC 152), *river-bed* (OC 97), *scaffolding* (OC 211), and *hinges*
(OC 341) of our thoughts and actions. They do not agree or disagree
with reality; they constitute *what we mean by reality*.[1]

Framework facts come nearest to being the "metaphysics" of
Wittgenstein's final philosophy, but it is a long way from the metaphysics of the *Tractatus* and an even longer way from traditional metaphysics. Such facts do not tell us anything about the ultimate nature

---

[1] This should not, of course, be thought of in traditional terms of idealism
or realism. Wittgenstein is not saying that "we make reality" or "reality is prior
to us." Both statements do not make sense in his terms since they presuppose
either a transcendental subject or a transcendental object (or, as is usually the
case, both, since one of these does not appear without the other), both of which
have disappeared from his later philosophy. The terms *object* and *subject*, for
the later Wittgenstein, acquire all their meanings from their uses in different
language activities.

of the world, for it is this picture of such an ultimate nature which has been rejected. But neither, on the other hand, are they the creation or projection of a subject. Instead they belong to common language activities, and these are a final basis, not to be further grounded or explained. Facts which in ordinary life we take as the ground, *are* the ground, the only legitimate and available certainty. We come to rest in the "majesty of the commonplace."

In terms of traditional ontology this, of course, can only appear as "relativism." But it is these terms which Wittgenstein has given up. "Relativism" presupposes something which cannot be known, and it is just this which Wittgenstein wants, not to deny, but to look at differently. The result might be seen as completing the work of Kant, for Kant stopped short of dropping the thing-in-itself and the transcendental subject, even though these were scarcely more than "limit points" in the final Kantian philosophy.

It is likely to come as a surprise that it is just such commonplace facts as "My name is so-and-so," "All human beings have parents," or "This is a tree" which, when they are used in this way, have for Wittgenstein the status of certainty. Just such facts as we normally take for granted. There is, for him, for example, no greater certainty than the certainty with which we know our own names, and this by no means overlooks the possibilities of amnesia or other aberrations.

What puzzles him, and what he tries to clarify throughout, is that sentences which express these ordinary certainties appear to have a dual character. On the one hand, they are what we rely upon, what we take for granted, what stands fast; but, on the other, it is only in connection with specific situations, where doubt may enter, that the same sentences really tell us anything or convey any actual knowledge. It is as if what we are most sure about stays in the dark and is only illuminated when some unusual situation challenges it. When we affirm or try to establish the truth of such certainties in isolation, without the illumination of the odd situation, they seem to lack sense.

Here the topological language of *inside* and *outside* may be helpful. As long as a statement like *This is a tree* answers to a legitimate doubt, Wittgenstein says, we seem to understand what it means. But when we lift it out of any context, then it seems as if we have to supply some "universal space" for it, and the philosopher, like a crazy man, is seen staring at the tree and repeating over and over again *This is a tree*, as if trying to impress a universal context on himself, a context in which things, as it were, carry their identities around with them and so we might be mistaken about anyone of them. The universal context, however, fails because even to permit the remotest possible truth for *This is not a tree* in a situation where every sane human being would say *This is a tree* is, as we will see, to destroy the meaning of the latter sentence itself. (It is as if, with these sentences, the *meaning* and the *truth* of the sentence are so inextricably united that to attempt to separate them, so as to find out *what* is supposed to be true, self-destructs the sentence.)

Normal everyday certainty (for example, that *This is a tree*) is, Wittgenstein holds, all we can get, and the attempt to get a still greater certainty is, in one way, parasitic on the normal certainty and, in another way, stretches the normal certainty to the point where it loses its meaning. There is no greater certainty than the ordinary kind—the kind we find in the case, for example, where somebody cannot see clearly whether something is a tree or not, and somebody else is in a position to tell him *This is a tree*, and this assurance carries with it the implication that this is what we normally would all say and act on.

Such normal certainty, Wittgenstein says, is not, of course, immune to *insanity* (OC 217, 281, 419, 572, 674), *drugs* (OC 676), *delusions* (OC 624), *mental disturbances* (OC 71), *unheard-of happenings* (OC 517), *bewilderment and confusion* (OC 304, 420), *blindness* (OC 418), or what we might call *"awakening"* (OC 578, 645). All these may come from outside to upset *any* certainty. But the point is that, if they do, they will also upset at the same time more or less our whole system of judgments, thought, language, and action. What good is the attempt to find certainties which would be impregnable to even these difficulties if it turns out that the very terms in which the supposed super-certainties are cast would fail to stand up through the difficulties? How can we hope to preserve certainties through madness and delusion when the very framework of normality itself has given way?

The traditional appeal to the ontological did, indeed, seem to put us in touch with a certainty immune to *any* threat, since it seemed to reach through to the in-itself, established inviolably apart from any aberrations which might happen to us. And the terms *object, substance, reality, fact* (central in Wittgenstein's own earlier philosophy), expressed just such a picture of an absolute ground. It was the impossibility of giving any final meanings to just these terms (since other ways of conceiving of them always remained *at least possible*) which destroyed for Wittgenstein the ground of the in-itself.

There is in the later philosophy no certainty which can remain unaffected through every eventuality, including drugs, madness, dreams, delusions, and illuminations. Such eventualities break down the framework of what counts as normal and reasonable, depriving us of the basis for any certainty at all, of any kind. The ordinary meanings are the focal meanings, and if they collapse, we cannot expect other meanings to survive.

The everyday certainties (as contrasted with the illusory super-certainties) are not to be understood as one more metaphysical ground, for they are not anchored in a world outside of normal human situations, for *what do we know about that?* What Wittgenstein attempts to express is that ordinary certainties are nonetheless certain for not holding through every catastrophe. Certainty is a logical category, not a factual one.

ii

In turning now to the question of *doubt* and Wittgenstein's discussion of the argument of G. E. Moore, it is helpful to begin with a distinction which he makes between *subjective certainty* and *objective certainty*. Wittgenstein's point is that the expression *I cannot doubt* may have either one of these two meanings:

First, the case of *subjective certainty*: In this case *I cannot doubt* expresses subjective conviction, and I *may* be mistaken no matter how certain I feel. Here *I cannot doubt* means the same as *I know for certain*.

Second, the case of *objective certainty*: In this case there is no sense to doubting and no sense to knowing either. Here *I cannot doubt* means *It makes no sense to talk about doubt in this case*. And this does not mean *I know for certain*, for where doubting is impossible, so is knowing.

How did Moore come to suppose that the impossibility of doubt is equivalent to knowing for certain? Wittgenstein's suggestion is that he confused these two cases. He treated the logical impossibility as if

it were an instance of (and so could establish) a psychological impossibility.

This becomes clearer if we look at Wittgenstein's discussion of
Moore's argument. Moore claimed (in his essay "Proof of an External
World") to know for certain, while holding up his hand, that *Here
is a hand*, a knowing allegedly based on his inability to doubt this. The
critical step was the transition from his *inability to doubt* to his *knowing for certain*. This gave to *knowing* a status in a situation where, in
Wittgenstein's terms, there was actually *nothing to know*.

In looking at Moore's argument we can, first of all, set aside
Moore's subjective state, because, Wittgenstein says, no matter how
strongly Moore feels, there is always the possibility that he is wrong
(i.e. that he only *thinks* he knows for certain), and, therefore, no
matter what he says we simply do not have to believe him. What
really counts is the logical impossibility of doubting.

To make Moore's claim to knowledge meaningful, Wittgenstein
says, we would have to suppose a further doubt. Moore's knowing
for certain, in other words, will make sense if a further doubt is *not*
impossible, but can be smuggled back in. We need to imagine a super-
doubt, a God-like doubt (or, if we prefer, a half-wit doubt or insane
doubt) against which the certain knowledge is supposed to hold and
which will make sense out of the certain knowledge. This may be the
further hidden structure in Moore's argument: a super-knowledge established against a super-doubt. (What leads us, in part, to suspect
this, is the question: Otherwise why bother at all with *knowing for
certain?*)

Such a super-doubt, in Wittgenstein's view, is *idle* (OC 117),
hollow (OC 312), *senseless* (OC 56, 310), *illusory* (OC 19), *based on
a false picture* (OC 249), and *witout consequences* (OC 338). Such a
doubt only makes sense when it is no longer a super one, but becomes
an ordinary one as the result of unusual circumstances—as, for example,
in the situation of an amputee in a hospital who isn't sure that he still
has his hand when he wakes up from an operation. In the absence of
such a situation Moore's staring at his hand and repeating over and
over *Here is a hand* seems to be answering the idle illusory doubt. (It
is as if he were trying to produce the *feeling* of knowledge, and it
might even be hard to do it.)

Super-doubt is, after all, a doubt familiar in philosophy, and we
may be inclined to say: "Surely it is at least possible that we are

completely deluded even about everyday certainties when there are no unusual circumstances. Is not a presumptuous doubt, or even an insane doubt, still a doubt? Was Descartes's demon-based or dream-based doubt no doubt at all?" For Wittgenstein such doubts *are* an illusion, but this has to be shown. (OC 19, 249.)

The argument may be stated like this: If we really doubted what we *think* we doubt in such a "super-case," so much else would be thrown into doubt along with it that we would no longer have any terms left in which to express the supposed original doubt. Suppose, for example, that I doubt that this is a hand while I am looking at it; then, the argument goes, I might just as well doubt that I am looking, or that I can see, or that I have eyes, or that my eyes are open, or that any of these words have any meaning, etc. All these propositions stand on the same level, and there is no reason why any of them should hold if the others don't. A doubt cannot arise about my hand being my hand while I am looking at it, just because this is that kind of a statement which we need as part of the framework for our genuine doubts.

What Moore has overlooked, Wittgenstein says, is that doubt makes sense only in terms of what is not doubtful, or, to put it another way, we can doubt some things only by not doubting others. (OC 115, 341, 519, 625.) If the entire house is bound to collapse when we open the window, the question of whether the window can be opened no longer makes sense.

For Wittgenstein, absolute, isolated, and complete doubt is an illusion, whether conceived in the manner of Moore or of Descartes. Doubt is possible *only in some terms*, since there has to be something that is doubted and therefore some kind of an identification of it must be possible. Doubting, in other words, is not an introspectively identifiable mental activity, separable from any content or conditions.

When Wittgenstein says that doubts must make sense (OC 2, 56, 310, 372), he means that there are meaning-conditions for doubt to be doubt. Two such meaning-conditions are mentioned: (1) doubts have grounds (OC 122, 288), and (2) doubts presuppose what is not doubted (OC 115, 219, 354, 450, 519, 341). Moore's doubt and Descartes's doubt fail to meet these conditions.

These meaning-conditions show that doubts come to an end, not because there is some psychological act which we cannot perform, or because we have run up against absolute truths, but because a doubt which has no content has no reason to be called a doubt. (A mere psychological act cannot be called anything.) Doubts end, not because we cannot doubt that we doubt, but because there is no longer sufficient basis left for calling it doubt.

Putting this "positively," what we cannot doubt, we cannot doubt, not because it is too true, too real, or too simple to doubt, but because we have accepted it as part of our world-picture and hence as part of the terms in which our doubts themselves are cast. Trying to doubt the conditions which make doubt possible is not running up against an ontological barrier, but a grammatical or logical one. As Wittgenstein puts it:

> But I did not get my picture of the world by satisfying myself of its correctness; nor do I have it because I am satisfied of its correctness. No; it is the inherited background against which I distinguish between true and false. (OC 94.)

The reason why, then, we would not understand somebody who held up his hand under normal circumstances and said "I doubt that this is a hand," is, for Wittgenstein, first and foremost, because *This is a hand* is a framework fact, the kind of fact which we take for granted in expressing ordinary doubts and, therefore, not itself subject to doubt without destroying the sense of other doubts. Just this is what we mean by saying that we are dealing, therefore, with a framework fact.

In order to try to establish a still greater certainty Moore had to imagine (at least tacitly) a still greater doubt. But both the super-certainty and the super-doubt were illusory. The illusions seem to have arisen because Moore took what was essentially a gramatical point (the senselessness of doubting certain things in ordinary circumstances) and tried to use it to establish an epistemological point (the supposed certainty of immediate experience). Then indeed it looked as if he had established something he knew for certain beyond the certainty reserved for ordinary mortals.

We can now summarize Wittgenstein's main criticisms of Moore's argument under two main headings:

(1) Moore's first mistake was in trying to ground maximum certainty subjectively; *I know* is not an answer to *It cannot be known* because

(a) it remains possible that he only *thinks he knows* since
the greatest feeling of certainty is not incompatible with
being wrong (OC 12-16, 21, 30, 178, 245, 404, 489, 549,
580), and
(b) we do not have to believe him (OC 22, 520);

(2) Moore's second mistake was a misuse of the word *know*, for
(a) knowledge must have grounds, and there are no grounds
here, since the propositions he is trying to establish are
already as sure as any evidence for them could be (OC
111, 245, 250),
(b) "knowledge" and "certainty" belong to different categories
(OC 308, 569.), and
(c) the knowledge claimed involves a doubt which is idle,
senseless, illusory (OC 2, 19, 56, 117, 249, 310).

iii

We turn now to Wittgenstein's view that ordinary certainties are
not a matter of knowledge, but are, in some way, prior to knowledge.
But if they are not knowledge, what are they?

Wittgenstein says that they play the role of *unmoving foundations*
(OC 403), what is *removed from doubt* (OC 341), what *stands fast*
(OC 151, 235), and what is *solid for us* (OC 151). They are

. . . a foundation for all my action . . . wrongly expressed by
the words "I know." (OC 414.)
. . . [a] direct taking-hold [which] corresponds to a *sureness*,
not to a knowing. (OC 511.)

We do not, in other words, *start* with knowing. There is no given
which is epistemologically primary. Rather we start with acting-with-
certainty. Our action is, as it were, embedded in a matrix of surety,
which is prior to knowledge, being the matrix of knowing-and-doubt-
ing and knowing-and-being-mistaken. Ordinary certainties are the
roads on which we walk without question, not because they are the
only possible roads or the *right* roads or even the *pragmatically justified* roads, but because they are the roads which we *are* on, and no
occasion has arisen for leaving them. As Wittgenstein puts it:

I have no grounds for not trusting them. And I trust them.
(OC 600.)

The first problem then is to separate these ordinary certainties from claims to knowledge. The kinds of certainties which we depend upon—that day follows night, that everybody grows older, that animals do not converse with people except in fairy stories—differ from knowledge in the following ways:

1—*Knowledge needs to be grounded* (OC 16, 18, 91, 243, 270, 504). This means that when we claim to *know* something, it has to be possible to state *how* we know it, or to show that we are in a position to know it (OC 550, 555). With regard to ordinary certainties, however, there is no ground (OC 307), and we do not have to be able to show how we know them (OC 84, 176).

> I cannot say that I have good grounds for the opinion that cats do not grow on trees or that I had a father and a mother. (OC 282.)

2—*Knowledge always carries with it the possibility of doubt* (OC 480). Knowledge and doubt have to make sense together. With regard to ordinary certainties, on the other hand, no doubt is possible, or at least no reasonable doubt, or no doubt that would not bring a large part of my world toppling down with it, if it were possible; and hence no knowledge is possible either.

The meaning-conditions for knowledge amount to the one main condition that knowledge has to be able to fail (OC 41, 58). What characterizes ordinary certainties, on the other hand, is that in normal circumstances it is inconceivable that they should fail because they are just what make up the normal circumstances and so also determine what constitutes failure. If abnormal circumstances should sweep such certainties away, it would be tantamount to "normality" or "reality" itself giving way.

In aiming to separate knowledge and certainty Wittgenstein tells us that, objectively or logically considered, they "belong to different *categories*" (OC 308). Knowledge requires the possibility of doubt and mistakes, while what is objectively certain rules these out. The distinction is between what is provided for *within* a language and what attacks the whole activity from *without*. The possibility of error is provided for; that of amnesia is not.

> If I were to say "I have never been on the moon—but I may be mistaken," that would be idiotic. For even the thought that

I might have been transported there, by unknown means, in
my sleep, *would not give me any right* to speak of a possible
mistake here. I play the game *wrong* if I do. (OC 662.)

An analogy may make this clearer: We might say that a football
remaining inflated in the course of a game is not part of the game,
but rather is one of the taken-for-granted certainties upon which the
game is based. We are not required in playing the game, in other
words, to take the possibility of the football becoming deflated into
account. In terms of the game it is, so to speak, inconceivable, and *we
make no error* if it should happen. That such balls are manufactured
in such a way that they do not usually deflate or break open or blow
up in the course of the game is part of the matrix of surety which
makes the game possible. (We can, on the other hand, easily imagine
a game in which the aim was to deflate the ball or in which there were
penalties for deflating it, etc.) Analogously, I may forget my name,
but I do not make provisions for such an eventuality, and it does not
figure as part of any activity in which I use my name. (If certain general facts about us were different, this might indeed have to be taken
into account.)

Objective certainty has no grounds *because it is itself what we
take as grounds* (like the ball and the field in football). Wittgenstein
says that we can give no grounds for going on the way we do, or
rather we

. . . could give a thousand [grounds], but none as certain as
the very thing they were supposed to be grounds for. (OC
307.)

We confidently put one foot in front of the other, altogether disre-
garding the possibility that the earth may open up in front of us or
that we may pitch over fatally stricken. Does this procedure, this
walking-with-sureness, require justification because it is not guarded
against *every* eventuality? Is there not a natural fideism here, for which
no one, not even the philosopher, need apologize?

In order to get this new perspective into focus Wittgenstein says
a step is needed "like the one taken in relativity theory" (OC 305).
This analogy suggests that knowledge-and-error (or knowledge-and-
mistakes) go together, making up a continuum of certainty in which
they are grounded and fused, as in relativity theory space-and-time

together make up the continuum in which they are fused and grounded. They are separable because they are first united.

Wittgenstein's dictum that *there is a sureness which is not a knowing*, but which is prior to knowing-and-not-knowing, challenges the primacy of epistemology across the board, whether empiricist or rationalist, realist or idealist. In his view philosophers have been bewitched by the word *know* (OC 435), a word which he says won't "tolerate a metaphysical emphasis" (OC 482). The philosophical tradition has given this word a preeminence which, he says, it does not deserve. The alternative, however, is not skepticism or irrationalism, but rather to put knowing back into its proper place by recognizing that there are meaning-conditions for knowing also, so that *making sense is not based upon knowing, but rather knowing itself must make sense.*

iv

What are the characteristics of ordinary certainties, and how do they relate to logical and mathematical certainties, on the one hand, and to experience and evidence on the other?

Before dealing with these questions, let us look at the way Wittgenstein describes ordinary certainties. He sees them as:

1—a foundation for all my action (OC 414)
2—the foundation of all operating with thoughts (with language) (OC 401)
3—an unmoving foundation of his language-games (OC 403, 411)
4—the foundation of all judging (OC 308, 614)
5—the substratum of all my inquiring and asserting (OC 88, 151, 162)
6—the inherited background against which I distinguish between true and false (OC 94)

These formulations have an ontological ring, and it might seem that they point to a new ontology. But here we must remember several points: (1) that it is quite immaterial what propositions play this role, (2) that propositions can move in and out of this role, and (3) that there is no further grounding for whatever propositions do happen to be cast in this way. The seemingly factual propositions which we take for granted constitute what we *call* reality and accepting them is what we mean by being sane and reasonable.

When something has been given the status of an empirical certainty or framework fact, it does not require explanation or justification. We are not concerned with whether it corresponds to the nature of things, for it is *what we mean by the nature of things*. It would make no sense to talk about the way things are, apart from the way we take for granted that they are. The certainties of our everyday lives —such as being sure what one's name is, where one lives, that we are on the earth, and that the earth has been here a long time—do not have to be backed up by evidence or experience.

It is a point which Wittgenstein stresses that empirical certainties do not lose any of their certainty for not having a transcendent basis or for not being matters of knowledge, nor again for being vulnerable to catastrophes or future changes. We are concerned with the role which they play, and in this respect they function as totally certain. Wittgenstein says they function like norms or rules (OC 167), not as *what* we judge, as what we judge *by*, even though any proposition may switch from one side to the other in the twinkling of an eye.

The *a priori* character, which Wittgenstein's early philosophy attributed to absolutely simple logical structures, shows up again here at the end as belonging to the working certainties of everyday life. These are now the framework facts, facts so established and important that they do not need support or credentials. They may have to move on to the stage at any moment, and they may be deposed altogether, but their significance is undoubted.

Wittgenstein puts at least some empirical certainties on the same footing as statements of arithmetic. He says, for example, that seeing that this is my hand, or recognizing objects with certainty, and arithmetic propositions (in so far as they rest on our not miscounting or miscalculating and our senses not deceiving us as we calculate) are "on the same level." Both types of statements are measures of the world, ways of structuring the world, frameworks for our lives and activities.

> I want to say: The physical game is just as certain as the arithmetical. But this can be misunderstood. My remark is a logical and not a psychological one. (OC 447.)
> I want to say: If one doesn't marvel at the fact that the propositions of arithmetic (e.g. the multiplication tables) are 'absolutely certain,' then why should one be astonished that the proposition "This is my hand" is so equally? (OC 448.)

Are empirical certainties then independent of experience? Only to the extent that we do not have any experience which contradicts them. Wittgenstein points out that it would be foolish to say that experience has taught me that objects do not disappear without reason or that cats do not grow on trees or that people do not have sawdust in their heads. Everything we know backs up these ideas; they fit in with all kinds of other things; and we never have any reason to question them. But it would be odd to say that we learned them from experience. We swallowed them down when we learned various language activities.

At one point Wittgenstein says that experiences do not teach us fundamental certainties because these are just the ways in which we interpret the experiences.

> One wants to say "*All* my experiences show that it is so." But how do they do that? For that proposition to which they point itself belongs to a particular interpretation of them. "That I regard this proposition as certainly true also characterizes my interpretation of experience." (OC 145.)

In other words, empirical certainties are ways of looking at experience. For example, if we take it as certain that everything is learned from experience, this itself is a way of looking at experience and not itself something learned from experience.

Are ordinary certainties established by evidence? Here the prior question is: What is to count as evidence? And it is this question which ordinary certainties answer. In other words, the same problem of certainty arises in connection with the evidence as in connection with that which it is supposed to be evidence for. We may attempt to use evidence to justify a certainty, but if then there is no way to justify the evidence, we will not be any better off, for

> It would be nonsense to say that we regard something as sure evidence because it is certainly true. (OC 197.)

It characterizes ordinary certainties, furthermore, that the evidence for them is no more convincing than they are themselves.

> My having two hands is, in normal circumstances, as certain as anything I could produce in evidence for it.
> That is why I am not in a position to take the sight of my hand as evidence for it. (OC 250.)

Finally, Wittgenstein makes two other points about empirical certainties or framework facts: (1) that they have a tacit or implicit character and (2) that they belong to systems. With regard to the first point, they are, he says, inherited or acquired along with what we learn. They tend to remain invisible, deriving their importance from what is around them, like the axis around which a body rotates, the immobility of which is determined by the movement around it. (OC 152).

With regard to the second point, these certainties do not stand in isolation, but belong to vast systems, in which they are inter-dependent and inter-connected. He speaks of them as having

a peculiar logical role in the system of our empirical propositions . . . (OC 136.)

Elsewhere he speaks of "our whole system of evidence" (OC 185), "the system of our empirical judgments" (OC 137), "our system of assumption" (OC 134), "the entire system of our language-games" (OC 411). We learn, he says, a totality of judgments, systems of beliefs (OC 140), and doubts, as a system (OC 126, 247).

What is the nature of these systems? Wittgenstein did not live to answer this question. He may well have been aware that there was a gap here. Toward the end of his notes we find this entry under date of April 4th, a little more than three weeks before his death, which occurred on April 29, 1951:

Why is there no doubt that I am called L.W.? It does not seem at all like something that one could establish at once beyond doubt. One would not think that it is one of the indubitable truths. (OC 470.)

The next entry, on the following day, April 5th, reads:

[Here there is still a big gap in my thinking. And I doubt whether it will be filled now.]

If, as seems likely, the parenthetical remark refers to the immediately preceding entry, then the "big gap" may well have had to do with the question of what kind of systems we have here.

Having burnt his fingers in both the *Tractatus* and the *Brown Book* on this question of trying to find an order of the *a priori*, Wittgenstein may well have hesitated before trying again. And perhaps it is no wonder that the next entry says:

> It is so difficult to find the *beginning*. Or, better: it is difficult to begin at the beginning. And not try to go further back. (OC 471.)

These sentences could be taken as the epitome of Wittgenstein's whole philosophy, for his major accomplishment was to find a new beginning. But they also represent something even more remarkable, for, taken in conjunction with the immediately preceding remarks, they show that at the very end of his life he was still thinking about the right beginning.

Wittgenstein's Place in Western Thought

ὥσπερ γὰρ καὶ τὰ τῶν νυκτερίδων ὄμματα πρὸς τὸ
φέγγος ἔχει τὸ μεθ᾽ ἡμέραν, ὅτω καὶ τῆς ἡμετέρας ψυχῆς
ὁ νῦς πρὸς τὰ τῇ φύσει φανερώτατα πάντων.

(. . . for, as the eyes of bats are dazzled by sunlight, so it is
with human intelligence when face to face with what is by
nature most obvious.)

ARISTOTLE

. . . the farewell of all *It is* comes to pass.

MARTIN HEIDEGGER

To perceive that there is nothing to be perceived is true perception.

HUI HAI

Before our very eyes "nothing" will be transformed into what
matters most.

LEV SHESTOV

CHAPTER 14

Wittgenstein's Place
in Western Thought

i

Before we can speak of Wittgenstein's place in the history of Western thought we have to formulate his essential vision of the world —the central core of his philosophy. Without this it is impossible to see his true significance. For although parts of his philosophy can be understood, to a certain extent, piecemeal, the unity of his thought and its inner relatedness is bound to elude us until we see how it is focused around a single central point.

It must be said that Wittgenstein always knew where he was going and what he had to do in philosophy. He was not searching for a vision; he had one from the beginning. What he was searching for were the ways to understand it and to express it. The difficulty was always an "enormous difficulty of expression" (N p. 40). And the despair was the despair of ever being able to make it clear to himself and to others. It was not the central vision which created the dark and somber tone of his philosophy, but rather what appeared to be the almost insuperable difficulty of saying it clearly.

Thus in the Preface which he wrote to the *Tractatus* he began by expressing only a very modest hope for that book:

> Its purpose would be achieved if it gave pleasure to one person who read and understood it. (T p. 3.)

By the end of his life, in the Preface to the *Philosophical Investigations*, *even* this modest hope had lessened:

> It is not impossible that it should fall to the lot of this work, in its poverty and in the darkness of this time, to bring light into one brain or another—but, of course, it is not likely. (PI p. x.)

239

The possibilities of misunderstanding, it must have seemed, were endless, beginning with Bertrand Russell's misunderstanding of the *Tractatus* and down to the experiences of his later years when

> I was obliged to learn that my results (which I had communicated in letters, typescripts and discussions), variously misunderstood, more or less mangled or watered-down, were in circulation. (PI pp. ix-x.)

The low opinion which he had of professional philosophy reveals all too well how little he thought could be expected from other philosophers. And this is not surprising in the light of his own experience. For his contemporaries had repeatedly misunderstood him: first in taking him as a "positivist," and then, when his philosophy had altered so drastically, as a "therapist,"—as if his principal aim at first had been to get rid of metaphysics through some form of "scientism" and then, when that had failed, to "cure" people of it through some kind of linguistic psychoanalysis. It must indeed have seemed to him that he was writing for some other age and for people who had not yet been born. For it must have seemed that no one would even *listen* to the main points, but everyone always heard only what he wanted to hear.

We can see how misunderstandings arose—by our leaving out what we did not *want* to see, selecting and emphasizing what fitted in with our own predilections. For example, Wittgenstein wrote:

> The philosopher's treatment of a question is like the treatment of an illness. (PI 255.)

How easy it was then to think of philosophy as "therapy" in a superficial sense. But the illness Wittgenstein was trying to treat was his own, as well as other people's. He did not think of the philosopher as one who was himself exempt from the illness, who was himself healthy and so could set out to cure others. Instead the philosopher suffered from the same maladies, the same troubles:

> The philosopher is the man who has to cure himself of many sicknesses of the understanding before he can arrive at the notions of the sound human understanding.
> If in the midst of life we are in death, so in sanity we are surrounded by madness. (RFM p. 157.)

How will the sicknesses be cured? Wittgenstein says by "a changed mode of thought and life."

The sickness of a time is cured by an alteration in the mode of life of human beings, and it was possible for the sickness of philosophical problems to get cured only through a changed mode of thought and of life, not through a medicine invented by an individual.

Suppose the use of the motorcar produces or encourages certain illnesses, and mankind is plagued by such illness until, from some cause or other, as the result of some development or other, it abandons the habit of driving. (RFM p. 57.)

The "changed mode" would be in the direction of something more natural than we know now. The significance of what is "natural," as this term is used by Wittgenstein, should not be overlooked.[1] In the *Notebooks* of 1915 we find this revealing remark:

. . . the feelings expressed in these sentences are quite natural and unartificial, so there must be some truth at the bottom of them. But what truth? (N p. 48.)

In the Preface to the *Investigations* he says that he wanted to get his thoughts into a "natural order" (*natürlichen Folge*), but was unsuccessful because the thoughts themselves had a "natural inclination" (*natürliche Neigung*) which prevented this (PI p. ix). The "naturalness" he was striving for was overcome by another "naturalness" to which he had to submit. Words like "healthy" and "pure" seemed to be connected with "natural," and these in turn with "good will." In the Preface to the *Philosophical Remarks* he speaks of wanting that book to be written out of "good will" and says that, in so far as it was not written out of "good will," but out of vanity (*Eitelkeit*), etc., he would want to see it condemned. The extent to which the book is "purified" of such things as vanity will be no greater, he says, than the extent to which the author himself is "purified" of them (PR p. 7).

These statements show the extent to which Wittgenstein believed that philosophy reflects the life of the philosopher. He can only be

---

[1] Of Gottfried Keller, who, according to Paul Engelmann, was "one of the few great writers whom Wittgenstein revered whole-heartedly" (Engelmann, *Memoirs*, p. 86), a critic has written that his "continued deep regard for nature expressed itself on almost every page of his works in his constant use of the adjective 'natürlich,' and its associates 'unverdorben,' 'gesund,' 'ursprünglich,' 'rein,' 'unbefangen,' 'einfach,' to designate a person or thing worthy of his favor." Herbert W. Reichert, *Basic Concepts in the Philosophy of Gottfried Keller* (N.Y.: AMS Press, 1966), p. 55.

as "simple" and "natural" as his life is. How vanity interferes he emphasized thus:

> Pretensions are a mortgage which burdens a philosopher's
> capacity to think. (OC 549.)

The inability to see clearly and to work out his thoughts better
was due to the "sickness of the time," as well as to his own failings,
but this did not mean that Wittgenstein did not know what had to
be done. On the contrary, as we have said, the central focus of his
philosophy was set from the beginning and did not change. Wittgenstein's thinking was a journey of discovery, but with a *fixed pole* which
did not alter even when, in a sense, the journey had to be undertaken
twice.

What was the central vision? It was the vision of what might be
called an incommensurable split between, on the one side, *language
and the world included in language,* and, on the other side, *the unsayable and the world as unsayable* (sheer existence, immediacy of
content, voiceless physiognomies, confronting the *I* and confronting us).

The starkness of this split (not even legitimately to be called a
"contrast"), which never left Wittgenstein's thought, might altogether escape us if there were not two striking parallels to it in the
previous history of philosophy: Plato's refusal to attribute any *reality*
to the sense world *per se* and Descartes's refusal to permit any *knowledge* of the outer world *per se.* In both these cases we cannot initially
even strictly speak of a "dualism" because only an incomprehensible
residuum is on one side. For Plato without the "being" which it reflects,
the sense world is "nothing," just as for Descartes without the "knowledge" which we have inwardly, the outer world is "nothing."

This helps us to understand how, analogously, the world apart
from meaning is "nothing" for Wittgenstein. We cannot even say
that there *is* such a "world" (any more than Plato could say that there
is a sense world or Descartes that there *is* an outer world). In each
case there is only a limit point of the unreal, the unknown and the unsayable, without so much as the possibility of saying what it is that
cannot be, cannot be known or *cannot be said.*[2]

When we look at the world, as Wittgenstein does, from the point

---

[2] The comparison between Plato, Descartes, and Wittgenstein, in its historical
dimensions, is discussed more fully below in the second section of this chapter.

of view of *meaning*, rather than from the point of view of *being* (as Plato does) or *knowing* (as Descartes does), then it turns out that existence *qua* existence has no meaning at all. Or, as it might better be put: what we want to mean by *existence* is just that which is other than language, not in the usual way in which everything that language talks about which is not language is other than language, but in the more drastic way that it lies outside of meaning as just what language cannot have any relation to at all. And this cannot *be* anything at all. (In short, *existence does not exist*.)

For Wittgenstein the *thatness* of phenomena (T 5.552; PI 386) and the *suchness* of phenomena (T. 6.522; PI 610) are beyond the limits of language. If there is a language for this we do not know it, and indeed nothing appears to be missing. When we speak, we necessarily speak of the *common* world in the *common* language (whether common by *structure*, as in the *Tractatus*, or by *convention*, as in the *Investigations*). But the red that we experience, that faces us, is something else again, something "unknown" (cf. PI 386-7).

Wittgenstein never forgot this "immediate beyond," this "beyond" which cannot be referred to, pointed at, or spoken about, which we are tempted to say is too *close*, too *obvious*, or too *real* for language. (The Cartesian error was to say too *private*, which set up a false comparison, as indeed any of these terms do if taken other than metaphorically). All meanings and all concepts are expelled from this speechless fullness as from what the astrophysicists call a "white hole." Though it may seem that language speaks of nothing else, actually (and this is what has to be seen) language never speaks of it at all. It is the inexpressible which "makes itself manifest" (T 6.522).

If this is hard to see and tends to elude us, the distinction here is, nevertheless, essential for understanding Wittgenstein because it is the distinction which lies at the center of his philosophy and gives it its cohesion and force. Wittgenstein's central problem was the impossibly difficult one of trying to express a difference so fundamental that it was not even a "difference"—between the *unsayable fullness-emptiness of the world* and the *world measured by language*, for the latter completely veils and renders doubly invisible the former and makes us blind to what *once seen is most striking and most powerful* (PI 129).

It may well seem that what we cannot say is nothing. But Wittgenstein did not say that "what cannot be put into words does not exist," but rather, something more interesting, that existence cannot be put into words and, therefore, that "what merely exists cannot be put into words." The world that we confront, in so far as it merely exists, is unsayable.

The absoluteness of the incommensurability here may be seen from the following table in which we have telescoped both periods of Wittgenstein's philosophy together in order to show the continuity of this theme.

Faced World	World Said
my world (T 5.62.)	the world (T 5.62.)
things manifesting (T 6.522.) phenomena as such	forms of objects (T 2.0251.) forms of life (PI 19.)
voiceless, speechless, unsayable	propositions as measure (N p. 41.) language-games as measure (PI 131.)
the "unknown language" (N p. 52.)	only language I understand (T 5.62.)
timeless, spaceless (T 6.4311-2)	systems of sameness and difference
the "room with no outside" (PI 399.)	forms of description (T 6.321.) criteria of identity (PI 253, 288.)
"something glorious" but nothing to compare it with (PI 610.)	logical pictures (T 2.182.) cncepts as ways of comparing
meaning as physiognomy (PI 568.)	meaning as use (PI 43.)

The reader must be warned: the *Faced World* cannot be talked about without being turned into the *World Said*. It is absolutely unsayable, even misleadingly spoken about in a negative way. Wittgenstein was intensely aware of this, and it produces what has been called the "poignancy of the incommunicable" in his writing. The temptation at first is to suppose that the *Faced World* is no more than the bare empty *thatness* mentioned in the *Tractatus* as not being even an experience, sheer existence as such (T 5.552). We then come to see that it includes also the *content* of the world, or the sheer qualitative immediacy, and that this is what he says manifests itself (T 6.522). And finally it dawns on us that it includes also the physiognomies that we see. In this way, starting from bare "existence," we come to realize that the unsayable for Wittgenstein is actually the fullness of the world facing us, which is there (as what we cannot speak) until it is spoken.[3]

Seeing this, understanding this, is the escape of the fly from the fly bottle, the breaking out of the Cartesian self into the open. Wittgenstein said that his aim in philosophy was to show the fly the way out of the fly bottle. It was because *he himself was out* that the phrase meant something more than the clarification of grammar. It meant showing *my world* as the locus of the *I* and thus also showing that *my world is the world* (the difference between them being entirely unsayable and certainly not sayable in terms of "privacy"). In this way the Cartesian self is "externalized" and released from its prison. The change in perspective which Wittgenstein's philosophy represents brings about such a freeing as soon as it is understood. What has to be seen are the *boundaries* of saying (whether as possible structures or conventional practices), for then it will at the same time be seen that the I-world and the phenomena as such *are not within these boundaries*. In this way, we point to what cannot be said.

To the Cartesian it must indeed look as if Wittgenstein went to great lengths "to prove that people have no insides." But from the point of view of his philosophy this appears instead as the restoration of *genuine integrated subjectivity* in place of the *objectified pseudo-subjectivity* of the Cartesian. It is the Cartesian who is the victim of a truly damaging philosophical schizophrenia in his supposed objective relation to his own inner states, for these inner states are, after all, *ourselves*, and do not merely "belong to us." The Cartesian is the unhappy solipsist locked away in metaphysical privacy. Wittgenstein's task was to show that what is valid in this is not the privacy, but the overwhelming unsayable immediacy which it misleadingly seeks to mediate and which is actually my world all around me, in the terminology of the *Tractatus*, and the phenomena as such surrounding all language-games in the terminology of the *Philosophical Investigations*.

---

[3] In the already quoted remark of G. E. M. Anscombe that "There is a strong impression made by the end of the *Tractatus*, as if Wittgenstein saw the world looking at him with a face," Miss Anscombe concludes her sentence with these words: "logic helped to reveal the face." It should be added now that logic (or grammar) cannot, of course, reveal the face as it looks at *I-alone*, or as it is *outside of all language-games*, for about *that* face we know nothing and nothing can be said, and, indeed, there is no such face.

ii

It has often been observed that the work of a great philosopher compels us to reexamine the whole previous history of philosophy in a new light, in effect to rewrite it. Wittgenstein is no exception. If (as many are coming to suspect) he stands at the beginning of a new period in Western thought, we may have to look at that history in a new way, and it is not too early to suggest how it may appear. The following table may serve this purpose:

	Plato ontology	
sense world no *being* as such		form world *being*
	Descartes epistemology	
outer world no *knowledge* as such		inner world *knowledge*
	Wittgenstein grammar	
phenomenal world no *meaning* as such		sayable world *meaning*

This table shows Wittgenstein's basic innovation to be taking *meaning* as more fundamental than either *being* or *knowledge*—that is, understanding *being* and *knowledge* both in terms of *meaning*, rather than accepting either as in any way at all prior to meaning. This is the consistent position of Wittgenstein throughout all of his writing and is the main key to his work.

The second important point is that Wittgenstein's position with regard to *meaning* can best be understood by analogy with Plato's position in regard to *being* and Descartes's in regard to *knowledge*. In each of these three cases there is an analogous residuum of what cannot *be* as such (the sense world), what cannot be *known* as such (the outer world) and what has no *meaning* as such (the phenomenal world). All three philosophers share a deep affinity as perhaps the supreme rep-representatives of *l'esprit geometrique*, but they are also widely separated because they embody three fundamentally different methods, which we may think of as the three basic methods in the history of Western philosophy.

These three methods corresponding to the three philosophical frameworks of Plato, Descartes and Wittgenstein are: (1) the Socratic *method of definition* (hinging on the distinction of particular-general); (2) the Augustinian *method of introspection* (which shifts the perspective to the inner-outer); and (3) the Kantian *method of presupposition* (which finds the principal division between the *a posteriori* and the *a priori*). The philosophies of Plato, Descartes and Wittgenstein, in effect, show us what the world looks like seen in terms of these three methods. Plato's *Cave* pictures the Socratic method, Descarte's *cogito* the Augustinian, and Wittgenstein's *language-games* the Kantian.[4]

How did these epochal changes in viewpoint come about? In the case of the transformation of the Platonic-Aristotelean framework we have to look to the medieval world itself, for it was during this period that the particular-general pattern of Greek thought metamorphized into the inner-outer framework of the modern world. We might call it the period of the birth of the modern subject. The new perspective of *outer-inner* or *object-subject* (fully secularized in Descartes) was, in effect, the final upshot of the religious influence on philosophy. The historian of Western philosophy will see in St. Augustine the primary figure in this "interiorization," just as he will see in Kant the pivotal figure in the modern transition away from this, since in Kant the subject is definitively split in two, the noumenal subject retreating out of reach.

Like the medieval world, the modern world also has had to

---

[4] To give a completer summary, we should recognize also another dimension of Western thought: the "monistic" versions of the Platonic and Cartesian "dualisms" as these appear successively in Aristotle, Averroes and Aquinas in the one case and in Spinoza, Leibniz and Hegel in the other. (Leibniz's pluralism is not as basic as his monism, since each monad mirrors not *a* whole, but *the* whole.) The relation of Aristotle to Plato foreshadows that of Averroes to Avicenna and Aquinas to Augustine and later that of Spinoza to Descartes and Hegel to Kant. In these pairs the second philosopher gives us a "monistic" revision of the first. It is by now a familiar pattern; a logically "pure" dualism (Plato, Augustine, Avicenna, Descartes, Kant), followed by a "monistic" version, in which, as it were, "unity" triumphs over "purity" (Aristotle, Averroes, Aquinas, Spinoza and Hegel). A "middle term" has to be found to bridge the gap: Aristotle's equivocal *substance*, Aquinas's *analogy*, Spinoza's *nature* and Hegel's *dialectic*. All this would suggest that it is almost inevitable that there will be a major monistic version of Wittgenstein, in which *phenomena* and *action* (Wittgenstein's two final terms) are brought together in some kind of a "circulation." The philosopher who accomplishes this will play the same role in relation to Wittgenstein as Aristotle did to Plato and Spinoza to Descartes.

struggle with the questions of the *subject*, the *particular* and the *immediate*, but now from the standpoint of science, rather than from the standpoint of religion. (As Wittgenstein so succinctly put it, physics is characterized by the fact that the words *I*, *this* and *here* do not appear in it (PI 410).) It has slowly become evident that while Cartesianism appeared to make both subject and object available to science, actually it made neither of them available at all. It was Kant's philosophy which finally revealed this by showing that both subject and object are beyond the reach of science because they are, in some way or other, *presuppositions* rather than *data*. The full implications (including the realization that the entire first person psychological situation, the so-called "inner world," *is* the non-objectifiable subject and a different kind of language use altogether, while the object is either a function of language or has no status at all) have had to wait for Wittgenstein.

Kant's innovation, the presuppositional method, dividing the world into the *a priori* and the *a posteriori*, is capable, we now see, of replacing the Cartesian division of *inner* and *outer* entirely. This is what Wittgenstein's philosophy showed, for it carried the Kantian method to the point of *wiping out the inner world of private objects altogether* (without at the same time falling into behaviorism, skepticism and relativism, which would have been inevitable if this had been interpreted within the Cartesian framework). Wittgenstein, who put *all* meaning into the presuppositional (even when, as in the later philosophy, this was regarded as only an *aspect* of the phenomenal), is the *ultimate Kantian*, as Descartes, who put all genuine knowledge into the inner world, was the *ultimate Augustinian*.

Kant, it seems clear now, is the primary figure in the transition from Descartes to Wittgenstein because Kant took the step of removing the object and the subject from the realm of the *known*; but, on the other hand, he stopped short of discarding them altogether. The Kantian philosophy, still oriented to the epistemological question, is forced to preserve the *ghost of the object* in the *ding-an-sich*, and the *ghost of the subject* in the *transcendental unity of apperception*. At these points Kant hangs on to the remnants of the Cartesian dualism (though not without misgivings, as his tamperings with the passages having to do with the thing-in-itself between the first two editions of the First Critique show).

The Kantian philosophy, nevertheless, breaks the spell of Cartesianism right up to the final step, by *backing the subject and object*

*out of the world altogether, even though it does not let go of them
altogether*. Reality as the noumena is a kind of appendage in Kant's
philosophy (and this already shows an odd situation—that *reality*
should be an *appendage*). It was obvious enough to Hegel, who made
the "noumena swallow up the phenomena" by taking the contradic-
tion between them as inner dynamic of the whole. Looking back on
this now, we can see in Hegel the last stand of the Cartesian dualism,
Cartesianism *in extremis*. Hegel believed that he had ended the history
of philosophy, but what he had ended was the Cartesian period. That
a new era might begin did not occur to him because he did not an-
ticipate abandoning the subject and object altogether (and still, as it
were, having anything left!).[5]

Kierkegaard's protest against Hegel—that the real subject with its
real problems has no place in Hegel's world—is actually a protest against
the whole modern period in philosophy, the entire Cartesian tradition.[6]
For in this tradition (as Hegel finally showed) subject and object were
only concepts to begin with. The Hegelian world-subject finally looks
like no subject at all, but only the apotheosis of the Cartesian "thinking self."[7]

It was Wittgenstein who completed the Kantian revolution by

---

[5] Did not Heidegger attempt to "reunderstand" Parmenides in the light of
Kant by conceiving the "meaning of Being" as the "presuppositions of Being"
(thus hoping to make a new beginning); while Husserl attempted to "reunderstand" Descartes also in the light of Kant by conceiving the Cartesian knowledge
from the standpoint of Kant's transcendental subject? In these cases we have Kant
working "backwards" on the history of philosophy, while Wittgenstein pushes
the Kantian point of view into an *entirely new* perspective.

[6] Attempts to establish a "real subject" in existentialism and various forms of
irrationalism and romantic vitalism fail because they define themselves only in
terms of the rationalisms which they reject. All the rhetoric of *activism, commitment, decisiveness, concreteness*, etc., cannot make up for this deficiency. Irrationalism is a mirror-image of rationalism, in somewhat the same way that materialism is a mirror-image of idealism. Marxist materialism, for example, makes
no sense apart from the idealism which it rejects but which is necessary to
define it. Until Marxists recognize this they will remain in a philosophical
dead-end.

[7] In this century we have also seen the disappearance of the object-as-such
from physics. The new basic unit in the quantum theory, for example, is the
observed-plus-the-minimal-observer. In this way objectivity is retained without
the in-itself. The minimal observer is, of course, no more a subject than the
human players in the case of Wittgenstein's language-games. The basic unit in
Wittgenstein's later philosophy is one in which human beings, language and
world are already inter-related and functioning together. We do not *start with*
objects and subjects; we *start with* language-games.

abandoning the Cartesian framework altogether and inaugurating, in all its strangeness and newness, an unknown world.[8] He accomplished this in two steps: first, in the *Tractatus* by dropping the Cartesian "thinking self" and keeping only a single point as metaphysical subject (just that one point which makes the whole world *my* world, without changing anything else at all) and keeping as objects only logical co-ordinates which themselves cannot even be meaningfully talked about; and then, second, in the *Investigations* by dropping even *this* subject and *these* objects and talking only about the grammar of the word "I" and language-games with the word *object*.

The final framework of Wittgenstein's philosophy is *phenomena* (not in-themselves, not object and never less than they seem) and *language as meaning-constituting actions* (not derived from subjects, "belonging to" subjects). That what has been dropped here will not be missed and, in fact, is only *what we did not need anyway*, will not be at first apparent, but slowly, or rapidly, will become apparent. Subject and object have disappeared, while philosophy survives.

Descartes's version of what is implicit in Augustine—the *absolute certainty of inner knowledge* (first formulated as an answer to skepticism by Augustine himself)—is paralleled by Wittgenstein's version of what is implicit in Kant—the *absolute impossibility of this kind of knowledge*. It is fitting that the *Philosophical Investigations* opens with a quotation from St. Augustine. Here the wheel comes full circle. Both men, however, are infused with the same spirit which expresses itself so differently. In the sense of respect for the subject and for the religious tradition, Wittgenstein was and remained an Augustinian.[9] We might even say that it was respect for the subject which led him to reject the Cartesian inner objectification.

If the movement of modern thought seems to have been to undo the movement of medieval thought, the up-shot is by no means a re-

---

[8] Michael Dummett's *Frege: Philosophy of Language* (N.Y.: Harper and Row, 1973) shows that the credit for the next to the last step belongs to Frege who for the first time put *meaning* ahead of *knowing* at the center of philosophy. It was Wittgenstein who carried this through completely, recognizing that even the terms *existence* and *knowing* must first have *meaning* and that the term *meaning* itself must be something quite ordinary. Thereby he dethroned all super-concepts.

[9] Norman Malcolm in his *Memoir* of Wittgenstein mentions that Wittgenstein "revered the writings of St. Augustine." His similar respect for Kierkegaard and for genuine subjectivity justifies calling him an Augustinian.

turn to the pre-medieval situation. There are no implications of a re-
vived classicism or humanism or paganism. The spirituality of the middle ages is not lost, but rather is preserved in a new form, free from
"scientific" or "humanistic" misunderstandings. For spirituality does
not hinge upon a certain interpretation of "inwardness." And, similarly,
the scientific achievement of the Cartesian era is not imperilled by
the coming age. A clearer understanding of the nature of science and
a purging of mythical elements is to be expected.

Wittgenstein speaks for an age free from the obsessions with
causality, *explanation*, *domination* and *control* which characterize our
age. He looks to a time when, instead of building ever greater and
more grandiose edifices for the expansion of the human ego (collective and individual), we will search for a new directness and purity of
thought and action.

In philosophy the Wittgenstein age spells the end of the point
of view which splits the human soul and exposes it to the pretensions
of inner "knowledge," as well as the end of the point of view which
gives the world a reality in itself apart from any reaction to it or com-
prehension of it.

Appendices

1. The Structure of the *Investigations*

2. The Protolanguage of the *Investigations*

3. Wittgenstein and Brouwer

4. Wittgenstein and Heidegger

5. Wittgenstein and Buddhism

THE STRUCTURE OF THE *INVESTIGATIONS*

The history of philosophy may be understood from the standpoint of the forms in which philosophy has been written. If we think, for example, of *dialogues, lectures, manuals, discourses, meditations, homiles, sermons, confessions, summas, essays, treatises, critiques, aphorisms* we see how the form itself tells us something of the nature of the philosophy.

The term *Tractatus Logico-Philosophicus*, a name said to have been suggested by G. E. Moore, gives us something of the flavor of that book—its short apodictic declamatory style, not altogether unlike in tone the tracts issued by the famous Tractarians. The numbering system adds an impression of logical organization belied on deeper acquaintance by the sheer complexity of the thoughts.

The *Philosophical Investigations* Wittgenstein calls an *album*, and an *album of sketches* (PI p. ix). This may give a decidedly false impression, for it is by no means a miscellany, a scrapbook or a commonplace book. In the first place Wittgenstein says it is a *precipitate (Niederschlag)* of sixteen years of investigation, and very many remarks assembled in that time were cut out. Then he tried to weld the thoughts together into a whole so that they "should proceed from one subject to another in a natural order without breaks." But this proved impossible and after "several unsuccessful attempts" he realized that "I should never succeed," for

> my thoughts were soon crippled if I tried to force them on
> in any single direction against their natural inclination (PI
> p. ix.)

What we have instead are fairly long chains about the same subject and then a sudden change, jumping from one topic to another. What is peculiar is this criss-crossing of the field of thought.

> The same or almost the same points were always being approached afresh from different directions, and new sketches made. (PI p. ix.)

255

Perhaps it is just this criss-crossing which most distinguishes the book
and which separates it from being a collection of aphorisms or any
kind of miscellany.[1]

Part I of the book does seem to follow a fairly clear order, breaking up into three main divisions, the first one of which goes over material presented in the *Tractatus*, putting it in a new way, while the
second two parts deal with material not discussed in the *Tractatus*.
These three main divisions are

A — new conception of language and meaning (PI 1-133)
B — "mental" phenomena and concepts (PI 134-427)
C — intentional aspects of "mental" phenomena and concepts (PI
      428-693).

A more detailed outline goes something like this:

A — new conception of language and meaning (PI 1-133)
      1—meaning as use and language-games (PI 1-25)
      2—names (seen in new way) (PI 26-64)
      3—essence of language (seen in new way) (PI 65-88)
      4—logic (seen in new way) (PI 89-115)
      5—philosophy (seen in new way) (PI 116-133)

B — "mental" phenomena and concepts (PI 134-427)
      1—"fitting" (PI 134-143)
      2—understanding (PI 144-155)
      3—reading (PI 156-178)
      4—knowing how to go on (PI 179-196)
      5—rules (PI 197-242)
      6—private sensations (PI 243-315)
      7—thinking (PI 316-362)
      8—images and imagining (PI 363-402)
      9—*I, consciousness, soul* (PI 403-427)

---

[1] An example of a miscellany in the history of philosophy is Clement of
Alexandria's *Stromateis* (ca. 190 A.D.), the Greek word here meaning *patchwork*.
Clement wrote that

> the form of my own miscellanies has the variegated appearance of a
> meadow, from the haphazard way in which things came into my mind,
> not clarified either by arrangement or style, but mingled together in a
> studied disorder. (Book vi, Ch. 1.) (The translation is from the Hort and
> Mayor edition (London: Macmillan, 1902), as quoted in the Editor's In-
> troduction, p. xii.)

Clement, for reasons of his own, including the desire to "hide" certain ideas,
deliberately chose a random style. Wittgenstein apparently was ruthless in selecting the remarks he wanted to keep, but was unable to get them into the "natural
whole" which he wanted.

C — intentional aspects of "mental" phenomena and concepts (PI 428-693).
   1—thinking and appliction (PI 428-436)
   2—satisfaction and expectation (PI 437-465)
   3—purpose and justification of thinking (PI 466-490)
   4—language and grammar (PI 491-512)
   5—understanding (PI 513-546)
   6—negation (PI 547-557)
   7—essential and inessential in language (PI 558-570)
   8—mental states and acts (PI 571-595)
   9—familiarity and recognizing (PI 596-610)
  10—willing (PI 611-629)
  11—intending and meaning (PI 630-693)

APPENDIX 2

THE PROTOLANGUAGE OF THE *INVESTIGATIONS*

From *static picture* to *dynamic gesture*—this is said to have been the development of the conception of language of Hugo von Hofmannsthal.[1] It might also describe the development of Wittgenstein's conception of language from the logical pictures of the *Tractatus* to the language activities of the *Investigations*.

The emphasis on the language of the body is already found in the quotation from St. Augustine with which Wittgenstein opens the book. St. Augustine writes of his elders:

> Their intention was shown by their bodily movements, as it were the natural language of all peoples; the expression of the face, the play of the eyes, the movement of other parts of the body, and that one of voice which expresses our state of mind in seeking, having, rejecting or avoiding something. (*Confessions*, Bk. 1, sect. 8; PI 1.)

It is especially interesting to find Wittgenstein in the Frazer Notes saying that

> In the old rites we have the use of an utterly complex gesture-language. . . . (NFGB p. 242.)

and also speaking of logic in connection with "primitive means of communication:"

> Any logic good enough for a primitive means of communication needs no apology from us. Language did not emerge from some kind of ratiocination. (OC 475.)

In various places scattered throughout his works Wittgenstein calls attention to gestures expressing primitive "logical operations":

> gestures of exclusion, rejection, expressing *negation* (PI 550)
> gestures of uniting, collecting, expressing *and* (PG17)

---

[1] See Hermann Broch's Introduction to the *Selected Prose of Hugo von Hofmannsthal* (N.Y.: Pantheon, 1952), Bollingen Series xxxiii.

gestures for *all* (RFM p. 7)
gestures for *and so on* (PI 208)
gestures for uncertainty (PG 28)
gestures of resignation (PI 330)

In the "Lectures on Aesthetics" aesthetic judgments are described as *gestures;* and in other places a theme or phrase in music is called a *gesture* (cf. Z 158) and he speaks of intonations as *gestures made with the voice* (Z 161).

Turning to looks and glances Wittgenstein describes the *language of the eyes:*

> We do not see the human eye as a receiver, it appears not to let anything in, but to send something out. The ear receives; the eye looks. (It casts glances, it flashes, radiates, gleams.) One can terrify with one's eyes, not with one's ear or nose. When you see the eye you see something going out from it. You see the look in the eye. (Z 222.)

Elsewhere he mentions the *vacant look*, which goes with concentrating on one's inner sensations in philosophy (PI 412); the *fixed look*, which we associate with robots and trances (PI 420); the *hostile look* (PI 652); and the difference between a *genuine loving look* and a *pretended loving look* (PI p. 228).

It seems clear enough that language in Wittgenstein's later philosophy has its roots in primitive and animal behavior, and this is stated in so many words in this:

> Our language-game is an extension of primitive behavior. (For our language-game is behavior.) (Instinct.) (Z 545.)

APPENDIX 3

WITTGENSTEIN AND BROUWER

One of the main factors in Wittgenstein's return to philosophy was a lecture delivered by the Dutch mathematician L. E. J. Brouwer in Vienna on March 10, 1928.[1] The lecture was entitled "Mathematik, Wissenschaft und Sprache." A second lecture was delivered by Brouwer four days later on March 14, 1928, entitled "Die Struktur des Kontinuums."[2]

Despite the emphasis on mathematics as human activity and on "constructivity," Brouwer's philosophy of mathematics was far removed from Wittgenstein's. The following passage from a 1952 paper defines Brouwer's conception of the foundation of mathematics:

> The first act of intuitionism completely separates mathematics from mathematical language, in particular from the phenomena of language which are described by theoretical logic, and recognizes that intuitionist mathematics is an essentially languageless activity of the mind having its origin in the perception of a move of time, i.e. of the falling apart of a life moment into two distinct things, one of which gives way to the other, but is retained by memory. If the two-ity thus born is divested of all quality, there remains the empty form of the common substratum of all two-ities. It is this common

---

[1] George Pitcher in his book *The Philosophy of Wittgenstein* contributes important biographical information about this:

> Professor Herbert Feigl has kindly informed me, in correspondence, that he and F. Waismann spent a few hours with Wittgenstein in a café after the lecture and that "It was fascinating to behold the change that had come over Wittgenstein that evening." Whereas previously he had been reluctant to discuss philosophy, and had even to be persuaded by Waismann and Feigl to attend the lecture at all, now "he became extremely voluble and began sketching ideas that were the beginnings of his later writings." In Feigl's opinion "that evening marked the return of Wittgenstein to strong philosophical interests and activities." (George Pitcher, *The Philosophy of Wittgenstein* (Engelwood Cliffs, N.J.: Prentice-Hall, 1964), p. 8, n. 8.)

[2] The first lecture was printed in the *Monatsheften für Mathematik und Physik*, XXXVI, Band I (Vienna, 1929), and the second in a pamphlet by the *Komitee zur Veranstaltung von Gastvorträgen ausländischer Gelehrter der exakten Wissenschaften* (Vienna, Oktober, 1930). Copies of these lectures were given to the present writer by friends of Brouwer who told him that Brouwer and Wittgenstein subsequently met two or three times privately.

substratum, this empty form, which is the basic intuition of mathematics. ("Historical Background, Principles and Methods of Intuitionism," *South African Journal of Science* (October-November 1952), pp. 140-1.)

No connection can be made between this and Wittgenstein's emphasis on mathematics as the formation of concepts and acceptance of paradigms.

In terms of fundamental world-view, however, Wittgenstein and Brouwer had a great deal in common and a similar temper of mind. This is shown by the following passage from an essay which gives the most comprehensive statement of Brouwer's over-all philosophy. Brouwer has just quoted from the Bhagavad-Gita and continues:

The categorical imperative prescribing the aforesaid attitude towards life has its counterpart in a sceptical prognosis that mankind, possessed by the delusion of causality, will slide away in a deteriorative process of overpopulation, industrialization, serfdom, and devastation of nature, and that when hereby first its spiritual and then its physiological conditions of life will have been destroyed, it will come to its end like a colony of bacteria in the earth crust having fulfilled its task. All this though timeless art and perennial philosophy continually suggest that the unknown forces governing the destiny of individual and community, are not subject to causality; that in particular the ways of fate cannot be paved with causality, and that security is as unattainable as it is unworthy; that intensification of organization increases vulnerability, that new vulnerability asks for protection through new organization, and that thus for organization which is believed in, there is no end of growth; finally that if the delusion of causality could be thrown off, nature, gradually resuming her rights, would be (except for her bondage to destiny) generous and forgiving to a mankind decausalized and subsiding to more modest and more harmonious proportions. ("Consciousness, Philosophy, and Mathematics," *Library of the Xth International Congress of Philosophy* (August 11-18, 1948), Vol. I, Proceedings of the Congress, p. 1242.)

Brouwer's attack on the "delusion of casuality" in this essay recalls Wittgenstein's reference to belief in the casual nexus as a "superstition" (T 5.1361) and to the "illusion" of today that the so-called laws of nature are the "explanations" of natural phenomena. (T 6.371.)

APPENDIX 4

WITTGENSTEIN AND HEIDEGGER

In his "Lecture on Ethics" (written some time between September, 1929 and December, 1930) Wittgenstein described as an experience of "absolute value" and *"my experience par excellence," wondering at the existence of the world* and being inclined to say things like "how extraordinary that anything should exist" or "how extraordinary that the world should exist."[1]

This suggested to many readers a central theme in Heidegger's philosophy.[2] For Heidegger had raised as fundamental the question: "Why is there any Being at all—why not far rather Nothing?" at the end of his essay "What Is Metaphysics?"[3] and repeated it again as "Why are there essents, why is there anything at all, rather than nothing?" at the beginning of his book *An Introduction to Metaphysics.*[4]

The idea that Wittgenstein's "absolute experience" was like Heidegger's fundamental question seemed to gain support from a comment made by Wittgenstein himself, given by F. Waismann under the heading "Zu Heidegger":[5]

---

[1] The "Lecture on Ethics" was printed in *Philosophical Review,* Vol. lxxiv, No. 1 (January, 1965), p. 8.

[2] As of 1971 there were twelve titles in a bibliography of articles comparing Wittgenstein and Heidegger. See D. A. Rohatyn, "A Note on Heidegger and Wittgenstein," *Philosophy Today,* Vol. 15, No. 1/4 (Spring, 1971), p. 69.

[3] included in Werner Brock, edt., *Existence and Being* (Chicago: Henry Regnery Co., 1949), p. 380.

[4] *An Introduction to Metaphysics* (New Haven: Yale Univ., 1959), p. 1.

[5] Friedrich Waismann, *Ludwig Wittgenstein und der Wiener Kreis: Gespräche, aufgezeichnet von Friedrich Waismann* (Frankfurt: Suhrkamp, 1967), p. 68.

This section from Waismann's book entitled "Zu Heidegger" was reprinted in German with an English translation as an Appendix to the "Lecture on Ethics" in *The Philosophical Review* referred to above. But, for reasons still unexplained, the title "Zu Heidegger" and the first sentence of the section, which is the one quoted above referring to Heidegger, were deleted. The deletion was pointed out by Michael Murray in "A Note on Wittgenstein and Heidegger," *The Philosophical Review,* Vol. lxxxiii, No. 4 (October, 1974), pp. 501-3. This is Wittgenstein's single reference, known so far, to Heidegger. Heidegger, for his part, quotes Wittgenstein in *Heraklit* (Frankfurt, 1970), p. 31.

I can readily understand what Heidegger meant by Being and dread.

Were not Wittgenstein and Heidegger talking about the same experience or taking the same question as fundamental? This thought was bound to occur. It is all the more important, therefore, to realize that they were *not* talking about the same experience or the same question at all.

When Heidegger wondered about the existence of anything at all *rather than nothing*, he wondered about it as a question *Why* against the backdrop of "nothingness." This was Heidegger's question *par excellence*.

It was not Wittgenstein's question *par excellence*. When Wittgenstein wondered at the existence of anything or of the world, it did not take the form of a question at all. In the "Lecture on Ethics" he did not ask "Why is there anything?" but instead *exclaimed* "How extraordinary that there is anything!" This was the difference: for Wittgenstein it was never a question, but an exclamation!

The Gnostic flavor of Heidegger's question: *Why is there anything rather than nothing?* (a question asked earlier by Leibniz and Schelling, but having its antecedents in the entire Gnostic tradition) is unmistakable, since it asks for a *justification* for the world. What could such a justification be? Is there any simpler one than Wittgenstein's inability to see the question in the face of the exclamation!

These remarks, of course, refer only to Heidegger's early philosophy. In Heidegger's later philosophy questioning ceases in order that we may be "open to Being" and so reach "the thinking that is without why." But this step takes Heidegger only to "waiting," and the exclamation in the face of what is beyond words still eludes him. Even in his later philosophy Heidegger still does not *think with his eyes*. Language is still both too important and not important enough for him. His eyes are not opened.

What about the dread which Heidegger experienced and which Wittgenstein said he could understand? Here again they were not talking about the same thing. Wittgenstein's dread was not dread in the face of nothingness, but dread at not being able to say (or respond adequately to) what immediately surrounds us, that fullness-emptiness which is beyond language and which evoked the exclamation "How extraordinary!" (And Wittgenstein believed that we are all in some way to blame for this failure and *will finally be held to account for it.*)

There are two kinds of ultimate experience here, though they are in no way side-by-side or on a par: one facing the nothingness, the other facing the fullness-emptiness. And these are perhaps the decisive possibilities for our age.

Heidegger's experience is more or less familiar and accessible, more or less known to all. It strikes a sympathetic chord. It reflects the spirit of the age, as the traditional self finds itself on the verge of annihilation, and as the world, which we cannot let go of, threatens to turn to the "nothingness" which has become the only touchstone of its "reality."

Wittgenstein's experience, on the other hand, is not familiar. It belongs to an age as yet to come when the self has already disappeared —not into the robot, but into the integrated subjectivity which no longer appears as the traditional "self." And the dread is that we may not be able to get there, for there is no bridge from where we are to that. (There is nothing but the dire need for the only way still open.)

The despair "in the darkness of this time" which Wittgenstein felt so strongly was connected with the overwhelming difficulty of communicating this new way of looking. He had to make it clear to himself, even though this did not guarantee making it clear to others.

What Heidegger's philosophy seems to suggest is that the impossibility of seeing the world in any way except in terms of nothingness does indeed threaten us with nothingness, and we must, therefore, wait for a new deliverance of Being. There is a sense that a new moment in thought is near, but what it is we do not know.

In Wittgenstein's philosophy, on the other hand, another alternative is present from the beginning, an alternative so simple that it is hard to see how it could have been overlooked, an alternative in which the nearest and most obvious is itself, when our eyes are open, seen to be beyond the nothingness.

· Appendix 5

WITTGENSTEIN AND BUDDHISM

The growing literature comparing Wittgenstein and Zen Buddhism[1] raises the question: How close is the affinity between them, and indeed between Wittgenstein and Buddhism in general?

A number of similarities between Wittgenstein and Zen are striking indeed:

1—the use of *shock effects* ("intentional nonsense," "rational madness") to jar students into seeing things differently;

2—the use of philosophical problems as *koans* or riddles which have to be, not solved, but *dissolved* by a complete change of viewpoint; and

3—the realization that it is the question, not the answer, which contains the mistake.

Underlying this is an affinity between Wittgenstein's attitude toward immediacy and the Zen attitude. What we have to realize is that there is *nothing between us and the world*—neither mind, nor experience, nor language, nor perception, nor inner impressions, etc. And similarly nothing between us and what we say. Hence the Zen doctrine: "When you say a word, say it quick," where quick does not refer to time but means *without intermediary*.[2]

The affinities go further, however, because Wittgenstein's later philosophy embraces three fundamental positions which belong to all

---

[1] In alphabetical order the main articles and books on this subject, as of now, are: (1) John V. Canfield, "Wittgenstein and Zen," *Philosophy*, Vol. 50, No. 194 (October, 1975), pp. 383-408; (2) Charles Hardwick, "Doing Philosophy and Doing Zen," *Philosophy East and West*, Vol. 13, No. 1 (October, 1963), pp. 227-234; (3) H. Hudson, "Wittgenstein and Zen Buddhism," *Philosophy East and West*, Vol. 23, No. 4 (October, 1973), pp. 471-481; (4) Warren Shibles, "Wittgenstein and Zen" in his book *Wittgenstein Language and Philosophy* (Dubuque, Iowa: Wm. C. Brown Co., 1969), pp. 84-100; (5) Paul Wienpahl, "Zen and the Work of Wittgenstein," *Chicago Review*, Vol. 12, No. 2 (Summer, 1958), pp. 67-72; and (6) Paul Wienpahl, *Zen Diary* (N.Y.: Harper and Row, 1970).

[2] This parallels the Biblical word *sudden*, which should be understood as *an eschatological and not a temporal category*. See David Daube, *The Sudden in Scripture* (Leiden: E. J. Brill, 1969). In both the Old Testament and the New Testament action in response to the divine happens "suddenly."

Buddhist teaching, those indicated by the Pali words: (1) *anicca*—no things; (2) *anatta*—no selves and (3) *tathata*—suchness.[3]

The most important differences between Wittgenstein's philosophy and Buddhism seem to center around his unwillingness to make the conceptual realm (or realm of language) any less "real" than the phenomenal realm. And to this is related Wittgenstein's strong sense of moral obligation. Although he would have understood the profundity of the laughter in Zen (and indeed at one time even said he could imagine a philosophy made up entirely of jokes), laughter was not his fundamental response to the world.

One way of looking at the historical difference between Western and Eastern thought is to see *appearance* and *reality* in something like reversed relations in the two traditions. What the West has called *reality* (self-identity guaranteed by concepts), the East has called *appearance* (conceptualization), while what the West has called *appearance* (phenomenality), the East has called *reality*. (In Buddhism, for example, it is said that "ignorance" and "consciousness" are interchangeable terms, which is virtually the opposite of what one finds in a Western philosopher like Hegel.)

With the meeting of East and West in recent centuries there are many signs that this age-old polarity is changing. The Western "reality" (the conceptualized world) finds itself confronted by Eastern "reality" (phenomenal immediacy) as something like its own limits, which are at the same time the limits of science and technology. And, on the other hand, the Eastern phenomenal "reality" is confronted by Western conceptual "reality" as something like an historical necessity for its own survival.

Philosophically the problem for both East and West is to encompass the difference in a way which preserves both. There can be *no priority of conceptual over phenomenal or of phenomenal over conceptual*. Both positions are now untenable. And the advocacy of either point of view by itself (curiously, often taking place now in the opposite part of the world) is inadequate.

---

[3] For summaries of Buddhist teachings see the following: Kamakami Sogen, *Systems of Buddhist Thought* (Calcutta: University of Calcutta, 1912); Richard H. Robinson, *Early Madhyamika in India and China* (Madison, Wis.: Univ. of Wisconsin Press, 1967); and D. T. Suzuki, *Outlines of Mahayana Buddhism* (London: Luzac and Co., 1907). *Suchness* is called by Suzuki the "essence of Buddhism" and the "ultimate principle of existence" (p. 125).

In this connection attention should be paid to Wittgenstein's type of phenomenalism (physiognomic phenomenalism) and his type of conceptualism (concepts as tools of language actions), for in these terms such a union may be possible. And his own philosophy indeed is such a union.

Sources of the Epigraphs

The sources of the epigraphs which appear at the beginnings of the chapters in this book are:

CHAPTER 1 (p. 1)

Th. Stcherbatsky, *The Conception of Buddhist Nirvana* (Shanghai, 1940; originally published Leningrad, 1927), p. 54. Stcherbatsky is speaking of the shift from the Hinayana to the Mahayana metaphysics.

Charles Peirce to William James, dated March 14, 1909. R. B. Perry, *The Thought and Character of William James* (Boston: Little Brown and Co., 1935), Vol. II, p. 439.

K. Venkata Ramanan, *Nagarjuna's Philosophy As Presented in the Maha-Prajnaparamita-Sastra* (Varansi-l, India, 1971), p. 86.

Hugo von Hofmannsthal, "From the Book of Friends," included in *Selected Prose*, trans. Mary Hottinger and Tania and James Stern (N.Y.: Pantheon, 1952), p. 362.

CHAPTER 2 (p. 10)

Bronislaw Malinowski, "The Problem of Meaning in Primitive Languages," included as Supplement 1 in C. K. Ogden and I. A. Richards, *The Meaning of Meaning* (N.Y.: Harcourt Brace, 1930), p. 316.

Simone Weil, *Oppression and Liberty*, trans. Arthur Wills and John Petrie (Amherst: University of Massachusetts Press, 1973), p. 96.

Heinrich Ott, "Language and Understanding," in *New Theology* No. 4, Martin E. Marty and Dean G. Peerman, edts. (N.Y.: Macmillan, 1967), p. 153.

CHAPTER 3 (p. 20)

R. W. Emerson, *Collected Works* (Cambridge: Riverside Press, 1904), Vol. VI, p. 143.

John of Salisbury, *Metalogicon*, I, 16; quoted in Desmond Paul Henry, *The Logic of Saint Anselm* (Oxford: Clarendon Press, 1967), p. 25.

Thomas Aquinas, *Summa Theologica*, Pt. 1, Q. 39, Art. 8; First Complete American Edition in Three Volumes (N.Y.: Benziger Bros., 1947), Vol. 1, p. 201.

CHAPTER 4   (p. 40)

John Jay Chapman, *Harper's Monthly Magazine* (December, 1936), p. 52; quoted in Arthur F. Bentley, *Inquiry into Inquiries* (Boston: Beacon, 1954), p. 113.

Immanuel Kant, *Critique of Pure Reason*, trans. Norman Kemp Smith (London: Macmillan, 1950), Analytic of Concepts, Transcendental Deduction, A 106, p. 135.

C. I. Lewis, *Mind and the World-Order* (N.Y.: Dover, 1956), p. 83.

Charles Peirce to William James, dated December 6, 1904. R. B. Perry, *The Thought and Character of William James* (Boston: Little Brown and Co., 1935), Vol. II, p. 433.

CHAPTER 5   (p. 54)

Eric Gutkind, *The Absolute Collective* (London: C. W. Daniel Co., 1937), p. 43.

Immanuel Kant, *Critique of Pure Reason*, trans. Norman Kemp Smith (London: Macmillan, 1950), Analytic of Principles, Postulates of Empirical Thought, A 225, p. 243.

Gordon Baker, "Criteria: A New Foundation for Semantics," *Ratio* 16 (December, 1974), pp. 156-189.

CHAPTER 6   (p. 68)

Plato, *Republic*, Bk. VI, 504C; James Adam, edt., *The Republic of Plato* (Cambridge: Univ. Press, 1965), Vol. II, p. 49.

Martin Heidegger, *Poetry, Language, Thought*, trans. Albert Hofstadter (N.Y.: Harper and Row, 1971), p. 191.

Goethe, quoted by Oswald Spengler, *The Decline of the West*, Vol. I, p. 97. Wittgenstein's choice of the term *Urphänomen* to describe language-games is certainly intended to associate them with Goethe's use of the term *Urphänomen*. (PI 654).

CHAPTER 7   (p. 88)

Paul Valery, quoted in Stanley Burnshaw, edt., *The Poem Itself* (N.Y.: Schocken, 1967), p. 78.

David Hume, *A Treatise on Human Nature* (Oxford: Clarendon Press, 1967), Bk. 1, Sect. iv, p. 13.

L. E. J. Brouwer, "Consciousness, Philosophy and Mathematics," *Library of the Xth International Congress of Philosophy* (Amsterdam, August 11-18, 1948); Vol. I, Proceedings of the Congress (Amsterdam, 1948), p. 1240.

Chapter 8   (p. 104)

Surangama Sutra (written in Sanskrit, ca. First Century A.D.). Lin Yutang, edt., *The Wisdom of India and China* (N.Y.: Random House, 942), p. 529.

Paul Valery, "Comments from the Notebooks," and "A View of Descartes," *Collected Works*; Vol. 9, *Masters and Friends*, trans. Martin Turnell (Princeton, N.J.: Univ. Press, 1968), pp. 312, 54.

A. C. Swinburne, "The Higher Pantheism in a Nutshell." Carolyn Wells, edt., *A Nonsense Anthology* (N.Y.: Dover, 1958), p. 30.

Chapter 9   (p. 126)

St. Augustine, *De Trinitate*, X, x, 14; quoted by Eric Przywara, edt., *An Augustinian Synthesis* (N.Y.: Sheed and Ward, 1954), p. 6.

George Berkeley, *Commonplace Book;* A. C. Frazer, edt., *Works of George Berkeley* (Oxford: Clarendon Press, 1901), Vol. 1, pp. 70-1.

Gertrude Stein, *The Geographical History of America and the Relation of Human Nature to the Human Mind* (N.Y.: Random House, 1939), p. 130.

Chapter 10   (p. 148)

Hugo von Hofmannsthal, *Selected Verse Plays* (N.Y.: Pantheon, 1964), p. xxxix.

Montaigne, *Apology for Raymond Sebond*, in Donald Frame, edt., *Complete Works of Montaigne* (Stanford, Cal.: Univ. Press. 1967), Essay II, 12, p. 422.

Gaurinath Sastri, *The Philosophy of Word and Meaning* (Calcutta: Sanskrit College, 1959), p. 8.

Chapter 11   (p. 168)

Goethe, quoted by Wittgenstein (VWC 134). The same passage from Goethe is also quoted by Spengler (whom Wittgenstein mentions in

the Frazer Notes) in *The Decline of the West*, Vol. I, p. 156.
Togan Koji, quoted in *Peonies Kana*, Haiku by the Upasaka Shiki,
trans. and edt. Harold J. Isaacson (N.Y.: Theater Arts Books, The
Bhaisajaguru Series, 1972), p. xxiii.
Wallace Stevens, "Description Without Place," *Collected Poems* (N.Y.:
Alfred A. Knopf, 1971), p. 344.

CHAPTER 12   (p. 192)

Lev Shestov, *Kierkegaard and the Existential Philosophy*, trans. Elinor
Hewitt (Athens, Ohio: Ohio Univ. Press, 1969), p. 25.
Eric Gutkind, "On the Possibility of Regaining a Ritual Existence," in
his *The Body of God*, trans. and edt. Lucie Gutkind and Henry Le
Roy Finch (N.Y.: Horizon Press, 1969), p. 70.
Ananda K. Coomaraswamy, *Time and Eternity* (Ascona, Switzerland:
Artibus Asiae, 1947), p. 87.

CHAPTER 13   (p. 220)

Friedrich Nietzsche, *Will to Power*, trans. Walter Kaufman and R. J.
Hollingdale (N.Y. Random House, 1967), Bk. III, Par. 522, p. 283.
Lev Shestov, *In Job's Balances*, trans. Amilla Coventry and C. A.
McCartney (London: J. M. Dent and Sons, 1932), p. 6.
Laotzu, *Tao Te King*, trans. Gia-Fa Feng and Jane English (N.Y.:
Vintage, 1972), Ch. 32.

CHAPTER 14   (p. 238)

Aristotle, *Metaphysics*, Book Alpha the Less, Bk. II, Ch. 1, 993b10;
Richard McKeon, edt., *Basic Works of Aristotle* (N.Y.: Random
House, 1941), p. 712.
Martin Heidegger, *On the Way to Language*, trans. Peter B. Hertz
(N.Y.: Harper and Row, 1971), p. 54.
Hui Hai, *The Path to Sudden Attainment: A Treatise of the Ch'an
(Zen) School of Chinese Buddhism by Hui Hai of the T'ang Dynasty*,
trans. John Blofeld (London: Buddhist Society, 1948), p. 16.
Lev Shestov, *In Job's Balances*, trans. Amilla Coventry and C. A.
McCartney (London: J. M. Dent and Sons, 1932), p. 337.

Bibliographies

(These bibliographies are intended to supplement those which appeared in my *Wittgenstein—The Early Philosophy* (N.Y.: Humanities Press, 1971). With a few exceptions no books listed there are included here. The list comprises only complete books in English, omitting all articles or single chapters in books, and all publications in other languages. Books by Wittgenstein himself will be found listed at the beginning of this book, where the Abbreviations for the references are given.)

I. About Wittgenstein's Later Philosophy

Hallett, Garth, S. J. *Wittgenstein's Definition of Meaning as Use*. N.Y.: Fordham University Press, 1967.

Hardwick, Charles S. *Language Learning in Wittgenstein's Later Philosophy*. The Hague: Mouton, 1971.

Kaal, Hans, and McKinnon, A. *Concordance to Wittgenstein's* Philosophische Untersuchungen. Leiden: E. J. Brill, 1975.

Kielkopf, Charles F. *Strict Finitism: An Examination of Ludwig Wittgenstein's* Remarks on the Foundations of Mathematics. The Hague: Mouton, 1970.

Morick, Harold, edt. *Wittgenstein and the Problem of Other Minds*. N.Y.: McGraw Hill Book Co., 1967.

Pitcher, George, edt. *Wittgenstein*: The Philosophical Investigations. Notre Dame, Ind.: University of Notre Dame Press, 1968.

Pole, David. *The Later Philosophy of Wittgenstein: A Short Introduction with an Epilogue on John Wisdom*. London: University of London, The Athlone Press, 1958.

Price, Jeffrey Thomas. *Language and Being in Wittgenstein's* Philosophical Investigations. The Hague: Mouton, 1973.

Rollins, C. D., edt. *Knowledge and Experience: Proceedings of the 1962 Oberlin Colloquium in Philosophy*. Pittsburgh, Pa.: University of Pittsburgh Press, 1966.

Saunders, John Turk, and Henze, Donald F. *The Private-Language*

Problem: A Philosophical Dialogue. N.Y.: Random House, 1967.

Specht, Ernst Konrad. *The Foundations of Wittgenstein's Late Philosophy.* Translated by D. E. Walford. Manchester: Manchester University Press, and N.Y.: Barnes and Noble, 1969.

II.   About Wittgenstein in General

Ambrose, Alice, and Lazerowitz, Morris, edts. *Ludwig Wittgenstein: Philosophy and Language.* London: George Allen and Unwin, and N.Y.: Humanities Press, Inc., 1972.

Bartley, William Warren, III. *Wittgenstein.* Philadelphia: J. B. Lippincott Co., 1973.

Bogen, James. *Wittgenstein's Philosophy of Language: Some Aspects of Its Development.* N.Y.: Humanities Press, 1972.

Dilman, Ilham. *Induction and Deduction: A Study in Wittgenstein.* Oxford: Basil Blackwell, 1973.

Engel, S. Morris. *Wittgenstein's Doctrine of the Tyranny of Language: An Historical and Critical Examination of His* Blue Book. The Hague: Martinus Nijhoff, 1971.

Fann, K. T., edt. *Wittgenstein: The Man and His Philosophy.* N.Y.: Delta, 1967.

Hacker, P. M. S. *Insight and Illusion: Wittgenstein on Philosophy and the Metaphysics of Experience.* Oxford: Clarendon Press, 1972.

Hunter, J. F. M. *Essays After Wittgenstein.* Toronto: University of Toronto Press, 1973.

Janik, Allan, and Toulmin, Stephen. *Wittgenstein's Vienna.* N.Y.: Simon and Schuster, 1973.

Kenny, Anthony. *Wittgenstein.* Cambridge, Mass.: Harvard University Press, 1973.

Klemke, E. D., edt. *Essays on Wittgenstein.* Urbana, Ill.: University of Illinois Press, 1971.

Leitner Bernhard. *The Architecture of Ludwig Wittgenstein.* Halifax: The Press of the Nova Scotia College of Art and Design, 1973.

Mundle, C. W. K. *A Critique of Linguistic Philosophy.* Oxford: Clarendon Press, 1970.

Pears, David. *Ludwig Wittgenstein.* N.Y.: Viking Press, 1970.

Pitkin, Hanna Fenichel. *Wittgenstein and Justice: On the Significance of Ludwig Wittgenstein for Social and Political Thought.* Berkeley, Calif.: University of California Press, 1972.

Rhees, Rush. *Discussions of Wittgenstein*. N.Y.: Schocken Books, 1970.
Vesey, Godfrey, edt. *Understanding Wittgenstein*. Royal Institute of Philosophy Lectures, Volume Seven, 1972-1973. N.Y.: St. Martin's Press, 1974.
Winch, Peter, edt. *Studies in the Philosophy of Wittgenstein*. N.Y.: Humanities Press, and London: Routledge and Kegan Paul, 1969.

III. Background

Ambrose, Alice. *Essays in Analysis*. London: George Allen and Unwin, and N.Y.: Humanities Press, 1966.
Drury, M. O'C. *The Danger of Words*. Studies in Philosophical Psychology Series. N.Y.: Humanities Press, 1973.
Dummett, Michael. *Frege: Philosophy of Language*. N.Y.: Harper and Row, 1973.
Frege, Gottlob. *On the Foundations of Geometry and Formal Theories of Arithmetic*. Translated by E.-H. W. Kluge. New Haven: Yale University Press, 1971.
Goodstein, R. L. *Essays in the Philosophy of Mathematics*. Leicester: Leicester University Press, 1965.
Grossmann, Reinhardt. *Reflections on Frege's Philosophy*. Evanston: Northwestern University Press, 1969.
Hanson, N. R. *Patterns of Discovery: An Inquiry into the Conceptual Foundations of Science*. Cambridge: University Press, 1958.
High, Dallas M. *Language Persons and Belief*. N.Y.: Oxford University Press, 1967.
James, William. *The Principles of Psychology*. N.Y.: Henry Holt and Co., 1890; reprinted N.Y.: Dover Publications, 1950.
Johnston, William M. *The Austrian Mind: An Intellectual and Social History, 1848-1938*. Berkeley, Calif.: University of California Press, 1972.
Malcolm, Norman. *Dreaming*. Studies in Philosophical Psychology Series. London: Routledge and Kegan Paul, and N.Y.: Humanities Press, 1959.
Malcolm, Norman. *Problems of Mind: Descartes to Wittgenstein*. N.Y.: Harper and Row, 1971.
Needham, Rodney. *Belief, Language, and Experience*. Oxford: Basil Blackwell, 1972.
Rhees, Rush. *Without Answers*. London: Routledge and Kegan Paul, 1969.

Thiel, Christian. *Sense and Reference in Frege's Logic*. Dordrecht, Holland: D. Reidel Publishing Co., and N.Y.: Humanities Press, 1968.

Trigg, Roger. *Reason and Commitment*. Cambridge: At the University Press, 1973.

Winch, Peter. *The Idea of a Social Science and Its Relation to Philosophy*. Edited by R. F. Holland. London: Routledge and Kegan Paul, and N.Y.: Humanities Press, 1958.

INDEX
of
REFERENCES to

PHILOSOPHICAL INVESTIGATIONS and TRACTATUS

(All references are to numbers of sections unless otherwise indicated.)

Philosophical Investigations

p.ix—1, 239, 240-1, 255
1—29, 258
2—70, 82, 92
3—74
4—74
5—70, 71, 74, 164
6—28, 29, 71, 74
7—2, 29, 69, 74, 78, 83, 94
8—82
9—28, 29
10—29
11—8, 23, 30
12—190
15—25
18—46
19—3, 91, 93, 244
20—27, 29
21—70
23—4, 23, 29, 69, 75, 91, 93
24—80, 83
26—74
27—23
28—25
29—24
30—2, 25-29, 70
31—23
32—85
33—85
36—213
38—24, 25, 34, 163
43—2, 33, 177, 244
44—37
45—34
47—29
48—82
50—2, 42, 64, 151
54—158
55—45
56—59, 180, 134
57—42

65—2
66—163
68—45
73—44
75—34
79—25, 34
81—12, 42, 202
82—29, 30
86—190
87—25
88—202
90—7, 149, 154, 162, 188
92—8, 154, 188, 189
93—164
96—42, 44
97—8
98—16, 151, 154
99—15

100—202
102—13, 17
108—8, 151, 154, 188
109—161, 164, 169, 213
110—44, 162
111—86
112—161
115—161
116—28
120—189
122—8, 29, 31, 162, 164
124—169
125—161
126—174-5
127—8, 164
128—154, 243
130—2, 8, 68, 69, 72
131—244
132—29, 163, 164, 190
133—28, 29, 164-5
135—44

INDEX
of
NAMES OF PERSONS

INDEX
of
SUBJECTS